AMERICA

AMERICA

IMAGINE A WORLD
WITHOUT HER

DINESH D'SOUZA

REGNERY
PUBLISHING
A Salem Communications Company

ISBN 978-1-62157-203-9

Library of Congress Cataloging-in-Publication Data

D'Souza, Dinesh, 1961-
  America / Dinesh D'Souza.
      pages cm
  Includes bibliographical references and index.
  1. Political culture--United States. 2. United States--Politics and government-
-Moral and ethical aspects. 3. Civilization, Modern--American influences. 4.
National characteristics, American. 5. United States--Relations. I. Title.
  JK1726.D76 2014
  973--dc23

Published in the United States by
Regnery Publishing
A Salem Communications Company
300 New Jersey Avenue NW
Washington, DC 20001
www.Regnery.com

Manufactured in the United States of America
10 9 8 7

Books are available in quantity for promotional or premium use. For information on discounts and terms, please visit our website: www.Regnery.com.

Distributed to the trade by
Perseus Distribution
250 West 57th Street
New York, NY 10107

For Gerald Molen,
whose life embodies the spirit of America

CONTENTS

CHAPTER 1

SUICIDE OF A NATION

With him the love of country means
Blowing it all to smithereens
And having it all made over new.[1]
—ROBERT FROST

Writing in the mid-twentieth century, the French existentialist writer Albert Camus posed for human beings a central question: to exist or not to exist. In Camus's words, "There is but one truly serious philosophical problem, and that is suicide." In a sense, this was Hamlet's question: "To be or not to be." For Camus, human beings had lived for millennia in a meaningful universe, a universe created by God, and one that gave significance and purpose to human life. But now, Camus wrote, we have discovered through science and reason that the universe is pointless, merely a constellation of flashing and spinning orbs and objects. God is absent from the world, which is another way of saying he does not exist for us. Consequently humans have to find ultimate meaning elsewhere, and there is nowhere else to look. So life becomes, in Shakespeare's words, "a tale told by an idiot, full of sound and fury, signifying nothing." Drawing on ancient myth, Camus likened the human predicament to that of Sisyphus endlessly rolling the rock up the hill, only to see it roll back down.

For Camus, the problem wasn't merely that the universe lacks meaning; it was that man desires meaning and there is no meaning to be had. Consequently our situation is kind of absurd. "The absurd is born of this confrontation between the human need and the unreasonable silence of the world." Most people, according to Camus, ignore this tragic reality. They deflect the meaninglessness of their lives by engaging in various trivial pursuits. But for morally serious people, Camus says, this deflection is not an option. He proposes that humans must take the absurdity of their lives seriously, and in doing so, they must consider whether to live in tragic absurdity or voluntarily end their lives. Suicide, for Camus, was an ethical choice.[2]

Of course people since ancient times have considered, and even committed, suicide. Typically, however, they did so out of personal despair, because life for them ceased to matter, or because they were in too much pain. Camus was original in that he raised existential despair to a universal human level—we are all in the same predicament—and because he considered suicide as not just something people do, but something we ought to regard as a moral option, perhaps even a moral imperative. Strange though this may seem, it is a view taken up, to an extent, by the most radical of environmentalists who see human beings as a blight on the planet.

As it is with humans, so it may be with nations. Nations, of course, rarely attempt suicide. I cannot think of a single country that has tried to destroy itself. Presumably this is because nations, like humans, have a survival instinct. The survival instinct of nations is the collective survival instinct of the people in those nations. Why, then, would a nation attempt to destroy itself or commit suicide?

Nations sometimes are conquered by other nations, or they collapse from within, but they never seek self-destruction. Yet Abraham Lincoln observed, a century and a half ago, that if America were ever to fall, it would not be by external means or even by internal collapse. Rather, it would be by the actions of Americans themselves. In his Lyceum Address, Lincoln said:

> Shall we expect some transatlantic military giant to step the Ocean and crush us at a blow? Never! All the armies of Europe, Asia and Africa combined, with all the treasure of the earth, our own excepted, in their military chest, with a Bonaparte for a commander, could not by force take a drink from the Ohio, or make a track on the Blue Ridge, in a trial of a thousand years. At what point then is the approach of danger to be expected? I answer, if it ever reach us, it must spring up amongst us. It cannot come from abroad. If destruction be our lot, we must ourselves be its author and finisher. As a nation of freemen, we must live through all time, or die by suicide.[3]

Surely Lincoln is not suggesting that America—or Americans—might voluntarily seek destruction. Undoubtedly Lincoln believed that such an outcome would be the unforeseen consequence of calamitous misjudgment and folly. Yet I intend to show in this book that the American era is ending in part because a powerful group of Americans wants it to end. The American dream is shrinking because some of our leaders want it to shrink. Decline, in other words, has become a policy objective. And if this decline continues at the current pace, America as we know it will cease to exist. In effect, we will have committed national suicide.

America's suicide, it turns out, is the result of a plan. The plan is not simply one of destruction but also one of reconstruction—it seeks the rebuilding of a different type of country, what President Obama terms "the work of remaking America."[4] While Obama acknowledges the existence of the plan, he is not responsible for the plan; it would be more accurate to say that it is responsible for him. The plan preceded Obama, and it will outlast him. Obama is simply part of a fifty-year scheme for the undoing and remaking of America, and when he is gone there are others who are ready to continue the job. What makes the plan especially chilling is that most Americans are simply unaware of what's going on. Their ignorance, as we shall see, is part of the plan.

It should be emphasized at the outset that the domestic champions of American decline are not traitors or America-haters. They are bringing down America because they genuinely believe that America deserves to be brought down. Their actions are the result of a powerful moral critique of America, one that has never been effectively answered. Nor is it easy to answer. Most people, confronted with the critique, go mute. Some respond with bluster; others want to change the topic. The ineffectiveness of these rebuttals makes independent observers believe this critique cannot be answered.

Consequently, the critique is widely taught in our schools and universities, and accepted as valid by the ruling powers in Washington, D.C. The critique leads to the conclusion that America must go down so that others can come up. It is now the accepted basis for America's foreign and domestic policy. The plan for national suicide is in effect. And if it continues to be implemented, it is merely a matter of time—years rather than decades—for the American era to be finished. American lives will be diminished, and the "American dream" will be an object of past recollection and contemporary sneering. In the minds of those who brought this about, this will be a very good thing. For them, as for Camus, suicide could be regarded as the moral course of action.

Thumb through the writings of the pundits and scholars, and talk of American decline is everywhere. "Is America Over?" reads the headline of the December 2011 issue of *Foreign Affairs*. Writing in *Political Science Quarterly*, Giacomo Chiozza warns that America, once-great, is now "facing the prospect of its final decay." Stephen Cohen and Bradford DeLong contemplate America's grim fate in a recent book *The End of Influence*. "The American standard of living will decline," they predict, and "the United States will lose power and influence." America can no longer dominate the world because "the other countries . . . will have all the money." Once an America booster, Fareed Zakaria now chants a different tune, suggested by the title of his book *The Post-American World*. Across the spectrum, commentators discuss how to prevent decline, or how to cope with decline. Virtually no one is saying that decline is a myth or that America's prospects are rising.[5]

There seem to be three obvious indicators of decline. First, the American economy is stagnant and shrinking relative to the growing economies of China, Russia, India, and Brazil. In a recent article, "The End of the American Era," Stephen Walt writes that "China is likely to overtake America in total economic output no later than 2025." The Organization for Economic Cooperation and Development (OECD), based in Paris, predicts that as early as 2016—when Obama leaves office—China, not the United States, will be the world's largest economy. When this seemingly inevitable event occurs, it will be the first time in many centuries that a non-Western, non-democratic, and non-English-speaking nation has headed the world economy. Since the American era coincides with American economic dominance, it seems fair to say that when the dominance ceases, the American era will officially have come to an end. And history shows that once nations lose their position at the top of the world, they never get it back.[6]

Second, America is drowning in debt. While China is the world's largest creditor nation, America is the world's largest debtor nation. At $17 trillion, the national debt is now bigger than the annual gross domestic product—in other words, it is bigger than the total sum of goods and services that America produces in a year. Nearly half of this debt has been accumulated during the Obama years, at the average rate of a trillion dollars a year. At this pace, Obama will more than double the deficit in two terms. Since a substantial portion of America's debt is owed to foreign countries, such as China and the Arab nations, debt produces a transfer of wealth away from America and toward the rest of the world. Today, instead of America owning the world, the world increasingly owns America. Moreover, if America continues to pile on debt in Obama proportions, it won't be long before the country is bankrupt. The striking aspect of this is not that the problem is so serious, but that the president seems remarkably indifferent, as if he's carrying on business as usual. As we will discover, he is. And the results are predictable. Rich countries, like rich people, can afford to act irresponsibly for a while, but eventually the creditors show up to take away your house and car.

Finally, America is losing its position in the world. The Obama administration is downsizing our nuclear arsenal when other nations are building and modernizing theirs. Under the START Treaty, America has gone from several thousand nuclear warheads to a limit of 1,550. In 2013, Obama proposed cutting that number even further to around 1,000, and he has said he intends getting rid of nuclear weapons altogether. Whether America's nuclear impotence will enhance world peace is debatable; that it will reduce America's military dominance is certain.

Besides nuclear hegemony, America is also relinquishing its hegemony around the world, especially in the strategically and economically vital Middle East. As political scientist Fawaz Gerges puts it in a recent book, *Obama and the Middle East*, "U.S. influence . . . is at its lowest point since the beginning of the cold war in the late 1940s. . . . America neither calls the shots as before nor dominates the regional scene in the way it did. . . . We are witnessing the end of America's moment in the Middle East."[7] The growing power of China, Russia, and other emerging countries has also restricted America's impact in Asia, Europe, and South America. America seems on the way to become a feeble giant, a second Canada.

Decline has consequences, not only for America but also for Americans. We are facing the prospect of a sharp drop not merely in America's role in the world, but also in America's standard of living. In some respects, America is exchanging places with the emerging countries. They are getting stronger while we grow weaker. They gain the influence that we have lost or relinquished. They are growing rapidly while we are risking an economic collapse that would plunge us into second- or even third-world status.

All this talk about America's decline or even collapse is surprising when we recall that, just a few years ago, America seemed to be on top of the world. In fact, America was the sole superpower. America's military might was unrivalled, its economy dominant, and its culture spreading contagiously on every continent. The American ascendancy began in 1945, after World War II. That's when America became a superpower. But America became the sole superpower only when the Soviet Union collapsed, in 1992. Thus the triumph of America in the second half of the twentieth century is accompanied by the sober realization that the American era is merely six decades old, and America has been the undisputed world leader for only two decades. When we consider that the Roman Age lasted a thousand

years, and the Ottomans and the British dominated the world for
several centuries, America's dominance seems brief, and already it
is precarious.

America's global ascendancy was predicted and indeed choreo-
graphed by the Founders, more than two centuries ago. The Founders who gathered in Philadelphia believed that they were creating a
formula for a new type of society. They called it the *novus ordo
seclorum*, a new order for the ages, or in Tom Paine's words, America was "the birthday of a new world." The Founders knew they were
in a unique position. Alexander Hamilton noted that, historically,
countries have been founded by "accident and force" but America
was an opportunity to found a nation by "reflection and choice." In
one sense the Founders were creating a universal example; thus
George Washington could say that the cause of America was also
the "cause of mankind."[8] At the same time, the Founders had created
a specific nation they believed would become the strongest, most
prosperous, and most influential society on the planet—and they
have been proven right.

What they could not have known, however, is that they were also
creating the last best hope for Western civilization. For many centuries, Europe was the embodiment and defender of the West. The
leadership of the West shifted from century to century—from the
Portuguese in the fifteenth century to the Spanish in the sixteenth
to the French in the seventeenth to the British in the eighteenth and
nineteenth—but nevertheless the baton passed from one European
power to another. It was only in the twentieth century that Europe
itself lost its preeminence. The main reason was that World War II
left all the three major European powers—Britain, France, and
Germany—in ruins.

In 1964, the political scientist James Burnham published *Suicide
of the West*. Burnham noted that "Western civilization has been in a

period of very rapid decline, recession or ebb within the world power structure." Burnham wasn't talking about the Western standard of living. Rather, he meant the decline of Western power and influence. Burnham noted that early in the twentieth century the West—led by Britain—controlled approximately two-thirds of the real estate on the planet. A "galactic observer" could not fail to see that "in 1914 the domain of Western civilization was, or very nearly was, the world." But within a few decades, Burnham said, the area under Western control had dramatically shrunk. One by one the West gave up its colonial possessions, sometimes voluntarily, sometimes after a fight. Either way, the countries of Asia, Africa, the Middle East, and South America were gaining their independence, which is to say, freeing themselves from Western control. "If the process continues over the next several decades more or less as it has gone on," Burnham wrote, "then—this is merely mathematical extrapolation—the West will be finished." And since historical contractions of this magnitude are seldom reversed, Burnham grimly concluded that "the West, in shrinking, is also dying."[9]

Burnham missed one critical development—the transfer of leadership from Europe to the United States. Unlike the British and the French, America was not a colonizing power. (In fact, America had once been a colony of Britain.) America sought no colonies for itself in the manner of the British and the French. Indeed, in the decades after World War II, America encouraged Britain to grant independence to its colonies. Thus America's influence in the world, unlike Europe's, was not based on conquest but rather on attraction to American ideals and the American way of life. Milton writes in *Paradise Lost*, "Who overcomes by force, hath overcome but half his foe."[10] America's influence was greater because its institutions and values were adopted rather than imposed. Still, America's triumph was accompanied by the sobering realization that if America fell, there would be no one left to pick up the baton. The end of the American era would seem to signal also the end of Western civilization.

If America is going down, what is causing this to happen? Clearly the cause isn't external. There is no Nazi or Communist menace strong enough to destroy the United States. The radical Muslims are a serious threat, both to American lives and American interests, but they do not control the U.S. economy nor can they threaten America's existence. At best, they are an external drag. Disconcertingly, however, the most powerful drag on America seems to be coming from inside America. We are being brought down from within.

Who or what is responsible for this? In my previous two books, I focused on one man, Barack Obama. Obama's presidency can be summed up in the phrase, "Omnipotence at home, impotence abroad."[11] Domestically, the Obama Democrats have been expanding the power of the state and reducing the scope of the private sector. Internationally, they have been reducing the footprint of America in the world. How to explain this dual motion? I stressed the anti-colonial ideology that Obama adopted from his father, as detailed in Obama's own autobiography *Dreams from My Father*. The core idea of anti-colonialism is that the wealth of the West has been obtained by theft. Consider the world as it must have looked in the mid-twentieth century to Obama's Kenyan father, Barack Obama Sr., or to my own dad, living in India. These men looked around the world and they saw affluence in the West and indigence everywhere else. They saw luxury in Paris and London and impoverishment in Nairobi and Mumbai. When they paused to consider why, the answer seemed obvious: the rich countries became rich by invading, occupying, and looting the poor countries. At this time, Britain still ruled Kenya, India, and many other countries. It was the heyday of colonialism. Thus the anti-colonial explanation seemed unavoidable, irrefutable. It is still widely believed and taught in schools and colleges as the standard account of how the West grew rich and how other countries remained poor.

Anti-colonialism is a Third World ideology, but it came to the United States during the Vietnam War. Consequently Obama learned his anti-colonialism not just from Barack Obama Sr. but from a whole host of anti-colonial radicals in America. I call these men Obama's founding fathers, and they include the former Communist Frank Marshall Davis, the domestic terrorist Bill Ayers, the Palestinian scholar Edward Said, the self-described Brazilian revolutionary Roberto Mangabeira Unger, and the incendiary preacher Jeremiah Wright. While Obama's primary mentor was his dad, he learned chapter and verse of the anti-colonial ideology in America, in Hawaii, and at Columbia University and Harvard Law School, and in Chicago.[12]

Since the 1960s, anti-colonialism in America has been integrated into a larger ideology. For decades, that ideology used to be called "liberalism." The ideology fell into such disrepute in the 1980s and 1990s, however, that liberals stopped calling themselves liberals. Now they call themselves "progressives." The term progressive suggests a commitment to progress. Progress implies change, and Obama's 2008 campaign slogans all focused on "change." But change in what direction? Presumably change here means improvement, things getting better. But what improvement? Better for whom? It has been said that if termites could talk, they would call what they do "progress." So we should reserve our enthusiasm for progressivism until we find out what progressives believe and what kind of change they want.

The term "progressive" harkens back to the progressive movement of the early twentieth century. Modern progressives invoke that movement, but they have formulated a much more comprehensive radicalism that goes far beyond anything that Theodore Roosevelt

or Woodrow Wilson envisioned. Roosevelt and Wilson were traditional American patriots who wanted to enact reforms, but not
remake an America they believed was fundamentally good, indeed
great. The new progressive ideology proceeds from a powerful left-
wing critique of America, one that grew out of the 1960s and has
been refined and elaborated since then.

This critique builds on a single idea: theft. Clearly this is also the
core idea of anti-colonialism. Listen to Frantz Fanon, a leading anti-
colonialist whom Obama said he read avidly in college. "The wealth
of the imperial countries is our wealth too. . . . The well-being and
progress of Europe have been built up with the sweat and the dead
bodies of Negroes, Arabs, Indians, and the yellow races. . . . Europe
is literally a creation of the Third World. The wealth which smothers
her is that which was stolen from the under-developed peoples." This
awareness, Fanon writes, produces "a double realization: the realization by the colonized peoples that it is their due and the realization
by the capitalist powers that they must pay."[13] Modern progressivism
incorporates this theft accusation into a systematic critique of America and the West.

According to the progressive critique, America was founded in
an original act of piracy: the early settlers came from abroad and
stole the country from the native Indians. Then America was built
by theft: white Americans stole the labor of African Americans by
enslaving them for 250 years. The theft continued through nearly a
century of segregation, discrimination, and Jim Crow. The borders
of America were also extended by theft: America stole half of Mexico
in the Mexican War. Moreover, America's economic system, capitalism, is based on theft since it confers unjust profits on a few and
deprives the majority of workers of their "fair share." Finally, America's foreign policy is based on theft, what historian William Apple-
man Williams termed "empire as a way of life." Why are we in the

Middle East? Clearly it is because of oil. America's actions abroad are aimed at plundering other people's land and resources so that we can continue to enjoy an outsized standard of living compared to the rest of the world.

The progressive indictment is a powerful one, encompassing past and present. It is not merely a political critique; it is also an historical one. Since the 1960s, progressive scholars have been doing a new kind of research. They call it "history from below." History, they say, has traditionally been told from the viewpoint of the great actors, the kings and statesmen who were seen to define events. This is history written by "winners." Meanwhile, the little people get ignored and the losers never get to tell their side of the story. "History from below" is intended to correct the imbalance. So thoroughly has it been institutionalized that it has now become the mainstream way to tell the American story.

Consider Howard Zinn's classic text, *A People's History of the United States*. This is probably the most influential history book of the past half century. Zinn makes no effort to conceal his perspective. "I prefer to try to tell the story of the discovery of America from the viewpoint of the Arawaks, of the Constitution from the standpoint of the slaves, of Andrew Jackson as seen by the Cherokees, of the Civil War as seen by the New York Irish, of the Mexican war as seen by the deserting soldiers of Scott's army, of the rise of industrialism as seen by the young women in the Lowell textile mills, of the Spanish-American war as seen by the Cubans, the conquest of the Philippines as seen by black soldiers on Luzon, the Gilded Age as seen by southern farmers, the First World War as seen by socialists, the Second World War as seen by pacifists, the New Deal as seen by blacks in Harlem, the postwar American empire as seen by peons in Latin America."[14]

Zinn is not afraid to give a one-sided picture. He does not believe there is such a thing as objective history; therefore, he wants to present *his* side. And what is his side? Zinn believes in global economic equality, looking forward, as he puts it, to "a time when national boundaries are erased, when the riches of the world are used for everyone."[15] Zinn makes his case, however, with a large compendium of facts, and I for one cannot fault his emphasis on "history from below." It is both interesting and morally commendable to look at the world from the point of view of the ordinary man, the little guy. How do the great events of the past and present affect him or her? Nations cannot be judged solely by how they make provision for the high and mighty. Rather, what matters is what kind of life a nation makes possible for the newcomer, the commoner, the low man on the totem pole. In this book I too will be doing "history from below," challenging Zinn and the progressives, but on their own terms.

Incredibly, the "theft" indictment of America has never been comprehensively answered. In fact, I am not aware of any previous attempt to answer it. America has champions and boosters, but so far they have relied heavily on slogans of liberty and patriotism and rah-rah-rah. But they have not squarely faced the progressive critique nor have they refuted it. Perhaps it is irrefutable. Didn't we seize the country from the native Indians? Didn't we steal the labor of the blacks? Isn't it true that having taken the land of the Mexicans, we won't now let them come back and work as agricultural laborers on what used to be their land? The progressive critique seems anchored in accepted facts.

The core of progressivism, of Obama's philosophy, is a moral critique of capitalism. This is different from the twentieth-century debate between capitalism and socialism, in which capitalism prevailed. In the last century, capitalism won the economic debate on the grounds of efficiency. But capitalism has never fully met the charge that it is unethical. In the 2012 presidential campaign, we heard about how America is divided into two groups: makers and takers. The makers are supposed to be the productive people, and the takers the ones who rely on the government. Presumably if takers outnumber makers, then progressives will continue to win elections.

This analysis, however, misses the appeal of progressivism to makers no less than to takers. Consider the fellow who parks cars at an expensive resort and earns $12 an hour. How many cars did he park yesterday? Let's say a hundred. And it costs around $25 to park a car overnight at the Ritz Carlton or the Beverly Hilton. So how much did the hotel make on the parking? It made $2,500. And how much did the hotel pay the parking guy? Around $100. So from the point of view of the parking guy, he's being cheated. He's the one who is parking the cars. Yet virtually the entire profit goes to the hotel. Why does he get so little? Who gets the remaining $2,400? Our indignant parking guy imagines some rich fellow using the money to take his girlfriend to Hawaii. The parking guy doesn't view himself as a "taker." Rather, he's a "maker." It's the rich guy who is the "taker," depriving his employees who do the work of their "fair share." The parking lot attendant wants to know, "Where's my American dream?"

We cannot convince the parking guy—and countless others like him—by simply chanting, "Free markets!" "Capitalism!" "America— Love It or Leave It." We have to actually show where the other $2,400 went. In other words, we have to show why the rewards of the free market system are not only efficient but also fair. If we cannot do this, we must admit that the actual outcomes of the capitalist system cannot be ethically justified.

If the facts adduced by the progressives are true, the conclusion is both startling and unavoidable. If America is founded on theft, and continues to sustain its wealth through rip-off and plunder, then America as a nation is morally indefensible.

So what should be done about this? A few progressives—the real radicals, the ones who are not afraid to speak their inner mind—do not hesitate to say it: America should be destroyed. For my *America* film I interviewed the radical activist Ward Churchill. I asked him where today is the "evil empire." He said, "You're in it." He added that the world would be better off if America, like Nazi Germany, were destroyed. I asked him bluntly if he would be satisfied if a bomb could be detonated that would wipe out America. In a calm tone, he replied, "Yes." So this is the extreme progressive view.

But there is also a rival view, which we can call the mainstream progressive or Obama view. This view agrees with the diagnosis of America but provides a different remedy. The mainstream progressive remedy is guilt and atonement. Americans, in this view, should feel guilty about what they have done and continue to do. Moreover, Americans—especially those who are productive and successful—must realize that their wealth is illegitimate and *must be returned to its rightful owners*. Obama clearly believes this. He aggressively peddles the theft critique, especially through his "fair share" rhetoric, and his own presidency is a tribute to the power of the theft argument. How, for example, did Obama get elected as a complete unknown? How did he get reelected when the economy was doing so badly? Why do the media give him a perpetual honeymoon? There is a one-word answer: slavery. America's national guilt over slavery continues to benefit Obama, who ironically is not himself descended from slaves.

Much of the progressive expansion of government—from the welfare state to affirmative action—can be understood as America's form of reparations for the crimes of history: not just slavery but also segregation, Jim Crow, and racism. Many blacks today still believe America owes them, and some advocate racial reparations in the form of cash payments. What does Obama think about reparations?

Consider a revealing statement by one of his former students. He said that when Obama taught at the University of Chicago, Obama "told us what he thought of reparations. He agreed entirely with the theory of reparations. But in practice he didn't think it was really workable." In order to have reparations, a society would have to settle such questions as "who is black, how far back do you go, what about recent immigrants," and so on. Considering such complexities, Obama rejected the idea of reparations for slavery. And this was also his position when running for president.[16]

But while Obama rejects race-based reparations, I believe he has found a way to achieve global reparations. This involves large transfers of wealth from America to the rest of the world. It also involves wealth redistribution within America. Why should America, which has 5 percent of the world's population, consume 25 percent of the world's resources? Why should successful people in America have so much more than other Americans? Obama insists these inequalities are undeserved; as he famously told a crowd of supporters, "If you've got a business—you didn't build that. Somebody else made that happen." Obama seems convinced that wealth is at best appropriated or at worst stolen rather than earned. He seeks to use his power to take it back. He intends to redistribute the money in America and around the world. In his view, he's giving back to people what has been illicitly taken from them.

Obama's approach is supported by a theme in philosophy that goes under the name of "stolen goods." The basic idea is simple: if you are in possession of stolen goods, you have to return them. If you have acquired wealth by stealing, or if you inherit goods that your ancestors stole from others, it's not enough to say sorry or to provide token compensation. No, you must return what isn't yours, and if you've used the wealth to accumulate more, then you must return that too.[17] So if it is true that America was built on stealing, and that America's abundance is the product of theft, then America as a nation is indefensible, inexcusable, and under obligation to undo the crimes she has committed and continues to perpetrate on her own citizens and on the rest of the world. Undoing America's crimes—and if necessary undoing America in the process: this is a summary of the progressive agenda. This is the progressive case for American suicide.

In this book, I intend to refute the progressive critique and provide a new understanding of what America means and why America is worth preserving. I will examine the historical critique by asking a simple question: As a result of the events of American history, are the people on the bottom better off or worse off? In other words, are the native Indians today better or worse because of the arrival of Columbus and Western civilization? Are blacks today better or worse because their ancestors were hauled here as slaves? Are Mexicans who now live on the American side of the border better or worse than Mexicans whose land was not conquered during the Mexican War? This is a way of examining history by considering its current impact.

I also intend to argue that America invented something new in the world. There are very few truly world-changing inventions. Fire is one of them. The wheel is another. The invention of agriculture is a third. In this book I will show that America is a society based upon perhaps the most important invention of all time: the invention of wealth creation. For most of human history, wealth was presumed to be finite. Consider a boy on the playground with ten marbles. How can he get more marbles? There is only one way. He has to take someone else's marbles. In the same way, wealth was mostly in land and the only way to get land was to take it. Conquest, in other words, was the natural mode of human acquisition. That's how most countries were founded, through force and conquest. Slavery and feudal economic exploitation were simply extensions of the conquest ethic. You get stuff by grabbing it or, as Abraham Lincoln once put it: You work and I eat.

Conquest was not merely the way of the world; conquest was seen as a legitimate way to acquire wealth. It is still seen that way in much of the world. This idea is hard for us in America to understand. The ethics of conquest are rooted in the ethics of tribal solidarity. Our tribe is the most worthy of our allegiance, and therefore its interests are paramount. Our job is to ensure the protection and welfare of our tribe. Therefore we should attempt to subjugate other tribes, before they do the same to us. The ethics of conquest are the ethics of a football game; we want our team to possess the ball at all times, and we cheer when our guys knock down and run over the other guys. If we recall the Old Testament, we see how the victories of Israel over its enemies are considered by the Israelites to be unambiguously good. It's either them or us, and it may as well be us.

Recognizing that conquest had been the universal ethic, America developed a new ethic, the ethic of wealth creation. America is founded on the understanding that wealth can be created through innovation and enterprise. Through the system of technological capitalism, we can go from ten marbles to twenty marbles without taking anyone's marbles. Obviously there were inventors and merchants around before America. But America is the first society to be based on invention and trade. America is the capitalist society par excellence. I will show how this new system of wealth creation is fair and just, and how it produces a better life for little guys in America and around the world. I will not shy away from addressing the progressive arguments that earning is itself exploitation, that profits are plunder, and that America's global actions are a disguised form of thievery.

I intend to turn the progressive critique on its head. I will demonstrate that the progressives are the real thieves, in that they use the power of the state to seize the property and possessions of people who have earned them. In the name of the ordinary citizen, progressives have declared war on the wealth creators. Yet they are not on the side of the ordinary citizen, because their policies lead to stagnation, impoverishment, indebtedness, and decline—all in evidence today. It is progressives who rely on government seizure and bureaucratic conquest to achieve their goals and increase their power. We work, and they eat. As we shall see, the progressives have a comprehensive scheme—one that relies on deceit—to win political support for their wealth confiscation. Most recently, in order to quell dissent, the progressives are implementing a chilling policy of national surveillance and selective prosecution—using the power of the police to harass and subdue their opposition. Ultimately what the progressives seek is a suicide of national identity, a dissolution of the American era. This involves not merely a diminution of America but a diminution of Americans.

I intend to blow the whistle on these people, starting with Obama and continuing with Hillary Clinton and the whole progressive menagerie. Once the ordinary American understands how moral terms have been inverted, and how he is being conned by his self-styled partisans, he will rise up and repudiate his new oppressors who are none other than his old oppressors under a new name. America remains now, as it has long been, a solution to the global problem of scarcity and the human problem of how to achieve prosperity and happiness. The world needs America, but only Americans can restore the formula for prosperity and human flourishing to the benefit of untold millions, here and everywhere, now living or yet to come.

CHAPTER 2

A TALE OF TWO FRENCHMEN

*The idea of right is simply that of virtue
introduced into the political world.*[1]
—ALEXIS DE TOCQUEVILLE, *DEMOCRACY IN AMERICA*

nti-Americanism, like Americanism, is a home-grown phenomenon. I am defining anti-Americanism, not pejoratively but clinically, as a strong antagonism to American ideas and institutions. Here I am not concerned with the anti-Americanism of some Bolivian radical, Russian apparatchik, or Iranian mullah. That could be written off as ignorant prejudice or arising from conflicting national interests. Rather, I am speaking of the anti-Americanism of Americans who know their country well, and have well-considered objections to its conduct. While it can sometimes be offensive, anti-Americanism of this sort should not be shunned but rather welcomed, to see if the criticisms are correct. In the words of Edmund Burke, "To love our country, our country ought to be lovely."[2]

Progressives sometimes sound anti-American, but they are not simply advocates of destruction. In destroying one America they seek to construct another. In other words, their unmaking is a prelude to a remaking. So there is a vision of America that progressives affirm. It just happens to be very different from, indeed antithetical to, the vision that conservatives affirm. Contrary to what we hear, the great American divide is not a clash between conservatives who advocate liberty versus progressives who oppose liberty. Rather, the two sides each affirm a certain type of liberty. One side, for example, cherishes economic liberty while the other champions liberty in the sexual and social domain. Nor is it a clash between patriots and anti-patriots. Both sides love America, but they love a different type of America. One side loves the America of Columbus and the Fourth of July, of innovation and work and the "animal spirit" of capitalism, of the Boy Scouts and parochial schools, of traditional families and flag-saluting veterans. The other side loves the America of tolerance and social entitlements, of income and wealth redistribution, of affirmative action and abortion, of feminism and gay marriage.

I recently debated Bill Ayers—1960s radical and Obama mentor—at Dartmouth College. Our topic was "What's So Great about America." Ayers began by celebrating what he considered to be great about America. He did not, in this context, make any reference to the Founding Fathers. He didn't mention Abraham Lincoln. Rather, he invoked a protest tradition in America, going back to the nineteenth-century socialists and continuing through the twentieth-century progressives right up to, well, himself. Similarly in a recent book, Howard Zinn calls for America's existing pantheon of heroes—such as the Founding Fathers—to be replaced by such figures as the Seminole leader Osceola, who fought a guerilla campaign against the U.S. government, anarchist and social activist Emma Goldman, and the Iraq war protester Cindy Sheehan.[3] This is their America; this is the America progressives celebrate on the Fourth of July.

If patriotism isn't the dividing line, neither is American exceptionalism. Again, both sides believe America is exceptional but one side believes America is exceptionally good while the other believes that America is exceptionally evil. One group considers America the good society; the other considers America the evil empire. Even here, conservatives bemoan certain aspects of modern America while progressives celebrate them, such as government-administered national healthcare or forced acceptance of the homosexual lifestyle.

How can we compare and contrast these two Americas—the one that conservatives uphold and the very different one that progressives cherish? Oddly enough, we can do so by comparing the journeys of two Frenchmen to America. Their outsider perspective helps Americans see ourselves more clearly. The first, Alexis de Tocqueville, was an aristocrat who traveled widely in America in the early nineteenth century. A young man in his mid-twenties, Tocqueville was accompanied by a fellow aristocrat, Gustave Beaumont, who had a special interest in America's prison system. Together they journeyed from New England to Philadelphia to New Orleans to Wisconsin, covering more than seven thousand miles over a period of ten months. Tocqueville's visit occurred a few decades after the founding, so he was in a position to observe how the principles of the revolution had imprinted themselves into American life. He carefully observed American mores, eventually publishing his findings in his classic book *Democracy in America*. Intended originally for a French audience, this work is today more widely read and studied in America.

The other Frenchman, Michel Foucault, was an intellectual who first came to America in 1975. Over the next several years he made extended visits to the San Francisco Bay Area while teaching at the University of California at Berkeley; and later, in the early 1980s, lectured at Dartmouth where I met him as an undergraduate. Foucault obviously saw a very different America than Tocqueville, an America reshaped by the tumult of the 1960s. Moreover, Foucault's interests were very different from Tocqueville's. What Tocqueville found most appealing, Foucault found most repulsive. Indeed traditional America illustrated many of the things that Foucault considered most objectionable about Western civilization. But Foucault should not be written off as an anti-American. On the contrary, Foucault found himself wildly enthusiastic about America to the point that his French colleagues considered him madly pro-American. For Foucault, America in the late 1970s and early 1980s was great because it allowed people the chance to transcend all sexual limits; adults could not only have sex with each other, but also with young boys. Foucault regarded this as a noble ideal worth dying for. Together these two men illustrate the very different Americas affirmed by conservatives and progressives today.

Let's begin with Tocqueville, who observes at the outset that America is a nation unlike any other. It has produced what Tocqueville terms "a distinct species of mankind." Tocqueville here identifies what will later be called American exceptionalism. For Tocqueville, Americans are unique because they are equal. This controversial assertion of the Declaration—that all men are created equal—Tocqueville finds to be a simple description of American reality. Americans, he writes, have internalized the democratic principle of equality. They refuse to regard one another as superior and inferior. They don't bow and scrape in the way that people in other countries—notably in France—are known to do. In America, unlike in Europe, there are no "peasants," only farmers. In America, there are employees but no "servants." And today America may be the only country where we call a waiter "sir" as if he were a knight.

Equality for Tocqueville is social, not economic. Competition, he writes, produces unequal outcomes on the basis of merit. "Natural inequality will soon make way for itself and wealth will pass into the hands of the most capable." But this is justified because wealth is earned and not stolen. Tocqueville is especially struck by the fact that rich people in America were once poor. He notes, with some disapproval, that Americans have an "inordinate" love of money. Yet he cannot help being impressed in observing among Americans the restless energy of personal striving and economic competition. "Choose any American at random and he should be a man of burning desires, enterprising, adventurous, and above all an innovator." What makes success possible, he writes, is the striving of the ordinary man. The ordinary man may be vulgar and have a limited education, but he has practical intelligence and a burning desire to succeed. "Before him lies a boundless continent and he urges onward as if time pressed and he was afraid of finding no room for his exertions." Tocqueville observes what he terms a "double migration": restless Europeans coming to the East Coast of America, while restless Americans move west from the Atlantic toward the Pacific Ocean. Tocqueville foresees that this ambitious, energetic people will expand the borders of the country and ultimately become a great nation. "It is the most extraordinary sight I have ever seen in my life. These lands which are as yet nothing but one immense wood will become one of the richest and most powerful countries in the world."

There is one exception to the rule of the enterprising and hardworking American. At one point, Tocqueville stands on the Ohio-Kentucky border. He looks north and south and is startled by the contrast. He contrasts "industrious Ohio" with "idle Kentucky." While Ohio displays all the signs of work and well-maintained houses and fields, Kentucky is inhabited "by a people without energy, without ardor, without a spirit of enterprise." Since the climate and conditions on both sides of the border are virtually identical, what accounts for the difference? Tocqueville concludes that it is slavery. Slavery provides no incentive for slaves to work, since they don't get to keep the product of their labor. But neither does slavery encourage masters to work, because slaves do the work for them. Remarkably slavery is bad for masters and slaves: it degrades work, so less work is done.

While Americans cherish their freedom, Tocqueville emphasizes that they do not consider themselves immune from moral obligation or moral law. "It was never assumed in the United States that the citizen of a free country has a right to do whatever he pleases." Americans, however, derive their obligations not from government mandate but from religious morality and social pressure. There are innumerable sects in America, but "all sects preach the same moral law in the name of God." Moreover, religion balances entrepreneurial striving: the latter teaches how to better yourself, for your own good, while the former teaches obligations to others, for the good of the community. Therefore quite apart from its theological function, Tocqueville writes that, for Americans, religion "must be regarded as the first of their political institutions." As the quotation at the beginning of this chapter suggests, Tocqueville sees "rights" as steering people to do what is right—for him, the free society is also the decent society in which people can simultaneously do good and do well.

Everywhere in America, Tocqueville is struck by how Americans look to themselves rather than the government to get things done. Initially people try to do things for themselves. If they can't, they rely on family. (Tocqueville notes that from the outset it was families, not individuals, who settled America.) Americans also employ what Tocqueville calls the "principle of association" to form countless voluntary groups—religious groups, recreational groups, philanthropic groups, educational institutions, and so on. Unlike in Europe, Tocqueville observes that in America "when a private individual meditates an undertaking, however directly connected it may be with the welfare of society, he never thinks of soliciting the cooperation of the government; but he publishes his plan, offers to execute it, courts the assistance of other individuals, and struggles manfully against all obstacles.... In the end the sum of these private undertakings far exceeds all that the government could have done."

At one point Tocqueville is amazed—he thinks it must be a joke—to see a large group of men gather together and vow to avoid intoxicating drink. Then he realizes that temperance is best achieved through this kind of voluntary social effort than through compulsory laws. "There is no end which the human will despairs of attaining through the combined power of individuals united into a society."

Tocqueville finds the same participatory spirit when it comes to democracy—the people get involved. Their involvement, however, is most active and effective at the local level. This is the spirit of the New England town meeting. Democracy works well here because people know their own problems and how best to solve them. Tocqueville takes a different view of the federal government. He terms it "an immense and tutelary power" which seeks to control people by promising "to secure their gratifications and to watch over their fate." Its power may seem mild at first but it could gradually expand until it becomes "absolute." Its promises are illusory. "It would be like the authority of a parent if . . . its object was to prepare men for manhood; but it seeks, on the contrary to keep them in perpetual childhood." In sum, an overweening federal government would make itself the provider and arbiter of the happiness of Americans, but what it would really do is "to spare them all care of thinking and all the trouble of living."[4]

Michel Foucault first came to America in the mid-1970s, after a meteoric career in France. Born in Poitiers, Foucault attended the prestigious Ecole Normale Superieure in Paris. There he got good grades, but also attempted suicide, evidently on account of depression caused by his latent homosexuality. Throughout his life, Foucault seems to have had a deathwish. In *The Passion of Michel Foucault*, his biographer James Miller reports that Foucault fantasized about being a martyr—not a martyr for God but a martyr for the "lyrical core of man, his invisible truth, his visible secret." Foucault also said that "it is in death that the individual becomes at one with himself....Let us hasten the appointed time when death permits us to rejoin our selves."[5] In other countries people who seriously believe such things are given medical treatment; in France they are lionized as philosophers.

In the early 1950s, Foucault joined the Communist Party, leaving it when Stalin's crimes were exposed by his successor Khrushchev. Foucault then taught in Tunisia, where he roomed with his homosexual companion Daniel Defert. Returning to the University of Paris in 1968, Foucault turned the philosophy department into a center of radical leftism. Once Foucault proved he could out-radical the radicals, he was honored with election to the prestigious College de France. While Tocqueville came to America as a young man without a reputation, Foucault came to America when he was perhaps the most influential intellectual in Europe, a position he attained upon the death of Jean-Paul Sartre.

Foucault did multiple teaching stints at Berkeley; he first came in 1975, then returned in 1979, again in 1980, and again in 1983—and during this time he lived in San Francisco, regularly sampling its gay neighborhoods. Eventually Foucault got AIDS, and it is during this time that I met him. He came to lecture at Dartmouth while I was a student there. I worked for the press office at the college, and got to take Foucault around campus and to his public event. I recall him as brooding and obsessive, and he had a rancid, sneering laugh that signaled both despair and a personal sense of superiority. He delivered his lecture in a soft monotone, reading from notes, and when it was finished I had no idea what he had spoken about. One of my friends unkindly remarked, "He's the kind of philosopher who gives bullshit a bad name." Now I realize why Foucault seemed so fragile and his voice so soft—Foucault had contracted AIDS, and he would die of it the following year.

Foucault spent more time in America than Tocqueville, but he wrote nothing substantial or interesting about this country. Part of the reason could be that he found America dull and vulgar; he would not be the first modern Frenchman to feel that way. But I believe the reason goes deeper. If we read Foucault's work, we see how he found America to be characteristic of what he considered most repressive about Western modernity.

Foucault hated capitalism and free trade, detecting in ostensibly free exchange a hidden form of oppression. "It is only too clear," Foucault said, "that we are living under a regime of dictatorship of class which imposes itself by violence, even when the instruments of this violence are institutional and constitutional." And what exactly are the symptoms of this class dictatorship? For Foucault, it came down to a belief and a fact. The belief, which happens to be a wrong belief, is that wealth under capitalism is a zero-sum game. The fact, which happens to be true, is that many people in the West are forced to take jobs for money. But so what? Foucault considered capitalism to be cruel and exploitative for making people work to get a paycheck. Foucault insisted that work should promote self-fulfillment. In this he was echoing the early Marx, and proving himself a true child of the 1960s. He was also foreshadowing the recent comments by Nancy Pelosi and Harry Reid to the effect that many Americans feel "locked" into their jobs and now can, thanks to Obamacare, quit and write poetry or do nothing at all.[6] Foucault also hated American foreign policy on the grounds that it was repressive and tyrannical. Foucault vehemently denounced America's involvement in Vietnam, and he participated in anti-war demonstrations organized by the French left in the late 1960s and early 1970s.

Foucault argued that the "real political task in a society such as ours is to criticize the workings of institutions, which appear to be both neutral and independent; to criticize and attack them in such a manner that the political violence which has always exercised itself obscurely through them will be unmasked, so that one can fight against them." This was the focus of his life's work. Yet Foucault did not recommend that power be reconstructed on the basis of justice. He considered "justice" itself to be an illusory idea. For Foucault, it was all about power and the only way to fight power was with power. In a discussion with fellow leftist Noam Chomsky, Foucault acknowledged that the strongest force motivating a proletariat is envy. Envy, said Foucault, leads not only to the desire for power but also to the desire for revenge. "The proletariat doesn't wage war against the ruling class because it considers such a war to be just. The proletariat makes war with the ruling class because, for the first time in history, it wants to take power. . . . When the proletariat takes power it may be quite possible that it will exert toward the classes over which it has just triumphed a violent, dictatorial, and even bloody power. I can't see what objection one can make to this." Chomsky was so disgusted that he later termed Foucault the most amoral man he had ever met.[7]

Foucault's enthusiasm for violent dictatorship went beyond the retaliatory repression of the Western proletariat. In the late 1970s, Foucault went to Iran to witness the pro-American Shah being ousted by the Ayatollah Khomeini. Foucault met Khomeini and praised him lavishly. He also rhapsodized about the Iranian revolution, insisting it would not result in a theocracy. "By Islamic government," he wrote, "nobody in Iran means a political regime in which the clerics would have a role of supervision or control." Iran, Foucault insisted, would be a fount of liberty. "With respect to liberties, they will be respected to the extent that their exercise will not harm others; minorities will be protected. . . . Between men and women, there will not be inequality with respect to rights. With respect to politics, decisions should be made by the majority." Overall, Foucault found the Khomeini revolution a spontaneous eruption of moral passion. He called it "spiritual politics," in contrast with ordinary politics. His point was that Iran was pushing the normal limits of what could be achieved through political action. "Pushing limits" was something Foucault considered a necessary antidote to Western oppression.

Foucault seemed unaware that the Ayatollah Khomeini had been giving sermons for decades outlining what type of Islamic government he favored. These ideas had been assembled in a book, *Islamic Government*, that Khomeini published a few years before he came to power. Upon taking control, Khomeini moved swiftly to implement his program, unleashing a reign of terror. At first, Foucault delighted in the execution of former officials and supporters of the Shah. Revolutions, Foucault said, should be expected to do such things. It was only when the Khomeini regime started executing liberals, leftists, and homosexuals, using the very technologies of surveillance, propaganda, and force that Foucault condemned in other contexts—only at this point did Foucault lose his enthusiasm. He stopped talking about Iran, moving on to other topics. Never, however, did he apologize for backing a tyranny far worse than that of any American institution. Instead of warning about the dangers of Islamic tyranny, he continued to warn about the dangers of liberal democracy.[8]

Why did Foucault find himself attracted to Khomeini in the first place? I suspect the reason has little to do with Iran. Sure, Foucault visited Iran a couple of times, but he seems to have seen Iran through the lens of his prejudices. In this Foucault was simply one in a long line of Western intellectuals who visited totalitarian countries and praised their system of government. Over the course of a century, progressive intellectuals visited Stalin's Russia, Mao's China, Castro's Cuba, and Ortega's Nicaragua and found themselves entranced by the peasant paradise they supposedly encountered. Somehow the repression was invisible to them—the information was available, but they ignored it. Evidently they projected their own discontents with the West onto these other countries and saw them for something quite different than they actually were.[9] So too Foucault somehow converted his hatred for America and the West into admiration for America's deadly adversary. From Foucault's perspective, Khomeini was commendable for calling America the "great Satan"; after all, that was pretty much Foucault's view also. Foucault's blindness can be summed up in Saul Bellow's remark, "A great deal of intelligence can be invested in ignorance when the need for illusion is deep."

Foucault's anti-Americanism might have remained undiluted if not for some of his actual experiences in America. Those experiences actually convinced Foucault that, at least in one crucial respect, he was wrong about America. Previously Foucault had considered Europe to be the center of sexual liberation, and America to be a relatively uptight, puritanical country. (This is still a view held by many.) Foucault's experiences in San Francisco completely changed his mind. Instead of seeing America as the epicenter of control and repression, Foucault came to see it as offering a new type of liberation.

Foucault's work focuses on the distinction between the "normal" and the "abnormal." In his early work Foucault wrote about madness. Madness, he wrote, was once considered normal in the West, as madmen freely roamed about during the Middle Ages, but now the West institutionalized mad people, criminalizing them for simply being different. Foucault proceeded to examine the prison system, and here he arrived at the startling insight that people are thrown into prison merely for being "abnormal." For Foucault, the prison system was a metaphor for modern life, in which we—who consider ourselves to be free agents—are in reality subjected to various forms of subtle institutional control. This control makes us conform to what is normal, expected, and obligatory, and avoid what is abnormal, eccentric, and forbidden. From madhouses and prisons, Foucault generalized that pretty much all institutions—schools, banks, factories, retail stores, healthcare centers, and military barracks—resemble madhouses and prisons. Foucault's work was devoted to unmasking these hidden and not-so-hidden forms of power, and to championing transgression and deviancy as mechanisms for breaking down power systems.

One may have guessed by now that this rigmarole was basically Foucault's lengthy apologia for homosexuality, and arguably in his case, also pedophilia. Foucault, you see, was a homosexual who liked to have sex with teenage boys. He devised an elaborate theory about how Western civilization had made a bogus distinction between heterosexual and homosexual, and also between adults and children, and how in reality everybody is sexual from birth and has the ability to fluidly move from heterosexual to homosexual inclinations, leaving nothing out—not even pedophilia. Foucault praised the way homosexual culture manipulates the male-female distinction, and repudiates conventional morality, replacing it with what Foucault termed "laboratories of sexual experimentation."[10]

Foucault's biographer James Miller reports that Foucault spent his days teaching, and his nights plunging into San Francisco's violent sadomasochistic culture. Here was a guy who was in slacks and tweed in the morning, and leather in the evening—complete with jockstrap, tit-clamps, handcuffs, whips, paddles, riding crops, and cock-ring. (I am not making this up; Miller is very specific.) Foucault liked to get drugged before sex. He said in 1975, after first trying LSD, "The only thing I can compare this experience to in my life is sex with a stranger." In San Francisco, he discovered he could have both. Foucault especially enjoyed sadomasochistic sex, including master-slave routines, which he saw as a kind of game. "Sometimes the scene begins with the master and slave, and at the end the slave has become the master. . . . This stragic game as a source of bodily pleasure is very interesting." Foucault viewed S & M as a "limit experience" that suited his general philosophical affinity for breaking rules and testing boundaries. At one point, Foucault lamented that heterosexuals were missing out. While a good deal of heterosexual energy was "channeled into courtship," Foucault remarked that gay sex was "devoted to intensifying the act of sex itself." Of the gay bathhouse culture, Foucault wrote, "It is regrettable that such places do not yet exist for heterosexuals."[11]

Foucault knew he was taking health risks. Even as late as 1983, when Foucault knew that AIDS was devastating the gay neighborhoods, he declared, "To die for the love of boys—what could be more beautiful?" Miller writes that Foucault may not have recognized, until the very end, that he had AIDS. Foucault's longtime companion Daniel Defert denies this, reporting that Foucault had a "real knowledge" he was infected. The point, however, is that he didn't seem to care. It's one thing to risk your own life, but Foucault seems to have been willing to risk the lives of others as well. Apparently he felt that others too should enjoy "limit experiences" even if those experiences killed them.[12]

Tocqueville and Foucault—two very different men, separated not only by different temperaments, but also by a century and a half.

Tocqueville visited a very different America than Foucault did. In a way they each celebrated a certain type of freedom. Tocqueville celebrated the spirit of 1776—a spirit of enterprise and voluntary organizations and religious freedom. Foucault celebrated the spirit of 1968—not freedom of enterprise or America as a force for freedom in the world, but rather pelvic freedom, freedom from traditional moral constraints. What is the difference between these types of freedom? Which is better? To answer these questions we must probe deeper the roots of 1776 and the roots of 1968.

CHAPTER 3

NOVUS ORDO SECLORUM

Great Britain hath no more right to put their hands
in my pocket without my consent, than I have to
put my hands into yours for money.[1]
—GEORGE WASHINGTON, 1774

I n 1978 I left India as a teenager. I left because I was weary of
the nepotism and corruption in India, the ignorance and venal-
ity of the politicians, the bribes one had to pay every day. In
India, as in most countries, your destiny is to a large degree given
to you. It depends on what kind of family you are born into, whether
you are male or female, and what caste you are. I wanted to be the
architect of my own destiny, a virtual impossibility in my native
country. Most of all I was frustrated by the lack of opportunity even
for someone bright and willing to work hard. Basically there was no
future for me in India; I had to look elsewhere. I wasn't alone: pretty
much everyone I knew was trying to get out. To Canada they went,
or Australia, or Dubai, or to sea.

For me, there was really one place to look. America, I had been
told, was a place big enough to take me in and to give me a chance

to realize my aspirations. In India, as in most places, life happens to you; in America, I came to believe, life is something you do. "Making it" doesn't just mean succeeding. It means making your life. I came to America alone, without family or relatives here, and without money. In America I have not only achieved my ambitions; I have outpaced them. I originally intended to become a corporate executive of some kind; instead I found my true vocation as a writer, speaker, and filmmaker. I came to discover America, and here in America I have discovered myself. In this country I have not only found success; I have also been able to write the script of my own life. In America your destiny isn't given to you; it is constructed by you.

My story may be unusual in certain respects, but it is also part of a larger American narrative. Over the centuries, tens of millions of immigrants have come to America, initially from various parts of Europe, now mostly from places like China, Korea, Sri Lanka, Haiti, and Mexico. Why do all these people come? First, they want to escape the places they are from. Something about those places suffocates their aspirations or undermines their dignity. Second, they come because they know America is different. America doesn't just offer them a more prosperous life; it also offers them a fuller and better life—a life that is unavailable elsewhere in the world.

Consider the Irish peasant of the mid-nineteenth century, living in a village where scarcity is the norm. The family lives in a tiny cottage, wears tattered clothes, and seldom has enough to eat. The structure of society is basically feudal. Large landowners direct the lives of those who labor on their property. They in turn are answerable to local aristocrats, who kowtow before even more powerful aristocrats, who are ultimately subservient to the English throne. As a peasant, you learn to play by the rules—rules that regulate your work, your food, and your family life. If you prove recalcitrant, the big men will beat and break you—at best, they will throw you off their land, and then you must find some other landlord before whom to bow and scrape. This bowing and scraping is humiliating, to be sure, but you aren't alone in this: even people in the highest quarters of life must learn the courtier virtues, which means bowing and scraping before others even higher and mightier than they are.

And so it goes, a way of life that seems impervious to change. You might even have regarded it as eternal, but then came the potato famine, a famine worse than any before it, and now you are threatened with death by starvation. You grow tired of eating insects and roots, and soon even these are scarce. You look into your children's eyes, and you know death lurks nearby for them and for you. Your family somehow gets out, on a boat, leaving behind everything you have, and the only life you know. This is how you come to America. Future generations will say you were an immigrant, and you came voluntarily. Your fate will be contrasted with that of African Americans who were brought here involuntarily, in chains. The distinction is a valid one, of course, and yet it is only technically true that you came of your own accord. In fact you were pushed out of your own country, driven abroad by hunger and desperation, and you found America not because you had a dream but because you were fleeing a nightmare.

Even in America, nothing is easy. No one invited you and your fellow Irish to come here; no one is especially excited that you are here. Everything is unfamiliar—the landscape, the way people talk, the food, the work. To add to your woes, there is overt discrimination. Jobs are posted with signs: "No Irish need apply." When there is work to be had, it is strenuous and sometimes dangerous, there is no insurance if you get sick or hurt, and you can be fired or replaced on a whim. The word among the immigrants is that the slaves down South have it better, because they are looked after in old age and sickness, while you must solve those problems for your-self. At times you are so disheartened you wish you could go back, but there is no going back—there is nothing to go back to. So you push on, enduring rather than prospering, surviving rather than thriving. Yet gradually your situation improves. Slowly—and it could take a couple of generations—your family and the other families who have settled in the new country win the long hard battle against necessity. Now you have "arrived," and in a sense you are an "insider" poignantly viewing the new immigrants who come after you. You know exactly the travails, and also the opportunities, that await them.

In Ireland you were a native; in America, you are a foreigner. You cling to your old ways, even when they don't work very well, and you search for others who look and talk like you, who know the old Irish songs. In time, however, you realize you must attempt to become part of the new country. This is not an option; it is something you must do. You have lived long enough in America that you are no longer fully Irish; yet neither are you fully Americanized. You are like a man walking a tightrope from one building to another, and now you are precariously between the two structures. You nervously look back—you are tempted to retreat—but at this point the distance you have already traveled is more perilous than the one in front of you. So intrepidly you push forward. In a manner your ancestors in the old country would have thought impossible, you resolve to stop thinking of yourself as Irish; instead, you "become American." And to your amazement you realize that you can do this. If you thought about it, you would realize how strange it is. No one can move from some other country to Ireland and "become Irish," any more than they can move to India and "become Indian." To be Irish you need Irish ancestors and Irish blood. To be Indian you need brown skin and Indian parents. By contrast with Ireland, India, and other countries, America is defined not by blood or birth but by the adoption of the nation's Constitution, its laws, and its shared way of life. That's how the Irish, the Italians, and the Jews, and today the Koreans, the South Asians, and the West Indians, can all come to this country and in time "become American."

This chapter is about the spirit of the American founding, the spirit of 1776. I intended to begin with a brief discussion of the history of immigrants coming to the United States, but soon I realized that the history of the United States is the history of immigration. Decades ago Franklin Roosevelt was invited to speak to the Daughters of the American Revolution. This is a conservative group whose members claim to be descended from the country's earliest settlers. Even so, President Roosevelt began by addressing the group, "Fellow immigrants." With the exception of African Americans who were brought here as slaves, all Americans are immigrants or descended from immigrants. Even the native Indians came to America from somewhere else; most likely they came from Asia and crossed the Bering Strait over a land bridge to the North American continent. Strictly speaking, they too are immigrants.

What is the relevance of America's immigrant heritage? It is that America has been from the beginning a special type of country. It was a country originally uninhabited and then settled by people who inevitably came from somewhere else. Immigrants are different from the normal type of person. First, they tend to be, by disposition or circumstance, restless people—people who are not content with the given order of things. Second, they tend to be risk-takers; they are willing to leave almost everything behind to make their lives over anew. Third, by necessity they become improvisers, people who can adapt to new conditions and learn what is necessary to survive and prosper. Fourth, immigrants are self-reliant folk. They leave behind the old social supports—of caste or family—to make a new life dependent on their own efforts. These are the types of people for whom America was made, and these are the people who have made America what she is today.

The spirit of 1776 is an immigrant spirit. It is the spirit of getting away from the old world and starting again. The same spirit that motivated people, before 1776 and after, to leave their native lands and come to America, motivated America's decision to declare its independence from Great Britain. In a way, the whole country decided to pack up and leave Mother England. Together, Americans resolved to make a new political and economic system for a new kind of people. Americans in the late eighteenth century understood very clearly what it meant to risk everything—including life itself—upon a new venture of nation-building. They understood this because they were of immigrant stock—they or their ancestors had individually undertaken the same risks that they were now jointly undertaking in violently breaking away from the British empire and setting up their *novus ordo seclorum*.

The immigrant character of Americans—and the American founding—is the essential background against which we must assess the progressive and left-wing critique of the spirit of 1776. This is a critique that dubs the American Founders to be landed gentry, rich white men who owned slaves, and who set up a government for the protection of their ancestral and aristocratic privileges. Although this critique became mainstream in the 1960s—and is now widely taught in schools and colleges—it originated with the early twentieth-century work of historian Charles Beard. In his magnum opus, *An Economic Interpretation of the Constitution*, Beard argued that the Founders were wealthy landowners with interests in farming and manufacturing and that many of them owned slaves. From this he deduced that the Constitution was little more than a mechanism for these rich white folk to protect and extend their own privileges.

Beard regarded it as highly significant that women, slaves, and indentured servants were not represented at the Philadelphia Constitutional Convention.[2]

These themes have been taken up by progressive scholars like Howard Zinn and Noam Chomsky. Chomsky contends that the American Founders, just like the British, were wealthy aristocrats who despised the ordinary working man whom they considered part of "the rabble." Consequently, Chomsky writes, the Founders sought to protect slave-owners and property owners, and to pass their privileges on to posterity. The constitutional debates reveal Madison's scheme to, as Chomsky puts it, "protect the minority of the opulent from the majority." Zinn too stresses the affluence of the Founders. "George Washington was the richest man in America. John Hancock was a prosperous Boston merchant. Benjamin Franklin was a wealthy printer." Zinn concludes that "from the founding of the nation to the present day, the government has generally legislated on behalf of the wealthy; has done the bidding of corporations in dealing with working people, and has taken the nation to war in the interests of economic expansion and political ambition."[3]

How fair are these accusations? Certainly the Founders were among the more prosperous and better-educated citizens of their society, and a good thing this is, for who knows what America would look like had it been founded by the least successful and most ignorant citizens of the time. Admittedly, out of the fifty-five men who gathered in Philadelphia, no less than thirty owned slaves. Even so, these were not landed aristocrats who sought to conserve and extend their own titles and privileges. The proof of that is simple: Where are those titles and privileges? When I recently visited Mount Vernon, I asked about the whereabouts of the descendants of Washington's extended family. The guide said she had no idea, but there was one relative who lived in the area, although she may have moved. In

any other country, this would be astonishing. People would expect
the descendants of the founder of the country to be basking in fame
and wealth. This option was available to Washington, who could
probably have become monarch if he had wanted to, and established
a royal lineage. Instead he renounced the monarchy and opted for
a system of government that would give members of the Washington
family no special advantages. Jefferson's descendants live in the
same historical obscurity. The only time I have seen a public reference to Jefferson's progeny is when the descendants of his slave Sally
Hemings appeared on *Oprah* to insist upon their blood connection
to America's third president.

If progressives are mistaken about the spirit of 1776—if in reality
that spirit is not one of landed aristocracy but of the immigrants—
then does the critique of the American founding go away? On the
contrary, it assumes an even more powerful and interesting thrust.
In its revised conception, the progressive critique is an attack on the
immigrants themselves. The charge of theft, previously pinned on
putative aristocrats, is now launched against the immigrants and
their progeny. The immigrants are faulted for being greedy and
acquisitive and for establishing a society as greedy and acquisitive
as themselves. No wonder that such a society seized the land from
the native Indians. This was the original thievery. No wonder that
these hard, selfish people took advantage of the slave-trade to import
Africans to work for free. No wonder that the settlers set about grabbing half of Mexico by force and later establishing imperial rule over
the Philippines. America, like South Africa, established a *herrenvolk*
democracy—in other words, a democracy for the white settlers and
their ilk to the exclusion of blacks and other minorities. This too was
a kind of piracy, robbing dark-skinned minorities of their goods and
rights under the law. Capitalism, many progressives suggest, is a
system of organized theft of what working people have produced; it

is well-suited to the dog-eat-dog qualities that immigrants display. And it is totally in character for these immigrant capitalists to want to use America's military power to subjugate and dominate the rest of the world.

Throughout this book, I will be examining and answering these charges. We cannot assess them, however, without asking what is new about the spirit of 1776. In a sense, this is an answer to the ignorance of President Obama. Asked in 2009 whether he believed America is exceptional, Obama replied that he believed America is exceptional in the same way the British believe Britain is exceptional, or the Greeks believe that Greece is exceptional. Obama's real point was that America was no more exceptional than any other country.[4] In the spirit of presidential education, I venture to prove him wrong. Here I content myself with specifying the two unique principles that were articulated by Thomas Jefferson in the Declaration of Independence in 1776 and then integrated into the Constitution and the political architecture of the American founding. These principles are represented in two significant phrases: "created equal" and the "pursuit of happiness."

According to Thomas Jefferson, the American Revolution was motivated by "the palpable truth that the mass of mankind has not been born with saddles on their back, nor a favored few booted and spurred, ready to ride them legitimately, by the grace of God."[5] This may seem like verbal extravagance on Jefferson's part, except that before the American Revolution, all governments in all countries were based on a favored few, booted and spurred, claiming their authority to saddle, ride, and rule the mass of mankind. This is not to say that citizens everywhere had no rights. England, for instance, granted rights to citizens in a tradition stretching back to the Magna Carta. The operative term, however, is "granted." In England, as in other countries, it was the king or the ruling class that conferred rights and privileges from above. If the people enjoyed rights and protections, those were the king's to give, and were granted out of his magnanimity. In England the Crown was also considered the owner of all real property in the realm, and property rights were simply temporary grants of use conferred by the monarch. By themselves—and absent this bestowal of royal title and privilege—the people had no rights and owned nothing.

The American Revolution inaugurated the first government in the world that was based on the principle that sovereignty and rights are in the people and not in the king or the ruling class. It is sometimes said that while European countries located sovereignty in "divine right," America located sovereignty in "the consent of the governed." But this is not correct. Consider Jefferson's famous proclamation, in the Declaration, that "all men are created equal and endowed by their Creator with certain unalienable rights." Notice that Jefferson—who was a man of the Enlightenment, and by no means an orthodox Christian—nevertheless locates the source of equality and rights in a single source: the Creator. Why does he not locate the doctrine of equality in the people, in the consent of the governed? Because never have "all men" or all people ever given their consent to such a proposition. Moreover, even if they did, all people don't become equal—any more than they become tall or intelligent or morally good—by mutual or common agreement!

What Jefferson means is that all people are equal in having a shared human nature. Being human, they are of equal moral value in the eyes of their Creator. And it is because of this equality that legitimate government derives its authority to rule from the consent of the governed. Far from denying divine right, Jefferson appeals to it. In the American case, however, God sanctions a system in which sovereignty or ultimate authority derives not from the king but from the people. Royal sovereignty under God gives way to common sovereignty under God. America establishes the first government in history that is based on "We the people."

This is a momentous change. Instead of rights and privileges flowing "down" from the king to the people, they now flow "up" from the people to the government. In the old case the king granted limited authority and power to the people; in America, the people grant limited authority and power to their rulers. Elsewhere, the people are subjects and thus subjected to the laws, possessing rights only at the behest of the government. In America, there are no subjects, only citizens. Citizens are subject only to laws that they themselves make through their elected representatives. The representatives possess this power at the behest of the people, and they must obey the same laws as the rest of the people.

So the government that controls the people is, through majority rule, selected by the people. But who controls the government? The American answer to this question is: the Constitution. Once again, the American solution can be contrasted with English practice. England has no written constitution; instead, English law is based on a common law that has evolved over the centuries. The American Founders, however, adopted a Constitution which is a "higher law," a law that trumps even majority rule. Why is such a law necessary? When governments are given power through a democratic process, why do they need to be restricted and over-ridden by a higher law? The reason is that the American Founders recognized the limits of majority rule.

It may seem odd, in a democracy, that there should be any limits on majority rule. The reason for the limits is that the people as a whole have created the government, and the government must rule on behalf of the whole people. In the American context, of course, there are complications with the concept of the "whole people." The states, not the people directly, approved the Constitution. And even today, in presidential elections, the people choose their leader through the states. ("The state of Virginia goes for Barack Obama.") Even so, the point remains that government gets its moral legitimacy from the whole people, and in a sense, the only fully legitimate government is one that rules by consensus: the people decide as a whole. The problem is that, in practice, consensus is nearly impossible to achieve. So majority rule is the next best substitute. Still, majority rule must be set up in such a way that the majority rules on behalf of the whole. Madison writes that "the will of the majority" must be a "plenary substitute" for "the will of the whole society."[6]

Another way to put it is that the majority must not use its power to trample on minority rights. The Founders were very concerned about this. What if the majority decides, for instance, to confiscate the property of the minority? The Founders insisted that "tyranny of the majority" is just as dangerous as having a one-man tyrant. In some ways, it's more dangerous. It's bad enough to be oppressed by one man—even worse to be oppressed by the bulk of your fellow citizens. In *Notes on Virginia* Jefferson declared that "an elective despotism was not the government we fought for."[7]

Consequently the American Founders implemented multiple mechanisms for limiting the power of the central government—even an elected government—and for ensuring that this government did not become oppressive to all or even some of its citizens. The Constitution is a charter for limited government. Basically it says that the federal government can do this, this, and this. And beyond this, the federal government has no power to act. When Thomas Jefferson and later James Madison proposed that a Bill of Rights be added to the Constitution, Alexander Hamilton objected. In *Federalist* No. 84, Hamilton said enumerating such rights was "not only unnecessary" but could "even be dangerous." He asked, "Why declare that things shall not be done which there is no power to do?" He added, "Why, for instance should it be said that the liberty of the press shall not be restrained, when no power is given by which restrictions may be imposed?" Hamilton was concerned that specifying a list of restraints on federal power might encourage the government to claim unwarranted authority in areas where no specific restraints were listed.[8] But others wanted it in writing that government could not abridge certain fundamental rights, and so the Bill of Rights was adopted in the form of amendments to the Constitution.

In addition to limiting the size and power of the federal government, the Founders divided power between the federal government on the one hand, and states and local governments on the other. This principle is called "federalism." They also divided the federal government between a legislature, executive, and judiciary, which we know as a "separation of powers" and they instituted a system of "checks and balances" giving different branches of government (say the House and the Senate, or the president and the Congress, or Congress and the courts) authority to exercise competing authority on the same issue. This is a way of blocking schemes that don't enjoy broad support from going through.

In *Federalist* No. 51, Madison gave the underlying rationale for all this. Governments become oppressive, he writes, because of the infirmity in human nature. "If angels were to govern men, neither external nor internal controls on government would be necessary." But this is not the case: in place of angels, we have people like George W. Bush and Barack Obama. Such people have their own agenda; competing agendas form what Madison terms "factions." Each faction is likely to try and usurp the whole government and promote its own program. Consequently, factions must be thwarted, not by abolishing them, but by setting them against each other. "Ambition must be made to counteract ambition," Madison writes. This amounts to a "policy of supplying, by opposite and rival interests, the defect of better motives." This way the only projects that get approved are ones that serve the public good. The whole objective is to ensure that "the private interest of every individual may be a sentinel over the public rights."[9]

I mention all this because many of these carefully devised safeguards have been brazenly ignored in recent decades, with presidents and the federal government usurping authority reserved to the states, ignoring the Constitution when it limits the scope of governmental action, getting into wars without proper congressional authority, politicizing the courts, and so on. These offenses have been committed by Democrats and Republicans, progressives and conservatives, although the most flagrant violations are by Democrats and progressives who increasingly don't even pretend to feel inhibited by the Constitution. As a result, we now have a Leviathan state, far from the limited government the Founders envisioned. The government that was set up to protect our rights has in many cases become a danger to our rights. I will say more about this in a later chapter.

If one unique principle of the American founding was the idea that all men are created equal and endowed with unalienable rights, a second unique principle is the creation of a free market society with business as the national vocation and the innovator and entrepreneur as the embodiments of the American dream. Marx understood this. Writing in the mid-nineteenth century, he termed the United States "the most modern example of bourgeois society."[10] Yet America's commercial emphasis may seem unfamiliar to many today, because progressives have been attempting to redirect the energy of the American people—especially young people—away from the private commercial sector toward the government sector. When I first came to the United States in the late 1970s, the tone had been set by John F. Kennedy. Kennedy said to Americans: If you are young, if you are idealistic, then do what? Join the Peace Corps! Become a public servant. For JFK, there were nobler things to do with your life than work for a profit-making corporation. If you did that, you were a greedy, selfish guy. But if you became a bureaucrat, or went on a Peace Corps mission and lived in a hut in Africa, you were a morally wonderful person. We hear the same thing from Obama, who routinely tells young people in his graduation speeches: don't go for the brass ring, the corner office, the big promotion.[11] Presumably, he wants Americans to become community organizers or union bosses or go to work for the federal government. In the progressive lexicon, "business" is a term of derision and becoming a political activist or a federal bureaucrat is what the American dream is all about.

Not for the Founders. The Founders knew that, historically, in most cultures, business and trade were reviled. For nearly two millennia, across the world, the merchant and entrepreneur have been regarded as low-life scum. Confucius says, "The virtuous man knows what is noble. The low man knows what is profitable." In Japan, the social hierarchy placed the imperial family and the lords at the top, the warriors or samurai below them, then the farmers and artisans, and finally the merchants lowest of all. In the Indian caste system, the top rung is occupied by the priest, the next rung by the nobility, the next by the warriors, and down the list we go, until one step from the bottom, just above the hated untouchable, we find the merchant and the trader. Historian Ibn Khaldun, one of the great Islamic thinkers of the Middle Ages, has an essay arguing that looting is a morally preferable way to trade to acquire wealth. Why? Because trade is based on exploitation of the needs of others and is therefore base and shameful. Looting, by contrast, is courageous and manly, since you have to defeat a rival in open combat and take his stuff.[12] Even today in Europe, it's better to have inherited money than earned money. Inherited money is seen as innocent, like manna dropping from heaven, while earned money is seen as the result of some sort of exploitation.

The American Founders were well aware of this social hierarchy, and they inverted it. In a sense, they turned the whole totem pole upside down, so that in their new regime, the bottom-runged entrepreneur would now come to the top. The Founders began by rejecting the premise that undergirded property rights in England. Under English law, all property was owned by the king. Historian Forrest McDonald points out that according to English common law "every legitimate title to real property derived ultimately from a grant by the king." This same principle extended to the liberty to contract for work and keep the fruits of one's labor. That liberty too, McDonald notes, was considered a grant from the Crown.[13] While America's property and contract law was originally based on English law, the American Revolution changed all that. In the *novus ordo seclorum*, people would have a natural right—a God-given right—to their own property and to the benefits of their own labor and creativity. The Founders ensured the protection of this right in two ways.

First, the new regime set about to encourage new inventions and technology, which are the driving force of entrepreneurial capitalism. Capitalism is not merely a system for motivating work or distributing rewards in proportion to value created; it is also a system for creating new wealth, and there is no more obvious way to do that than through inventions and technology. The original Constitution—before the addition of the Bill of Rights—only mentions a single right, the right to patents and copyrights. Article 1, Section 8 of the Constitution gives Congress the power "to promote the Progress of Science and useful Arts, by securing for limited Times to Authors and Inventors the exclusive Right to their respective Writings and Discoveries." America may be the only country in the world to give patents and copyrights constitutional status. Commenting on this provision, Abraham Lincoln—himself a patent holder—said that the Founders sought to add "the fuel of interest to the fire of genius in the discovery and production of new and useful things."[14]

A second way the Founders sought to advance commerce and entrepreneurship is by encouraging a system of "natural liberty" in which people can buy and sell what they want, and work where they want, rising as far as their skills and talents take them. In other words, the Founders set up a market meritocracy. The twelfth book of *The Federalist* states that the new government in America has been set up to enable the efforts of "the assiduous merchant, the laborious husbandman, the active mechanic, and the industrious manufacturer" to "vivify and invigorate all the channels of industry and make them flow with greater activity and copiousness." Similarly Madison says in *Federalist* No. 10 that "the first object of government" is the "protection of different and unequal faculties of acquiring property."[15] Note that this is the primary goal of the new regime. Inequality of outcomes is not seen as a necessary evil that government should seek to remedy; rather, the government itself exists to guard citizens' right to accumulate unequal fortunes and property.

Some progressives regard the term "meritocracy" with suspicion, believing that it contradicts the equality provision of the Declaration of Independence. Thomas Jefferson, however, did not agree. Jefferson declared that "there is a natural aristocracy among men," and he went on to say he considered it "the most precious gift of nature." Jefferson's defense of aristocracy may seem surprising, because like most of the Founders he was a fierce enemy of the aristocracies of Europe. But Jefferson emphasized that he opposed those hierarchies because they were based on chance and inheritance. He called the European system an "artificial aristocracy" and a "tinsel aristocracy" because its claims to excellence were spurious. Jefferson supported differences that were based on achievement and merit.[16] We see clearly here how, from the point of view of Jefferson and the Founders, the Declaration of Independence does not mean we are equal in endowments, only in rights. Equality of rights not only permits inequality of success or outcomes; it provides the moral justification for inequality of outcomes. It is fair that some receive gold and silver medals when everyone competed in the contest according to the same rules.

Since the American founding, the American formula of democratic self-government—of making the people control the rulers, and not the other way around—has become a virtually unquestioned norm for the world. Even governments that violate democracy pretend to rule on behalf of the people. Moreover, America's focus on the entrepreneur has produced the most inventive and entrepreneurial society in history, which has benefited not just business-owners but workers and ordinary people. Already by 1815, historian Daniel Walker Howe points out, Americans were better fed and in better health than their English counterparts. Between 1830 and 1950, America had the fastest-growing economy in the world. By the mid-twentieth century, the American economy was so productive that a nation with around 5 percent of the world's population accounted for one-fourth of the global economy.[17] In America I am not surprised by how good the people at the top have it; I am amazed to see what a good life America has provided for its common man. Even people of little education and ordinary ability—I would go so far as to say even the unimpressive and the lazy—have nice homes and nice cars and take annual vacations. I do not believe that all this will be true in the future, but it has been true for the past half century.

Even today, the spirit of 1776 is very much alive, as American technology continues to lead the world and many Americans continue to guard their liberties and property from government usurpation. At the same time, the spirit of 1776 is no longer the only, and perhaps no longer the dominant, spirit in America. It now has a serious rival—the spirit of 1968, the progressive spirit—that intends to become its permanent replacement. If that happens then America will, in a way, have been un-founded and re-founded, and a new group of people will have to be dubbed America's founding fathers.

CHAPTER 4

AMERICA THE INEXCUSABLE

*I thought of myself as a revolutionary, committed to
overturning the whole system of empire.*[1]

—BILL AYERS, *PUBLIC ENEMY*

The terrorists who bombed the Pentagon did not think they
were doing anything wrong. They believed they were justified, because America was the bad guy, the Great Satan, and
they were fighting against the evil empire. Initially they intended to
strike against the symbols of American wealth and power. Ultimately they would have to find a way to dismantle the power structures themselves. For these hardened men, and their terrorist group,
extremism in defense of national liberation was no vice; moderation
in pursuit of justice was no virtue. To this day they have no regrets
over what they did. Am I referring to Osama bin Laden, circa September 11, 2001? No, I am referring to Bill Ayers, circa 1972. Three
decades before bin Laden and al Qaeda struck at the Pentagon and
other American targets from abroad, Bill Ayers and his Weather
Underground bombed the Pentagon and other targets from inside

America. Too bad for them the two groups didn't meet; they could have worked together toward their common aim.

"Everything was absolutely ideal on the day I bombed the Pentagon," Ayers recalls in his memoir *Fugitive Days*. "The sky was blue. The birds were singing. And the bastards were finally going to get what was coming to them." The bastards in this case were the U.S. military and the U.S. Congress. Ayers was getting ready to do to them what he believed they were doing to others. The Weather Underground's targets were the Pentagon and the U.S. Capitol. Ayers was sick of merely protesting the Vietnam War. It was time to take action, what Ayers terms the "propaganda of the deed." Why the Pentagon? "The Pentagon was ground zero for war and conquest, organizing headquarters for a gang of murdering thieves, a colossal stain on the planet, a hated symbol everywhere around the world." Why the Capitol? "We have attacked the Capitol because it is, along with the White House . . . a monument to U.S. domination over the planet." Al Qaeda could hardly have put it better.

Ayers had been radicalized by the Vietnam War—a war that he saw as part of a global struggle against U.S. imperialism. "My country stood on the wrong side of an exploding world revolution," he says. "I thought of myself as a revolutionary, committed to overturning the whole system of empire." To prepare himself, he and his friends studied the revolutionary manuals. "We read Castro and Guevara, Lenin and Mao, Cabral and Nkrumah, but on any point of ideology we turned most often to Ho Chi Minh." For Ayers, Vietnam was a simple story of the good guys versus the bad guys. "The basic story line for us . . . was that Vietnam was fundamentally united fighting an aggressive invader from the West, that the Vietnamese allied with the West were puppets artificially installed, and that Vietnam would ultimately win." Ayers wanted Vietnam to defeat the United States. "I'm not so much against the war as I am for a Vietnamese victory. I'm not so much for peace as for a U.S. defeat."

Despite the centrality of Vietnam, however, Ayers was fighting a larger battle. "We had been insistent in our anti-Americanism, our opposition to a national story stained with conquest and slavery and attempted genocide." And finally the culprit was being held to account. Ayers found himself, he writes, in "a world in flames—mass demonstrations in the South, revolution in Latin America, upheaval across Asia, liberation in Africa, roiling tension in our cities, nuclear annihilation and mass murder hanging precariously over our heads." Ayers concluded, "Seen through one lens, the madness was the war in Vietnam, and the monster was the politics and policy of that war. Through another, the madness was an aggressive and acquisitive foreign policy, and the monster the military-industrial complex. And through a third lens, our lens, the madness was the export of war and fascism into the third world, racism and white supremacy at home, the inert, impoverished culture of greed and alienation: the monster would be capitalism itself, the system of imperialism."

Today Ayers is a respected professor of education at the University of Illinois at Chicago. Normally terrorists get sent to prison or Guantanamo; in this case, he got tenure. In fact, Ayers is one of the leading voices in elementary and secondary education in the country today. While Osama bin Laden is in his grave, and his successor Ayman al-Zawahiri is a hunted man, Ayers attends academic conferences and is well-paid on the speaker circuit. I recently debated Ayers at Dartmouth. His speech echoed the themes of an earlier rant he delivered at the University of Oregon. There he crowed, "The American Empire is in decline, economically, politically, and in some ways culturally. The empire is declining and the game is over."

Was Ayers rehabilitated by the progressives because he has sorrowfully repented and recanted? Actually, no. On September 11, 2001, the fateful day bin Laden struck the Pentagon and the World Trade Center, the *New York Times* published a profile of Ayers to coincide with the publication of his memoir. Ayers told reporter

Dinitia Smith, "I don't regret setting bombs. I feel we didn't do enough." Ayers has said that he might do it again. "I can't quite imagine putting a bomb in a building today . . . but I can't imagine entirely dismissing the possibility either."[2]

Ayers is a significant fellow in his own right, but he is also significant for his connection with President Obama. Ayers hosted a fundraising event for Obama in Chicago in 1995; the two of them have been friends for nearly twenty years. They have worked together, socialized together, and served on boards together. Even so, when the Obama-Ayers connection surfaced in the media, Obama and his aides pretended that Obama barely knew Ayers. Their only link, according to Obama aide David Axelrod, was that they lived in the same neighborhood and their kids went to the same school together. This of course was a bald-faced lie. Obama tried to cover his tracks, saying he should not be held responsible for what Ayers did "forty years ago, when I was eight years old." But of course the issue isn't just Ayers in the 1970s, but Ayers today. Obama failed to mention that Ayers has refused to apologize for his past, and that Ayers sees himself now as the same person with the same convictions he had then.

From Ayers's own words we see that he was galvanized into action by the Vietnam War. Here in America, Vietnam was largely interpreted through an anti-Communist lens, a way of stopping the dominoes from falling in Southeast Asia. Yet this is not how Ayers viewed Vietnam—rather, he saw it largely through the lens of anti-colonialism. And Ho Chi Minh, the leader of the North Vietnamese, saw the war in exactly the same way. In a sense they were right. Vietnam was a colony of the French, and when the French withdrew in the early 1950s, the Americans stepped in. In Ayers's day, there were numerous other anti-colonial struggles going on in Asia, Africa, and South America. Ayers candidly describes himself as a guerilla fighter for anti-colonialism, with the difference that his operations were being conducted inside America, within the belly of the beast.

We see from Ayers—a Chicago boy who came to see his destiny as linked with that of Che Guevara and Ho Chi Minh—how anti-colonialism started as a Third World phenomenon but was imported to America through the Vietnam War. Thanks to Vietnam, the most important political movement in the non-Western world in the past century also became one of the most important movements in America. Anti-colonialism became embedded within the American left, and thus Ayers could join a global effort to defeat America without setting foot outside his own country. Rather, he went underground in America. Anti-colonialism itself became the underground ideology of American progressivism, so that black and native Indian and feminist and gay activists in the 1960s and 1970s saw themselves as fighting in some sense the same battle being waged by the anti-Vietnam movement and by the Vietnamese guerillas themselves. What unified them all was the conviction of America the Inexcusable.

This was the theme of the class of 1968; it was their shared ideology. I could choose as representative of that ideology any of a vast assortment of characters, from MIT activist Noam Chomsky to Yippie showman Abbie Hoffman to Columbia hothead Mark Rudd to folk singer Joan Baez to actress and radical activist Jane Fonda to her former husband (and Students for a Democratic Society founder) Tom Hayden. Except for Chomsky—who rages on in his eighties—the others are now irrelevant. So I have chosen instead to highlight a different cast of characters: Bill Ayers, Frank Marshall Davis, Edward Said, Roberto Mangabeira Unger, and Jeremiah Wright. This is a group I've previously called "Obama's founding fathers." Their relevance is that they articulate the ideology of 1968 while also demonstrating how that ideology was imbibed by Obama right here in America—in Hawaii, at Columbia, at Harvard Law School, and in Chicago.

In my previous book *Obama's America* I discussed in detail this cast of characters; here I just want to give a sense of their depth of alienation from America, and their open hostility to America's foreign policy and free market system. Frank Marshall Davis, the former Communist who was Obama's mentor in Hawaii, was so radical that he opposed President Truman's Marshall Plan as a "device" for maintaining "white imperialism." Truman and Marshall, he wrote, were using "billions of U.S. dollars to bolster the tottering empires of England, France, Belgium, Holland and the other western exploiters of teeming millions." Indeed the objective of America after World War II was "to re-enslave the yellow and brown and black peoples of the world." While Davis spurned America he praised "Red Russia" as "my friend."[3] Young Obama—sitting in Davis's hut in Hawaii week after week for several years—took it all in. This portrait of devoted young Obama imbibing the ravings of a pot-smoking former Communist is the progressive version of a Norman Rockwell painting.

At Columbia, Obama studied under the Palestinian scholar and activist Edward Said. Before his death in 2003, Said was a vehement critic of America, a country with a "history of reducing whole peoples, countries and even continents to ruin by nothing short of holocaust." Said alleged that America replaced Britain and France as a global imperialist power after World War II. As a Palestinian, Said considered Israel the small colonial power and America the big colonial power. If Israel was the Little Satan, America was the Great Satan. "The United States," Said wrote, "virtually underwrites the occupation of the West Bank and Gaza and in effect pays for the bullets that kill Palestinians." Consequently the Palestinians have a right to use violence to fight back in what Said termed "one of the great anti-colonial insurrections of the modern period." The use of force is legitimate in this context "to repossess a land and a history that have been wrested from us." Like Ayers, Said believed in the propaganda of the deed, and there is a picture of him online throwing rocks at Israel. Of course the gesture is symbolic. Even so, for his support of Palestinian guerilla action, this former member of the Palestine National Council and associate of Yasser Arafat was termed a "Professor of Terror."[4]

Roberto Mangabeira Unger, Obama's teacher at Harvard Law School and friend since then, has sought to hide his association with Obama. "I am a leftist," he later told an Obama biographer, "and by conviction as well as temperament, a revolutionary. Any association of mine with Barack Obama . . . could only do harm." Unger advocates what he terms "world revolution," a basic takeover of financial institutions and their reshaping to serve global economic equity. For instance, Unger calls for "the dismembership of the traditional property right" in favor of what he calls "social endowments." Most remarkably, Unger calls for a global coalition of countries—supported by American progressives—to reduce the influence of the United States. He calls this a "ganging up of lesser powers against the United States." He specifically calls for China, India, Russia, and Brazil to lead this anti-American coalition. Unger says that global justice is impossible when a single superpower dominates. He wants a "containment of American hegemony" and its replacement by a plurality of centers of power. "Better American hegemony than any other order that is now thinkable," he admits. "But much better yet no hegemony at all."[5]

Finally there is Obama's long-time preacher Jeremiah Wright. We've heard about how Obama somehow sat in his church for two decades and yet heard nothing of Wright's radical ideology. Even progressives know this is bunkum. From Wright's infamous sermon "The Day of Jerusalem's Fall," delivered on September 16, 2001, we

get the standard anti-colonial theft doctrine. "We took this country
by terror away from the Sioux, the Apache, the Iroquois, the Comanche, the Arapaho, the Navajo. Terrorism. We took Africans from their
country to build our way out of ease and kept them enslaved and
living in fear. Terrorism. We bombed Grenada and killed innocent
civilians, babies, non-military personnel; we bombed the black civil-
ian community of Panama, with stealth bombers, and killed
unarmed teenagers and toddlers, pregnant mothers and hard-
working fathers. We bombed Qaddafi's home and killed his child.
We bombed Iraq; we killed unarmed civilians trying to make a living.
We bombed a plant in Sudan to pay back an attack on our embassy.
Killed hundreds of hard-working people, mothers and fathers who
left home to go to work that day, not knowing they would never get
back home. We've bombed Hiroshima, we've bombed Nagasaki,
we've nuked far more than the thousands in New York and the Pentagon and we never batted an eye. Kids playing in the playground,
mothers picking up children after school, civilians, not soldiers,
people just trying to make it day by day. We have supported state
terrorism against the Palestinians and black South Africans, and we
are indignant. Because the stuff we have done overseas is now
brought back into our own front yard."[6] Translation: we are the bad
guys and we deserved the 9/11 attacks.

Notice that Obama's founding fathers are not mere dissenters
who think that some of America's actions may have been mistaken
or counterproductive. Rather, this is a group that detests America's
role in history and in the world, loathes America's core institutions,
and seeks to undermine America and even do physical harm to
America and to Americans. Yet this is the group that has taught and
shaped President Obama. No wonder that Obama is different from
any previous president. He's a Democrat, but he is unlike Truman

or John F. Kennedy, or even Jimmy Carter. The reason? Obama is the first president whose ideology was shaped by the radical 1960s.

Bill Clinton was the first president who grew up in the 1960s, yet Clinton was also shaped by older influences, including Southern patriotism and Bible Belt conservatism. Clinton came of age in the era of the sexual revolution, and his personal behavior displayed the self-indulgence of the 1960s, yet Clinton's policies showed nothing of the animus toward America that we find in Davis, Said, Unger, Ayers, and Wright. I am sure if you asked Clinton, even today, whether he would like to see America remain number one, he would emphatically say yes and be astonished that he was even being asked the question. With Obama, however, who knows what he would say, and whatever he said, it would probably be quite different from what he actually felt. The reason Obama has evaded and lied about his associations is that he doesn't want people to know what he learned from them, and the degree to which their views of America are also his. Born in 1961, Obama was too young to have participated in the radicalism of the 1960s, but he is our first president who has learned, from the ideologues of that era, to think of his own country as America the Inexcusable.

How did we get the 1960s? One is tempted to locate the ideological roots of this era in the 1930s. The expansion of the welfare state that President Lyndon Johnson termed the Great Society seems to have originated in President Franklin Roosevelt's New Deal three decades earlier. It is true that FDR made some radical speeches that repudiate the principles of the founding. While the Founders considered the government to be the enemy of rights—several provisions of the Bill of Rights begin, "Congress shall make no law ... "—FDR insisted that the government is the friend and the guarantor of rights. While the Founders regarded economic liberty as a basic right, FDR justified the curtailments of economic liberty for some in the name of economic security for all. Even so, the New Deal's actual programs were relatively modest, and they were a response to an emergency situation, namely the Great Depression. According to historian David Kennedy, FDR feared that after the Depression America's economy might never grow again; he viewed the pie as fixed, and his redistribution programs were based on what turned out to be a false assumption. I am not blaming FDR: many reasonable people in the 1930s believed that capitalism had failed, and that something new had to be tried.[7]

In the 1960s, by contrast, capitalism was working well and the economy was booming. The welfare state represented a massive expansion and acceleration of government programs, and thus it did constitute a real shift away from the spirit of 1776. Moreover, the 1960s introduced other new elements—the attack on America as a rogue nation, the repudiation of traditional moral and social values—that were simply not present in the 1930s. So ideologically, the 1960s represent a coming together of diverse radical impulses, some from the past, some new, which led to a new way of living in America, a real breaking point. The spirit of 1968 is starkly opposed to the spirit of 1776.

Recall that this is the first time that America truly had a "generation gap," a chasm between parents and children. In previous generations, children wanted to be like their parents. They wanted, as quickly as possible, to grow up and become adults. In the 1960s, however, children regarded themselves as morally superior to their parents, even while indulging in irresponsible behaviors like lawlessness and drug-taking that their parents had never even considered. In short order, the children became incomprehensible to their parents, not only in their music, but also in their values. And while the parents grew older, the children, in a sense, never grew up. They remained, as it were, perpetual adolescents. Now they are graying and grayed adolescents, a breed the world has never seen before. So America is now divided into the group that is a product of the 1960s, and the group that never quite embraced the values of the 1960s. Over time, the generation gap has become an ideological gap. The parents, in a sense, represented the spirit of 1776 and their children the new spirit of 1968.

We think of the 1960s as reflected in its bohemianism, its sexual experimentation, its skepticism toward America, and so on, but all these traits are also evident in the Beatniks of the 1950s. "America I've given you all and now I'm nothing," Allen Ginsberg wrote in his poem titled *America*. "America when will you stop destroying human souls?" Ginsberg is not shy in that poem about advertising his homo-sexuality, his rejection of conventional religion, or his affinity for the Communists. "America I used to be a communist . . . I'm not sorry." "I won't say the Lord's Prayer." "America I'm putting my queer shoulder to the wheel." In his poem *Howl* Ginsberg raged against "robot apartments" and "invisible suburbs" and "demonic industries" and "monstrous bombs." His first line shows a recognizable self-indulgent hubris. "I saw the best minds of my generation destroyed by madness."[8] The best minds are clearly his and those of his icono-clastic friends. Together Ginsberg, Jack Kerouac, Neal Cassady, and others defined a "Beat" sensibility. Kerouac's *On the Road* came to symbolize not only the nomadic life but also nomadic values—values that departed from those of traditional America.

I met Ginsberg at Dartmouth in the 1980s—he came with his catamite Peter Orlovsky. While I tried to learn from Ginsberg about what motivated him—what caused him to become such a rebel—he kept urging me to read Orlovsky's new collection, *Clean Asshole Poems*. The title, Ginsberg assured me, was derived from India, where people wash with water and therefore have much cleaner rear ends than people in the West. Ginsberg had a particular fascination with me because of my Indian origin. He seemed to associate India with spiritual and sexual liberation, and my efforts to acquaint him with dowry, arranged marriage, or the caste system—Indian institutions that could scarcely be termed "liberating"—provoked little interest. What I did learn from Ginsberg is that the Beats were "ahead of their time," and that the bohemian culture that was confined to small precincts of San Francisco and Greenwich Village in the 1950s went mainstream in the 1960s. "Suddenly," Ginsberg told me, "we were everywhere."

How did this happen? It is tempting to answer: Vietnam, Civil Rights, feminism, the sexual revolution. Those were all huge events, and yet the 1960s cannot fully be explained by them. On the contrary, it is the spirit of the 1960s that explains why those movements evolved in the way they did. Consider Vietnam. It was a terrible war, but that can't account for why it produced so much alienation, since it was much less terrible than Word War II. It was a "colonial war" in the eyes of its enemies, but was it any different in that regard from the Korean War? Something more was going on.

Similarly feminism and the sexual revolution cannot explain the 1960s; indeed, both really began, and were made possible, by the technological revolution of the late 1940s and 1950s. Feminism and the sexual revolution were enabled by technology—not only the pill but also labor-saving household devices like the vacuum cleaner. Suddenly it became possible for women to control their fertility, and housework became a part-time occupation. These devices made possible a new way of life in the 1960s, but underlying the change was a shift in values that caused large numbers of people to seek this new way of life. While human nature has always been what it is, suddenly in the late 1960s an ever-increasing number of women started having sex (and babies) before marriage, and demanding that they be treated "just like men." We need to ask what made them want this for themselves.

While many former activists of the 1960s now admit their self-indulgences, they uniformly insist that they were also moved by a higher cause—the cause of Civil Rights. Yet the activists of the 1960s were on the periphery of the Civil Rights movement, which was a black-led and black-dominated movement. Sure, the Bill and Hillary types may have spent a summer in the South, having sex and picketing, but their influence on the Civil Rights Revolution was marginal. In Spike Lee's film *Malcolm X*, he depicts an actual incident in which a young white activist approached Malcolm X asking what she could do to help the cause of the black people. Malcolm X answered, "Nothing." The girl was crushed. Now this may seem like an insensitive answer, but it was actually honest. Malcolm X realized that the young woman couldn't do much, and doing much wasn't even her real goal. Mainly she wanted to feel good about herself and this is why she left in tears. Malcolm X told her the truth: she wasn't helping, couldn't help, and should probably just go home.

As we can see from the young woman's reaction to Malcolm X, there was angst aplenty in the 1960s, and we must look for its deeper cause, the cause that can help explain the emergence of the spirit of 1968. We are looking for the origins of a new sensibility in America that approached issues like Vietnam, feminism, Civil Rights, and the sexual revolution in a way that no previous generation—certainly not the preceding generation—would have. I got a valuable clue to the answer some years ago when I read Tom Brokaw's book *The Greatest Generation*. This book celebrates the virtues of the generation that grew up between the two world wars.[9] As I read Brokaw's book, I asked myself: What made the "greatest generation" so great? The answer is twofold: the Depression and World War II. The virtues of that generation were the product of scarcity and war. Hardship and need forged the admirable qualities of courage, sacrifice, and solidarity. But the greatest generation failed in one important respect: it could not produce another great generation.

Why not? The obvious answer is affluence. The parents of the greatest generation wanted their children to have the advantages they never had. And in giving their children everything they wanted, the frugal, self-disciplined, sacrificial generation of World War II produced the spoiled children of the 1960s—the Clinton generation. Ironically the generation that came to revile capitalism was produced by the largesse of capitalism. This outcome had been predicted a generation earlier by the economist Joseph Schumpeter. Schumpeter warned that capitalism produces a "gale of creative destruction" that topples traditional institutions and traditional mores. Specifically, Schumpeter predicted that the abundance of capitalism would erode the qualities of hard work, self-discipline, and deferred gratification that produced that abundance in the first place.

Why would young people raised in a level of comfort that is historically unprecedented turn so ungrateful, so mean-spirited, so dissolute? I believe a big part of the reason is that they lost the sense of purpose that had sustained earlier generations. I am not speaking here of religious values or even patriotic feeling. Rather, I am speaking of the simple sense of seriousness and satisfaction that people get when they struggle and prevail against grinding necessity. Earlier generations of Americans had to strive to provide food, clothing, and shelter for themselves and their children. This task could prove laborious, unending, backbreaking, but it also provided a goal and a horizon for life. It conferred dignity and a genuine sense of meaning and accomplishment.

By contrast, the children of the 1960s had nothing comparable to live for. As far as they could see, the struggle against necessity no longer existed. Nor did they appreciate what their parents went through; rather, they regarded their parents as soulless conformists who lacked true openness and idealism. The 1960s was motivated by repudiation of the old way and the quest for a new way. "Liberation" now came to mean liberation from old values—from the spirit of 1776. This took many shapes and forms—drugs, religious experimentation, sexual promiscuity, even bra-burning, as well as protesting, looting, and rioting. Perhaps most repulsive was the heartless ingratitude and even meanness that young people showed their parents. When frugal, hardworking, patriotic parents saw their teenage children giving them and all they held dear the finger, they saw, with a deep sadness, all that their hard work and savings had wrought. In the late 1960s, from the point of view of parents, America became a foreign country.

Yet by 1970 the movement had already lost its momentum, and by 1980 it was completely dead. America got out of Vietnam, women entered the workforce in record numbers, and the Civil Rights movement successfully enshrined equality of rights under the law. Americans had no more tolerance for hippies and bra-burning and riots and public sex. By the mid-1980s, the sit-ins and love-ins that had defined the 1960s themselves became archaic and incomprehensible. Michel Foucault was dead, and the gay bathhouses were closed. So what did the activists do? Many of them did what Bill Ayers did—they became teachers. Far from abandoning their ideology, they carried it with them into the school and college classroom.

As Ayers points out, teaching is for him simply activism by another name. During our Dartmouth debate, I asked Ayers whether he had given up trying, bin-Laden style, to bomb U.S. government buildings, and whether this meant he was no longer a revolutionary. Ayers answered that he was still a revolutionary, in the sense of seeking fundamental social transformation, but he had now figured out a better way to achieve that goal, namely through the classroom. Comparing his old life as a terrorist with his new one as a professor, Bill Ayers writes, "Revolutionaries want to change the world, of course, and teachers, it turns out, want to change the world too."[10]

By withdrawing temporarily from the political sphere, the activists of the 1960s intended to consolidate their power by raising up a new generation—a generation that might be even more successful than they had been. A conservative era was coming—the election of Reagan made that clear—but perhaps out of the ashes, through the efforts of its committed followers, the spirit of 1968 might rise again.

CHAPTER 5

THE PLAN

We must first see the world as it is,
and not as we would like it to be.[1]

—Saul Alinsky, *Rules for Radicals*

B y the end of 1968, the spirit of the 1960s was politically dead.
The radicals didn't know it, but the country had turned
against them. In California, the spiritual home of the 1960s,
Ronald Reagan had been elected governor, and he would go on to
win a second term. Reagan openly scorned the hippies, noting that
they "looked like Tarzan, walked like Jane, and smelled like Chee-
tah." When the radicals surrounded Reagan's gubernatorial limou-
sine, displaying signs saying "We are the future," Reagan scribbled
his response on a piece of paper and held it up to the glass: "I'll sell
my bonds."[2] In 1972, four years later, the radicals would nominate
one of their heroes, George McGovern, as the Democratic candidate
for president, but he would go down to resounding defeat by Richard Nixon, who ran on an anti-Soviet, law-and-order platform. The
Democrats were dubbed the party of "acid, amnesty, and abortion."

Watergate would give the Democrats an unexpected reprieve, but even that would prove short-lived, and in 1980 Reagan would win the presidency, and govern for two terms, ushering the United States into a new epoch of conservatism that would last a quarter of a century.

If the radicalism of the 1960s were to be revived, in any form whatsoever, it would take new leadership. Even before such leadership emerged, there would need to be a strategy to bring the carcass back to life. Strategies require a strategist, and such a strategist would have to be a man of uncommon perception. Such a man would have to fully face the debris of the 1960s—the world as it is—without fog or illusion. At the same time he would retain the dream of the 1960s—the world as he felt it ought to be—and work to close the gap between current reality and future possibility. Without sentimentalism, he would have to repudiate the failed approaches of the 1960s, preserving the ideals and the agenda, but introducing new techniques that could work in a new era. Such a man would have to be tough, wily, even deceptive, both an idealist and Machiavellian. Even more, he would have to be patient, so that his approach could be implemented when the time was right. Quite likely he would not even live to see his schemes come to fruition, but with time he might produce converts who would use his strategies to carry their shared ideals to the highest corridors of power. Such a man, if he existed, would be the last hope of the 1960s. In Chicago, there was such a man.

Saul Alinsky was born in Chicago in 1909. His parents were Russian Jewish immigrants. He attended the University of Chicago, where he got a degree in archaeology. During the Great Depression, however, he saw that "archaeologists were in about as much demand as horses and buggies." He studied criminology in graduate school and then became a labor organizer, working in the slums of Chicago.

He created the Industrial Areas Foundation and a network of activist organizations that soon expanded to other cities. Eventually he shifted his emphasis from labor organizing to organizing poor people and teaching them how to extract political and economic benefits from the government. In the late 1960s and early 1970s, Alinsky developed a comprehensive strategy for social transformation. He did this partly in response to Richard Nixon's attempts to woo the middle class—the "silent majority," as Nixon called it. While he championed the poor and the underdogs, Alinsky himself enjoyed the good life. He liked good food, good wine, good cigars, and golf. One of his favorite places was Carmel, California, where he died of a heart attack in 1972.

Alinsky was a paradoxical figure. A labor organizer, he also hung out with clergymen, mafia leaders, and corporate tycoons. Jewish by birth, and atheist by conviction, he worked closely with Catholic bishops and Protestant pastors. A reflexive patriot, he nevertheless hated much about America and sought to replace the country he lived in with a different kind of country that he could unreservedly love. Modest in style, Alinsky was arrogant about what he could achieve. "I feel confident," he once said, "that I could persuade a millionaire on a Friday to subsidize a revolution on Saturday out of which he would make a huge profit on Sunday even though he was certain to be executed on Monday."[3] Alinsky was an architect of revolution, a revolution that sought to undo the Reagan revolution, and even the American Revolution.

To do that he needed leaders, and over the years he inspired and tutored many influential writers and activists. One was Cesar Chavez, head of the United Farm Workers; another was the scholar and activist Armando Navarro, one of the champions of a separate homeland for Mexican Americans. A third was the former student-activist Tom Hayden, who along with his then-wife Jane Fonda organized anti-Vietnam demonstrations. Hayden want to Hanoi in 1965 to meet with North Vietnamese leaders. So did Staughton Lynd, another Alinsky acolyte who was active in socialist agitation and demonstrations against U.S. foreign policy. This roster is impressive enough, but it leaves out Alinsky's two most influential disciples. Rarely has a man been more fortunate in his students. Alinsky found two individuals, a man and a woman, who more than three decades after his death, might actually realize his goal of replacing the America that is with the America that Alinsky believed ought to be.

In the 1980s and 1990s, Barack Obama, a native of Hawaii, with his roots in Kenya and Indonesia, kept going to Chicago to find jobs as an activist and community organizer. Although Obama was president of the Harvard Law Review, and courted by high-paying law firms, he chose to take a low-paid job in Chicago. There he built his political career, first as a community agitator, then as a state representative, then as a senator from Illinois, before he ran for president. In an interview for my *America* film, I asked the social scientist Stanley Kurtz, who has studied Obama closely, why Obama, who had no roots in Chicago, kept returning there. Kurtz responded that Obama made Chicago his new home because he became an Alinskyite, and he wanted to master the techniques of Alinsky. I knew of course that Obama's first job in Chicago was working for the Alinsky network; there is a picture on the web of Obama teaching Alinsky's techniques to fellow community activists. Kurtz, however, has documented a deeper connection between Obama and Alinsky. He discovered that Obama during the mid-1990s even joined a radical political party called the New Party that had been founded by the Alinsky spinoff organization Acorn.[4] Yet this has received very little press coverage, in the manner that all information damaging to Obama receives very little press coverage. Obama himself suppresses his debt to Alinsky, saying nothing about it in his autobiography *Dreams from My Father*.

As I have argued earlier—and as Obama's own autobiography confirms—Obama got his dreams from his father, but the story doesn't end there. While Obama's anti-colonialist dreams may have originated in Barack Obama Sr.'s experience in Kenya, they were reinforced in young Obama's life through his experiences in Hawaii and the years he spent growing up in Indonesia. Then, young Obama learned chapter and verse of the anti-colonial ideology in New York at Columbia, in Boston at Harvard, and in Chicago through various Alinsky organizations. Obama learned from Alinsky how to convert radical ideology into political power, in other words, how to win and retain high office. Obama was such a good student that he became a teacher of Alinsky techniques, and ultimately he used those techniques to carry himself to the White House, and to win a second term. Describing Alinsky's influence on Obama, Alinsky biographer Sanford Horwitt said in an NPR interview, "Barack Obama is in the White House because he really learned a lesson on the streets of Chicago."[5]

Now, by a kind of arrangement, Obama intends to hand over the baton of leadership to his fellow Alinskyite, Hillary Clinton. Clinton was a Goldwater girl in the early 1960s. She became radicalized in high school by a teacher who introduced her to a Methodist magazine that promoted leftist causes from economic redistribution to gay rights. By the time Hillary entered Wellesley College in 1965, she was a committed leftist. Yet she was smart enough to realize that the tactics of the 1960s were juvenile. They were the tactics of people outside the tent, peering in. Hillary wanted to be inside the tent, peering out. She had met Saul Alinsky in high school, but she renewed her association with him in college, inviting him to speak at Wellesley, and writing her undergraduate thesis on him. Hillary viewed Alinsky as a theorist of power—able to take radical ideas mainstream. Interestingly when Hillary became first lady, Wellesley removed her thesis from public circulation. One of her professors got a call from the White House, requesting this, and Wellesley responded by adopting a rule that the senior thesis of any president or first lady should not be publicly available. The rule of course applied to a single case, that of Hillary.

When Hillary graduated, she was offered a job by Alinsky. She refused, and decided instead to go to law school. In her book *Living History*, Clinton portrays her decision as arising out of a "fundamental disagreement" with Alinsky. In Clinton's words, "He believed you could change the system only from the outside. I didn't."[6] Hillary wanted to complete her education and get the best credentials she could to get into the mainstream institutions of power.

Initially, Hillary's trail was not one of feminist trail-blazing. She did a brief stint as counsel to the House Judiciary Committee in the Watergate investigation, but that seems to have ended when her over-zealous tactics resulted in her ouster. She then married Bill and followed him to Arkansas, where he was later elected governor. When Bill was elected president in 1992, she accompanied him to the White House. She endured Bill's lecheries and backed him, with admirable stoicism, through the impeachment attempt. Since Bill's presidency, she has forged an independent identity, first as senator and then as secretary of state, qualifying her to become a formidable candidate for the White House in 2016. If that happens, Hillary the Alinskyite will have succeeded Obama the Alinskyite, and Alinsky will be, at least in part, responsible for the election of two American presidents in a row.

The Alinsky train really got rolling in 2008 when the Democratic nomination was contested by two Alinskyites, the man who wanted to be the first African American president and the presidential wife who wanted to be the first woman president. Ultimately the black Alinskyite beat the female Alinskyite, in part because in America the politics of race trumps the politics of sex.

Some Americans think that if they elect Hillary Clinton in 2016 they are also going to get Bill. We occasionally hear of how nice it would be to get back "Billary." Even some conservatives relish the prospect, because, they say, Obama doesn't have a clue and Bill is smart. Yet here is the case where Obama and Hillary—not Bill—may get the last laugh. Bill of course is a White House addict and he desperately wants to hang around the Oval Office, hobnob with foreign leaders at State Dinners, and issue White House pontifications. The only way for him to do this is to help get his wife elected.

To this end, Bill put aside his reservations about Obama. Bill has long regarded Obama as a lightweight unworthy of the Democratic presidential mantle. In 2008, he told Senator Ted Kennedy that Obama's only credential was that he was black and that "a few years ago this guy would be getting us coffee."[7] There is no evidence that Clinton has fundamentally changed his perspective. Even so, he campaigned assiduously for Obama's reelection. Why? To ensure that Obama would repay the favor, and four years later, when he could not run again, permit Hillary (rather than Joe Biden or someone else) to be his replacement. What Bill doesn't seem to realize is that Hillary has her own agenda. While Bill wants the fun of being back in the White House, and being listened to again, Barack and Hillary want to implement the plan that Alinsky devised for progressives to retain power and change America.

As a young man Alinsky saw the hardships of the Great Depression. He saw what he regarded as the failure of capitalism, and even more the injustice of capitalism. Many Americans saw their savings evaporate and their jobs disappear. As a labor organizer, he set up "people's organizations" in industrial slums, mostly in immigrant communities in Chicago. Alinsky became a socialist. He confessed his socialist convictions in his 1946 book *Reveille for Radicals*. Alinsky wrote that radicals like himself "want to advance from the jungle of laissez-faire capitalism. . . . They hope for a future where the means of production will be owned by all of the people."[8]

Alinsky's real influence, however, has less to do with his ideology than with his tactics. He developed what he called a "science of revolution," which is fully articulated in his second book, *Rules for Radicals*. This book was not published until 1971, a year before Alinsky's death, although Alinsky had been putting its teachings into effect much earlier. By the time the 1960s came along, Alinsky was a middle-aged man. He was not exactly a creature of the 1960s. He supported the Civil Rights movement, but he was not closely involved with it. He opposed the Vietnam War, but that wasn't the cause that drove him. He was sympathetic to the attempts of the 1960s radicals to break down traditional codes of morality, but at the same time he regarded the radicals as soft, ignorant, undisciplined, and ineffective—a "herd of independent thinkers" desperately in need of a better plan of action. The 1960s activists regarded themselves, not Alinsky, as the vanguard of revolutionary thinking, but as their organizations fell apart and their tactics failed, many of them turned to him for guidance.

Rules for Radicals was informed by Alinsky's close engagement with student radicalism, including the activists of Students for a Democratic Society and Bill Ayers's Weather Underground. Alinsky scorned the Weather Underground as representing "comic book leftism" which achieved nothing and then turned to violence. Alinsky argued that violent revolution was a chimera, and that what could be achieved in America was "orderly revolution." Orderly revolution requires getting the consent of organized groups and the power brokers of society. Alinsky was not impressed by the SDS either, regarding it as a group of naive middle-class students playing at being revolutionaries. He spurned their foot-stomping political "tantrums," dubbing them practitioners of "Rumpelstiltskin politics."[9] Bottom line: all these people were ineffective and didn't know how to bring about real change.

Alinsky argued that there are two kinds of radicals. He contrasted what he termed the "rhetorical radical" from the "radical realist." Rhetorical radicals like to talk. Anger is their touchstone of virtue. They are bombastic with their Marxist or Leninist slogans. Yet they don't get much done. Alinsky wrote, "I have learned to freeze my hot anger into cool anger." Cool anger is based on deliberation and experience, both of which "have made my actions far more calculated, deliberate, directive and effective." Alinsky realized that changing social systems is hard, and that radicals need patience and discipline—a kind of Puritan sensibility.

Alinsky began by recognizing who the radicals were. Despite their histrionic self-descriptions as victims, these were not underprivileged working people or downtrodden minorities—they were educated members of the middle class. "With rare exceptions, our activists and radicals are products of and rebels against our middle-class society." Alinsky agreed with the goals of the radicals—to destroy middle-class values. "All rebels must attack the power states in their society. Our rebels have contemptuously rejected the values and way of life of the middle class. They have stigmatized it as materialistic, decadent, bourgeois, degenerate, imperialistic, warmongering, brutalized and corrupt. They are right." At the same time, Alinsky disagreed with the strategy of the 1960s radicals. They habitually called the cops "pigs" and working people "racist" and traditional values "square." Alinsky pointed out, "We must begin from where we are if we are to build power for change. The power and the people are in the big middle-class majority. Therefore, it is useless self-indulgence

for an activist to put his past behind him. Instead he should use the
priceless value of his middle-class experience. . . . Instead of the
infantile dramatics of rejection, he will now begin to dissect and
examine the way of life as he never has before. He will know that a
'square' is no longer to be dismissed as such—instead, his own
approach must be 'square' enough to get the action started. . . .
Instead of hostile rejection he is seeking bridges of communication
and unity. . . . He will view with strategic sensitivity the nature of
middle-class behavior with its hang-ups over rudeness or aggressive,
insulting, profane actions. All this and more must be grasped and
used to radicalize parts of the middle class."[10]

The central problem is that middle-class people typically don't
want to be radicalized. They don't want to undermine their country.
They are patriots who would rather win wars than lose them. They
don't consider the people fighting on the other side to be the good
guys. They like capitalism, and just want to succeed within the system. They believe in law and order, and support the police to maintain it. They are not fans of public sex or public defecation, in the
manner of the most exhibitionistic hippies. They espouse traditional
values, even though they don't always live up to them. Alinsky realized that the task of the radical is to turn middle-class people against
themselves, to make them instruments of their own destruction. This
would not be easy.

So how did Alinsky figure out a winning strategy? He says he got
it from the philosopher Machiavelli, author of *The Prince*. Alinsky
wrote, "*The Prince* was written by Machiavelli for the Haves on how
to hold power. *Rules for Radicals* is written for the Have-Nots on how
to take it away." Yet I was startled to see that, with the exception of
a few maxims of realpolitik, *Rules for Radicals* actually draws very
little from Machiavelli. I began to wonder if Alinsky's invocation of
Machiavelli was a diversion. If so that would be a very Machiavellian

thing to do. I began to flip randomly through Alinsky's book in frustration when I came upon the dedication page. There I read perhaps the most unusual dedication in the history of American publishing.

Most books are dedicated to loved ones—family and friends—or to influential mentors. Alinsky, interestingly enough, dedicates his book to the devil. This is not a joke: *Rules for Radicals* is actually dedicated to Lucifer. Alinsky calls him "the first radical known to man who rebelled against the establishment and did it so effectively that he at least won his own kingdom." Now this is remarkable in itself, and yet it has attracted very little attention. Progressives who learn about it are initially surprised, and then tend to dismiss the dedication with a roll of the eyes and a weary "Oh brother." This, however, is intellectually uncurious. Alinsky was serious about his choice. In fact, he returned to the same theme in a *Playboy* interview he did in 1972. In it he said, "If there is an afterlife, and I have anything to say about it, I will unreservedly choose to go to hell." When the interviewer asked why, Alinsky said, "Hell would be heaven for me. Once I get into hell, I'll start organizing the have-nots over there. They're my kind of people."[11]

Back to the Lucifer dedication: Now why would Alinsky do this? The man was an atheist, so he didn't believe in an actual Satan. Yet Alinsky calls him the "first radical." Clearly a radical writing books called *Reveille for Radicals* and *Rules for Radicals* would have a lot to learn from the original radical. I turned for inspiration to Stanley Fish, one of the world's leading Milton scholars, whom I interviewed on the subject of Lucifer as he is portrayed in *Paradise Lost* and, more broadly, in the Western tradition. I asked Fish to elaborate on Lucifer's strategy against God.

Fish outlined a four-part strategy. First, polarization. Satan is deeply alienated from God. He doesn't seek to mend fences; he polarizes. He issues a declaration of war against God. As Milton's Satan puts it, "War then, war open or understood, must be resolved." Second—and this is rather ironic, coming from Lucifer—demonization. Incredible though it seems, Satan demonizes God. How? By making God into a tyrant, the symbol of "the establishment." This makes Satan into a champion of resistance, of counterculture. He claims to be combating what he terms "the tyranny of heaven." Third, organization. Satan is a mobilizer of envy; he draws on the very quality that motivated the bad angels to rebel in the first place. For Satan, envy against God is a great motivator, and he appeals to that envy among the other discontented angels. What's Satan's strategy for doing that? Satan is a community organizer. We see him in the early books of *Paradise Lost* building coalitions among the rebel angels, and motivating them to join him in a nefarious campaign against God and God's special creation man. It is a project undertaken, as he puts it, "to spite the great creator."

Finally, deception, or what Satan calls "covert guile." Satan knows he cannot defeat God by force; he has to rely on deceit and cunning. From the moment he approaches Eve in the garden, he relies on camouflage. He doesn't come as Satan; he comes as a wily serpent. And his rhetoric is serpentine: he tries to make Eve think he is on her side, even though he intends her destruction. Satan doesn't feel bad about these deceptions because he has already rejected God's moral order; consequently, he isn't bound by moral rules. "Evil, be thou my good." Remote though these ideas may seem from contemporary politics, we will see how Alinsky made full use of them. In fact, they are the cornerstone of the Alinsky strategy. Martin Luther King had a dream; Alinsky developed a scheme, and he got it from Lucifer.

One can see Lucifer's influence in Alinsky's contention that "ethical standards must be elastic to stretch with the times." Alinsky wrote that morality and ethics were fine for those who didn't seek to improve the world for the better. But for those who do, the ends always justify the means. "In action," Alinsky wrote, "one does not always enjoy the luxury of a decision that is consistent both with one's individual conscience and the good of mankind. The choice must always be for the latter." This is not to say that Alinsky eschewed appeals to conscience and morality. He used them, but only when they proved strategically effective. Morality for Alinsky is a cloak that the activist puts on when it suits him or her. One of Alinsky's ethical rules was that "you do what you can with what you have and clothe it with moral arguments."[12]

When the 1960s activists came to see Alinsky—with their long hair and unkempt clothing and bad odor—here's what he told them. You can be freaks, but you should not come across as freaks. You can be revolutionaries, but you should not look or act or smell like revolutionaries. Take baths. Use deodorant. Cut your hair. Put on ties and dresses if you have to. Don't use obscenities. Don't call the police "pigs" and U.S. soldiers "fascists." Feign an interest in middle-class tastes; in other words, pretend to be like the people you hate. Speak their language, even to the extent of using local colloquialism or slang. Meanwhile, work creatively and even unscrupulously to build these people's resentment against the big corporations and the military and the power structure. Don't hesitate to tell lies, but make sure they can't be easily found out. Create a sense of entitlement by making promises that cannot be delivered and then use the resulting frustration as a weapon to mobilize the people into action. This strategy can be summarized as: polarization, demonization, organization, and deception. In other words, the Lucifer strategy. In these ways, Alinsky said, the power of the white middle-class majority can be harnessed even to undermine the values and interests of the white middle-class majority.

Most of the radicals didn't listen to Alinsky. And even today we see the Occupy Wall Street types, just as disheveled and dirtball as their predecessors in the 1960s, taking over parks and cursing the system. One radical, however, who recognized the value of Alinsky's counsel to look good and even "square" was Hillary Clinton. It took her several years to internalize this advice and transform her own appearance. If you see early pictures and video of Hillary, she looks and sounds like a former hippie. Over time, however, Hillary started dressing like a respectable middle-class mother and speaking in a clipped, moderate sounding voice. Young Barack Obama, too, looked like a bit of a street thug—in his own words, he could have been Trayvon Martin. Over time, however, Obama started dressing impeccably and even practiced modulating his voice. "The fact that I conjugate my verbs and speak in a typical Midwestern newscaster voice—there's no doubt that this helps ease communication between myself and white audiences," he admits. "And there's no doubt that when I'm with a black audience, I slip into a slightly different dialect."[13]

Hillary and Obama have both learned the Alinsky lesson that you should aggressively pursue power while pretending to be motivated by pure altruism. How do they do this? They do it by denouncing money as a motive for a career, and by flamboyantly demonstrating to the public that they are not motivated by money. Note that Hillary, despite her Yale Law School credentials, meekly followed Bill Clinton to Arkansas and became a "good wife" during his scandals. Never has she pursued a lucrative law career, and the same is true with Obama. Obama spurned big-money law firms that courted him, preferring instead to work as a community organizer. These are the kinds of decisions—Alinsky knew—that fill people with wonder. What people don't realize is that Hillary and Obama are just as ambitious and self-motivated as any avaricious careerist. The only difference is that they are going after power instead of personal wealth. With power, they can direct the affairs of society, and in time positions of power can easily be converted into personal wealth.

More important, Hillary and Obama both adopted Alinsky's strategic counsel to sound mainstream, even when you aren't. Since Hillary ran for the U.S. Senate in New York, she has sounded a moderate tone. This is the "new Hillary," as the press dubbed her. Most of America has fallen for it. They think that because Hillary dresses "square" and sounds "square" therefore she must be "square" in her thinking. And it is the same with Obama. Like Hillary, Obama shows tremendous personal discipline. He is a master of giving the American people what they want to see and hear, while doing something entirely different. While Obama pursues radical policies, he sounds mainstream and lets people project things onto him that are not who he really is. In his own words, "I serve as a blank screen on which people of vastly different political stripes project their own views."[14] Lucifer was right: appearances make an easy substitute for reality. These are the ways in which our two Alinskyites make themselves palatable to the American middle class, which to this day has no idea how hostile Hillary and Obama are to middle-class values.

If Hillary Clinton is elected in 2016, the baton will have passed from one Alinskyite to another. In this case, Alinsky's influence will have taken on a massive, almost unimaginable, importance. Obama will have had eight years to remake America, and Hillary will have another four or perhaps eight to complete the job. Together, these two have the opportunity to largely undo the nation's founding ideals. They will have had the power, and the time, to unmake and then remake America. They may not be responsible for the suicide of America, but they certainly will have helped to finish off a certain way of life in America, and they will leave us with a country unrecognizable not only to Washington and Jefferson but also to those of us who grew up in the twentieth century. If they succeed there may be no going back. Then it will be their America, not ours, and we will be a people bereft of a country, with no place to go.

CHAPTER 6

THE RED MAN'S BURDEN

Let not America go wrong in her first hour.
—Christopher Newport, *The New World*

The road up the mountain was steep and winding, on our way to see the woman who wanted to get rid of Mount Rushmore. She was an American Indian activist, a leader of the Sioux Tribe. As we approached the destination for our interview—which is featured in my *America* movie—I thought about how Columbus's landing in America changed the world. Imagine if there was no America and Columbus kept going. He might have landed in his intended destination, India! That would have changed history a little, but only a little. The reason is that India was already a long-established civilization; at best, Columbus would have set up one more trading post. The America landing, by contrast, opened up a new continent not only to European occupation and settlement but also to the founding of a new country, the United States of America.

Today, in the schools, the progressives emphasize that Columbus didn't "discover" America. He couldn't have, since there were already people here. Rather, they say, Columbus "conquered" America. Yes, well. We're going to get into the issue of conquest, but let's begin by pondering the "discovery" question. Rarely do the progressive pedants ponder the significance that it was Europeans who landed here in America, not native peoples from this continent who landed on the shores of Europe. If native Indians could have conquered Europe and sailed up the Thames or the Seine, would they not have done it? Of course they would. But they didn't, because they couldn't. It's worth asking why things happened the way they did.

We were in the Black Hills region of South Dakota, where the carved faces of Washington, Jefferson, Lincoln, and Teddy Roosevelt emerge unexpectedly out of a mountain. It's an oddly thrilling sight, made even more special for me because I got to fly in a helicopter and see Rushmore from the sky, coming almost face to face with the four presidents. Mount Rushmore is a popular site for visitors, and the town has become a kind of "trading post," selling cowboy hats, holsters, and all kinds of wild west paraphernalia. During the day there are staged shoot-outs, and in the evening the beer flows in the bars and country singers sing songs from another era, such as "You picked a fine time to leave me, Lucille."

Charmaine White Face is a Sioux Indian and a spokesperson for the tribe's national council. She hates Mount Rushmore, and wants to see it disappear. White Face is a small woman, a little frail even, and I could hardly imagine her setting off explosives to blow up Mount Rushmore. She said she wouldn't get rid of it that way although there may be other native Indian activists who would happily light the fuse. White Face would prefer that Mount Rushmore not be maintained. A monument requires constant preservation, she points out. Rushmore, she says, should simply be abandoned. That way, nature would take its course, and erosion would first obscure and eventually eliminate those four iconic faces. To White Face, they are the faces of tyranny, conquest, and genocide.

Genocide is a strong word—it suggests not only murder on a massive scale but also the desire to wipe out an entire people. White Face believes it, and she believes it goes back to Columbus and the white settlement of the Americas. She's not alone. Russell Means, the American Indian activist, has said that "Columbus makes Hitler look like a juvenile delinquent." Writer Winona LaDuke deplores "the biological, technological and ecological invasion that began with Columbus's ill-fated voyage 500 years ago." Writer Tzvetan Todorov faults Columbus and other European invaders with producing "the greatest genocide in human history." Historian Glenn Morris accuses Columbus of being "a murderer, a rapist, the architect of a policy of genocide that continues today." Literary scholar Stephen Greenblatt claims that Columbus "inaugurated the greatest experiment in political, economic and cultural cannibalism in the history of the Western world."[1] The native American indictment can be summed up this way: the white man systematically killed us off, and then stole our country.

White Face wants the country back. Specifically, she wants the Black Hills to be returned to the Sioux, who had it before it was taken by the United States government in violation of its treaty obligations. There have been court cases about this, and the Sioux seem to have a valid claim. An 1868 treaty affirms that the Black Hills are "set apart for the absolute and undisturbed use and occupation of the Indians." Yet the treaty was abrogated by Congress in 1877. The courts have recognized this, and awarded the tribe money—lots of it. Currently there is more than $1 billion on offer to the Sioux. The money continues to gather interest. That's because the Sioux won't take it. The Sioux don't want money, insisting that the Black Hills are "not for sale."[2]

The Sioux position, conveyed by White Face, is that the land needs to be returned; it needs to become tribal land again. White Face showed me what used to be several ancient sacred sites "where the Great Spirits dwell" and she wants those sites restored, so Sioux people can once again commune with the spirits. I reminded White Face that before the Sioux, there were Cheyenne Indians and other tribes on that land. So if America stole the land from the Sioux, didn't the Sioux steal the land from the Cheyenne and other tribes? If the land is returned to the Sioux, shouldn't the Sioux turn around and give it back to those who had it before? White Face looked flustered. She said that, long before the white man came, American Indians had certain "dominant" tribes, and the Sioux happened to be one of them. Some tribes were in charge and that's all there was to that. If the land was returned to the Sioux, she said, perhaps the tribe would let the Cheyenne and others worship at the holy sites.

But how did these "dominant" tribes become dominant? White Face's euphemistic rhetoric aside, they became dominant by defeating the weaker and smaller tribes. So the Sioux indeed got land in the typical way that Indians got land—by defeating and displacing the previous inhabitants. Stronger warlike tribes like the Sioux, the Apache, and the Comanche have always done it and weaker pacific tribes like the Hopi and the Pueblo have always known it. Here, in a nutshell, we see the problem of asserting a "we got here first" land claim: almost inevitably, there was someone who was there earlier who can assert the same claim against you.

We'll come back to this, but for now, let's move to Columbus and the charge of genocide. The historical Columbus was a Christian explorer. Howard Zinn makes it sound like Columbus came looking for nothing but gold, but Columbus was equally driven by a spirit of exploration and adventure. When we read Columbus's diaries we see that his motives were complex: he wanted to get rich by discovering new trade routes, but he also wanted to find the Garden of Eden, which he believed was an actual undiscovered place. Of course Columbus didn't come looking for America; he didn't know that the American continent existed. Since the Muslims controlled the trade routes of the Arabian Sea, he was looking for a new way to the Far East. Specifically he was looking for India, and that's why he called the native peoples "Indians." It is easy to laugh at Columbus's naïveté, except that he wasn't entirely wrong. Anthropological research has established that the native people of the Americas did originally come from Asia. Most likely they came across the Bering Strait before the continents drifted apart.

We know that, as a consequence of contact with Columbus and the Europeans who came after him, the native population in the Americas plummeted. By some estimates, more than 80 percent of the Indians perished. This is the basis for the charge of genocide. But there was no genocide. Millions of Indians died as a result of diseases they contracted from their exposure to the white man: smallpox, measles, cholera, and typhus. There is one isolated allegation of Sir Jeffrey Amherst (whose name graces Amherst College) approving a strategy to vanquish a hostile Indian tribe by giving the Indians smallpox-infected blankets. Even here, however, it's not clear the scheme was actually carried out. As historian William McNeill documents in *Plagues and Peoples*, the white man generally transmitted his diseases to the Indians without knowing it, and the Indians died in large numbers because they had not developed immunities to those diseases. This is tragedy on a grand scale, but it is not genocide, because genocide implies an *intention* to wipe out a people. McNeill points out that Europeans themselves had contracted lethal diseases, including the pneumonic and the bubonic plagues, from Mongol invaders from the Asian steppes. The Europeans didn't have immunities, and during the "Black Death" of the fourteenth century one-third of the population of Europe was wiped out.[3] But no one calls these plagues genocide, because they weren't.

It's true that Columbus developed strong prejudices about the native peoples he first encountered—he was prejudiced in favor of them. He praised the intelligence, generosity, and lack of guile among the Tainos, contrasting these qualities with Spanish vices. Subsequent explorers such as Pedro Alvares Cabral, Amerigo Vespucci (from whom we get the name "America"), and Walter Raleigh registered similar positive impressions. So where did Europeans get the idea that Indians were "savages"? Actually, they got it from their experience with the Indians. While the Indians Columbus met on his first voyage were hospitable and friendly, on subsequent voyages Columbus was horrified to discover that a number of sailors he had left behind had been killed and possibly eaten by the cannibalistic Arawaks.[4]

When Bernal Diaz arrived in Mexico with the swashbuckling army of Hernán Cortés, he and his fellow Spaniards saw things they had never seen before. Indeed they witnessed one of the most gruesome spectacles ever seen, something akin to what American soldiers saw after World War II when they entered the Nazi concentration camps. As Diaz describes the Aztecs, in an account generally corroborated by modern scholars, "They strike open the wretched Indian's chest with flint knives and hastily tear out the palpitating heart which, with the blood, they present to the idols in whose name they have performed the sacrifice. Then they cut off the arms, thighs and head, eating the arms and thighs at their ceremonial banquets." Huge numbers of Indians—typically captives in war—were sacrificed, sometimes hundreds in a single day. Yet in a comic attempt to diminish the cruelty of the Aztecs, Howard Zinn remarks that their mass murder "did not erase a certain innocence" and he accuses Cortés of nefarious conduct "turning Aztec against Aztec."[5]

If the Aztecs of Mexico seemed especially bloodthirsty, they were rivaled by the Incas of South America who also erected sacrificial mounds on which they performed elaborate rites of human sacrifice, so that their altars were drenched with blood, bones were strewn everywhere, and priests collapsed from exhaustion from stabbing their victims.

Even while Europeans were startled and appalled at such blood-thirstiness, there was a countercurrent of admiration for what Europeans saw as the Indians' better qualities. Starting with Columbus and continuing through the next few centuries, native Indians were regarded as "noble savages." They were admired for their dignity, stoicism, and bravery. In reality, the native Indians probably had these qualities in the same proportion as human beings elsewhere on the planet. The idealization of them as "noble savages" seems to be a projection of European fantasies about primitive innocence onto the natives. We too—and especially modern progressives—have the same fantasies. Unlike us, however, the Spanish were forced to confront the reality of Aztec and Inca behavior. Today we have an appreciation for the achievements of Aztec and Inca culture, such as its social organization and temple architecture; but we cannot fault the Spanish for being "distracted" by the mass murder they witnessed. Not all the European hostility to the Indians was the result of irrational prejudice.

While the Spanish conquistadores were surprised to see humans sacrificed in droves, they were not shocked to witness slavery, the subjugation of women, or brutal treatment of war captives—these were familiar enough practices from their own culture. Moreover, in conquering the Indians, and establishing alien rule over them, the

Spanish were doing to the Indians nothing more than the Indians had done to each other. So from the point of view of the native Indian people, one empire, that of Spain, replaced another, that of the Aztecs. Did life for the native Indian get worse? It's very hard to say. The ordinary Indian might now have a higher risk of disease, but he certainly had a lower risk of finding himself under the lurid glare of the obsidian knife.

What, then, distinguished the Spanish from the Indians? The Peruvian writer and Nobel laureate Mario Vargas Llosa offers an arresting answer. The conquistadores who came to the Americas, he concedes, were "semi-literate, implacable and greedy." They were clearly believers in the conquest ethic—land is yours if you can take it. Yet these semi-literate greedy swordsmen, without knowing it, also brought with them something new to the Americas. They brought with them the ideas of Western civilization, from Athenian rationalism to Judeo-Christian ideas of human brotherhood to more modern conceptions of self-government, human rights, and property rights. Some of these ideas were nascent and newly developing even in the West. Nevertheless, they were there, and without intending to do so, the conquistadores brought them to the Americas.[6]

To appreciate what Vargas Llosa is saying, consider an astonishing series of events that took place in Spain in the early sixteenth century. At the urging of a group of Spanish clergy, the king of Spain called a halt to Spanish expansion in the Americas, pending the resolution of the question of whether American Indians had souls and could be justly enslaved. This seems odd, and even appalling, to us today, but we should not miss its significance. Historian Lewis Hanke writes that never before or since has a powerful emperor "ordered his conquests to cease until it was decided if they were just." The king's actions were in response to petitions by a group of Spanish priests, led by Bartolomé de las Casas. Las Casas defended the Indians in a famous debate held at Valladolid in Spain. On the other side was an Aristotelian scholar, Juan Sepulveda, who relied on Aristotle's concept of the "natural slave" to argue that Indians were inferior and therefore could be subjugated. Las Casas countered that Indians were human beings with the same dignity and spiritual nature as the Spanish. Today Las Casas is portrayed as a heroic eccentric, but his basic position prevailed at Valladolid. It was endorsed by the pope, who declared in his bull *Sublimus Deus*, "Indians . . . are by no means to be deprived of their liberty or the possessions of their property . . . nor should they be in any way enslaved; should the contrary happen it shall be null and of no effect."[7] Papal bulls and even royal edicts were largely ignored thousands of miles away—there were no effective mechanisms of enforcement. The conquest ethic prevailed. Even so, over time the principles of Valladolid and *Sublimus Deus* provided the moral foundation for the enfranchisement of Indians. Indians could themselves appeal to Western ideas of equality, dignity, and property rights in order to resist subjugation, enforce treaties, and get some of their land back.

It is against this backdrop that we should consider the question of whether the white man stole the Americas from the Indians. Let's begin by appreciating the ambiguity of the term "theft" in this context. The abolitionist Frederick Douglass in his autobiography tells the story of how as a slave he stole food from his master. Douglass impishly points out that in extracting meat from the tub, he wasn't really stealing. That's because as a slave he wasn't considered a human being; he was considered his master's property. But the master's provisions were also the master's property. So Douglass says that far from stealing from his master he was merely "taking his meat out of one tub and putting it in another."[8] The point of this anecdote is that concepts of "theft" only make sense when there is a built-in infrastructure of ownership, property rights, and morality.

"Theft" requires that someone legitimately own something, so that it is possible for someone else to illegitimately take it. If I steal your corn, and it turns out it wasn't your corn—you stole it from someone else—then I have indeed committed theft, but not against you, only against the person who actually owns the corn.

Theft, with respect to the Indians, is rendered problematic because the Indians themselves had no concept of property rights. The Indians held that no one actually owns land—land is the common property of all. Who then gets to use the land? Naturally it is the one who is occupying it. This picture was further complicated by the fact that there were two types of Indian tribes, the sedentary agricultural tribes and the nomadic hunting tribes. The sedentary tribes cultivated the land and seemingly by occupation they were its rightful owners. The hunting tribes, since they moved around, occupied no particular place. Over time, however, the hunting tribes used their martial skills to defeat and displace the sedentary tribes. They then became the new sedentary tribes, and their claim to the land was also based on occupancy. Of course there were constant clashes among tribes—no one wanted to be ejected from their land. Everyone understood, however, that there was no real basis for complaint since it wasn't "their" land in the first place. When everyone is a renter, use is solely according to possession. This is the conquest ethic in its purest form.

The white men who settled America didn't come as foreign invaders; they came as settlers. Unlike the Spanish, who ruled Mexico from afar, the English families who arrived in America left everything behind and staked their lives on the new world. In other words, they came as immigrants. We can say, of course, that immigration doesn't confer any privileges, and just because you come here to settle doesn't mean you have a right to the land that is here, but then that logic would also apply to the Indians. Let's recall that the Indians who were here also once came as immigrants. In the beginning there was no one here, and then the Indians came from Asia or someplace else and themselves "discovered" the new world.

Does this mean that the Indians "owned" America because they got here first? To see this question in its clear light, consider the biblical story of Cain and Abel. Abel was a shepherd while Cain was a farmer. Abel moved around with flocks, while Cain cultivated the earth. Now imagine that each day while Abel tended livestock, Cain built fences and said "This is mine and this also is mine" until Cain has enclosed all the existing land, while Abel continues as a shepherd. Does this mean that the descendants of Cain—owing to their original occupation of the earth—own the whole world? In his *Discourse on the Origin of Inequality*, Rousseau suggested that the first man to build a fence around something and say "this is mine" was the original con artist. Rousseau raises the question of how one can claim to own something in perpetuity simply by occupying and claiming it. To understand the legitimacy of property rights, we have to see the justice in Rousseau's comment. If ownership of the globe is not first-come, first-served, then how does an individual—or a tribe, or a nation—get to declare that it owns land and that everyone else who tries to occupy or use it is a usurper?

It would be nice to turn to an American Indian source for a doctrine of the origin of property rights, but no such source exists. The white man who displaced the Indians also brought with him that doctrine—not to mention courts of law to enforce it—which ultimately enabled the Indian to challenge the white man's occupation on the basis of the white man's own doctrine. What, then, was that doctrine? In the ancient and medieval world, just as in the Americas, there was no clear notion of property rights. People owned property, but the idea that they had a *right* to it would have been regarded as absurd. The ancient view of property was summed up in Cicero's analogy: Owning a piece of land or property is like occupying a seat in a public theater. It's your seat, but only while you are sitting in it. You don't own it, and even its possession comes with certain duties and obligations. The ancients also assumed that the amount of land, like the number of seats in a theater, is generally fixed, so it's not right to take up more space than you need.[9]

Philosopher John Locke was the first to formulate a coherent doctrine of property ownership. Interestingly he developed that doctrine by considering the contrast between Europe and the new world. Locke observed that an Indian chief, lording it over thousands of his tribe, nevertheless "feeds, lodges and is clad worse than a day laborer in England." Why is this? Locke reasons that it is not because of land, which the Indians have in abundance, more than they can possibly use. The difference, then, is not in land but in what people do with land. For Locke, the difference comes from human effort. It is human effort that converts unowned and largely useless land into owned and useful property.

Locke began with the simple premise that every person owns himself or herself. Every man has property in his own person which "no Body has any Right to but himself." Locke adds, "The Labor of his Body, and the Work of his Hands, are likewise properly his." It follows from this that nobody has a right to own somebody else or to forcibly seize the fruits of another person's labor. So where do property rights come from? Locke argues that when we "mix" our labor with land, we come to own the land as well. Why? Because land is abundant, and nature by itself is almost worthless. What good—Locke asks—are acorns, leaves, and moss? It is labor that adds value to land. Indeed labor adds virtually all the value that converts nature's provision into bread, wine, and cloth. Thus, Locke says, we have a right to acquire as much land as we can ourselves cultivate and develop.[10]

We can see what Locke is getting at by considering the purchase price reputedly paid for the island of Manhattan. Supposedly the Dutch bought Manhattan from a group of Indians for $24—or around $700 in today's dollars. This was in 1626. Today, it seems like an incredible bargain. But Locke might argue that the Dutch over-paid, because in 1626 there was no Manhattan. There was a piece of land—no better than any other piece of land—and its actual value would depend entirely on what was done with it. There are places in the world today where one can buy a large piece of land for $700. Prices in Manhattan are astronomical only because of everything that has been built there with human ingenuity and foresight over the intervening three and a half centuries. The Indians who sold Manhattan were not robbed. "Manhattan" is the creation of the new people who built it, not the original inhabitants who occupied it.

None of this is to excuse, or justify, the record of cruelty, displacement, and broken treaties involving the Indian. Even though I am an immigrant, and my ancestors were not here at the time, I cannot read about these without shame and distress. Tocqueville felt the same way. As he traveled through America, he saw in the winter of 1831 a band of Choctaw Indians being taken across the Mississippi. "The Indians had their families with them, and they brought in their train the wounded and the sick, with children newly-born and old men at the point of death." It was a wrenching sight. At the same time, Tocqueville writes, "It is by agricultural labor that man appropriates the soil. . . . The Indians occupied America without possessing it. . . . They were there to wait merely until others came." It was those others, Tocqueville realized, who would conduct the "experiment of the attempt to construct society on a new basis" and build "a great nation yet unborn."[11]

In a way, the tragic outcome was predictable. America was settled by successive waves of bold, energetic, entrepreneurial people who were ready to mix their labor with land and build a new kind of civilization. The Indians were here first, but they were only sparsely and sporadically occupying the land. Consequently, many settlers regarded America as largely unoccupied, although the Indians surely disagreed with that perspective. Too bad the two groups could not amicably work out a way to share and benefit from this vast country. They couldn't, I believe, because both groups continued to espouse at least elements of the conquest ethic. Neither wished to be taken from, but both were willing to take when they had the power and the inclination to do so.

Historically, it was a missed opportunity. When we study the history of white-Indian relations, we see that in the eighteenth century white attitudes toward the Indian were largely sympathetic. Indeed several leading figures of the founding period (Patrick Henry, John Marshall, Thomas Jefferson) proposed intermarriage between whites and Indians as a way to integrate the natives into the American mainstream. "What they thought impossible with respect to blacks," political scientist Ralph Lerner writes, "was seen as highly desirable with respect to Indians." Attitudes hardened, however, when the Indians sided with the British during the revolutionary war. During this period, Howard Zinn admits, "almost every important Indian nation fought on the side of the British."[12] After the revolution, naturally, the American leaders treated the tribes as hostile nations—which they were.

Today we think of Indians as tragic figures, woebegone on the reservation. But that's not how Andrew Jackson—Indian fighter and later president—saw them. Jackson knew the Indians were canny, organized, and strong. In short order they had the same guns and equipment as the white man. The Indians knew the territory, they knew how to fight, and at first they resisted the settlers on even terms. We should not regard the Indians as passive weaklings. Many of them had the spirit of the Shawnee chief Tecumseh, who famously cried, "Let the white race perish....Back where they came, on a trail of blood, they must be driven!...Burn their dwellings—destroy their stock—slay their wives and children that their very breed may perish. War now! War for ever!"[13]

This was not mere rhetoric—Indian massacres were a serious threat that settlers had to contend with. Some of this violence was unprovoked. Indians weren't retaliating for injuries done them; they were engaging in simple banditry and theft. As late as the 1840s, a traveler heading north from Mexico commented on the regularity of Comanche raids over the previous months. "Upward of ten thousand heads of horses and mules have already been carried off, scarcely has a hacienda or rancho on the frontier been unvisited, and everywhere the people have been killed or captured."[14] It was only over time, with the advance of Western technology, that the raiding threat subsided and the military advantage shifted decisively in favor of the settlers.

So the settlers fought the Indians, and made deals with them, and signed treaties with them, and sometimes broke those treaties, and eventually the settlers got the land they wanted. The Indians were forced to retreat and settle for reparations and reservations. For many decades now, the U.S. government has tried to make restitution to Indians for broken promises and repudiated agreements. Unfortunately, the result has been to make large numbers of Indians dependent on the federal government. Many Indians today live on reservations without working, subsisting off the federal dole. I drove across the Pine Ridge reservation with Charmaine White Face. We saw the dilapidated trailers the Indians lived in. In every village, there were stray dogs barking loudly. I saw in the Indians, especially the young men, the same look of hopelessness that I used to see among slum-dwellers in Mumbai. "This is a terrible place to live,"

White Face told me. I asked her if she trusted the federal government. She snorted. "Never! Look what they have done to our people.
They promise to protect you, and then they destroy you." I mentioned Obamacare. Her only response was, "Get ready."

So when Indian leaders like White Face say that their people are
being shafted, I know what she means. The Indians have gotten a
bad deal. I'm not saying it is a good deal. At the same time, we should
be clear about what the alternatives are. It makes no sense to say,
"Give us back Manhattan." We cannot give you back Manhattan
because Manhattan was never yours. You sold a piece of land that
was virtually worthless and on it others have built a great and glori-
ous city. It is unjust to demand back what was never yours in the
first place. Then you say, "Give us back the Black Hills." You point
out that there is uranium and other minerals in those hills, and now
that land is worth a fortune. Once again, no Indian tribe knew how
to mine uranium and no Indian tribe knew what to do with uranium
if they had it. Other Americans have added value to the Black Hills
by figuring out how to tap its resources, and now the Indians want
the land back so they can take advantage of what others have figured
out how to do. The Indians were cheated when the treaty was broken
and they deserve a fair restitution. If the courts simply return the
Black Hills, however, they will be giving back far more than was ever
taken. The same is true of the rest of America. The land now is not
the same as the land then, and demanding a return of land which
others have developed and whose value others have increased is not
justice; it is stealing.

The best option available to the Indians, it seems, is to assimilate
to the new civilization that the Europeans brought to America, and
to take advantage of the wealth-creation opportunities that have so
enriched the lives of wave upon wave of immigrants. This assimila-
tion option has been available to the native Indians in a way that,

for nearly two centuries, it was not available to blacks. Yet this is precisely the option that the native Indians rejected from the outset. Today, many Indians have assimilated, and some tribes have taken advantage of gaming rights and made huge fortunes through operating casinos. Still others live forlorn on the reservation, psychologically removed from the America that is around them. These are people who seem to prefer the joy of victimhood—and the exertions of claiming reparations of one sort or another—to the joy of entrepreneurial striving. They are doing this in the name of their ancestors, who were brave and resourceful people, and yet I sometimes wonder what their brave and resourceful ancestors would think if they could see the current state of the native Americans.

It seems easy for an armchair progressive activist to deplore Columbus's legacy. I see the sadness in the eyes of a Charmaine White Face, and I am tempted to agree. Then I ask myself: What would have happened if Europeans never came to America? Would the Indians have developed their own modern civilization? Would they have adopted Western ways? Or would they have continued living as before, and what would that look like? I suppose it would look like the lifestyle of aboriginal tribes that we see today in Australia or Papua, New Guinea. Essentially they would be living characters out of *National Geographic*. No Western clothes, no Western medicine, no Western technology. If I wanted to be blunt about it, I'd throw in rotting teeth, high infant mortality, and low life expectancy. Imagine people still living in tepees and chasing animals for their meals.

I know, it sounds wonderful as an idea—perhaps even as a short vacation. But try living like that; it would be almost as strange as trying to jump around all day like a frog. The native Indians know that, which is why none of them live like that. They could—the reservations are huge, and the Indians could create a simulacrum of their original lifestyle if they wanted to. But they don't. In refusing to do so, they are voting for their current life over their ancestral life. The choice is not without its regrets. They have endured great hardships over the years, and they will never stop mourning the legacy of Columbus. Even so, they have no interest in going back to the *National Geographic* life. They would rather live in modern America and enjoy the fruits of the civilization that Columbus and his successors brought to the continent.

CHAPTER 7

THE MYTH
OF AZTLAN

*I'd like to see the United States disappear. I'd like to see
it become part of Mexico, part of a huge
new nation dominated by a Chicano majority.*

—Chicano scholar and activist Charles Truxillo

S ome years ago, I witnessed a demonstration in southern California by a group of American Latinos waving Mexican flags.
Clearly these Americans identified more with Mexico than
with the United States. I was initially puzzled about why Americans
felt this way. If they wanted to move to Mexico, they certainly could.
I was not aware of any border restrictions preventing Americans
from getting into Mexico. Then I realized why these Latinos don't
make the move. They think they *are* living in Mexico—the part of
Mexico that was illegally seized and occupied by the United States.
For many Americans, the Mexican War in the mid-nineteenth century may seem like ancient history. But just as some Southerners
haven't gotten over the Civil War, these Hispanics haven't gotten over
the Mexican War. Unlike the Southerners, who seem reconciled to
having lost their war, the Hispanics want to undo the effects of the

Treaty of Guadalupe Hidalgo, the treaty that ceded half of Mexico to the United States. Even so, they don't want to become Mexicans again. Rather, these American Latinos seek to create a new country, encompassing northern Mexico and the southwestern United States, a place they call Aztlan. "Aztlan" is derived from Aztec, and is supposed to recall the land where the great Aztec empire once thrived.

During that demonstration, I engaged in conversation an illegal immigrant from Mexico, and he made a passionate plea that has stayed with me since. He said, "The United States grabbed half of Mexico out of a pure lust for land. Most of what we call the Southwest—Texas, New Mexico, Arizona, California, and parts of Utah, Nevada, and Colorado—was part of Mexico. We are Mexican people and this used to be our land, before the United States invaded our country and took it. We still consider the land to be ours by right. Yet the Americans won't let us return and do agricultural labor on land that once belonged to us. How wicked can people be that they take something that is yours and then they won't even let you work and support your family on the land of your fathers?"

I still recall the wistful face of the man who said that. The issue he raised wasn't one I'd considered before, nor has it gone away since. Today leading Hispanic intellectuals and activists form part of a progressive coalition that presses the same argument. These Hispanics, however, are not wistful; they are angry. And they are here not to beg but to insist. Contemporary activists like Angel Gutierrez, Rodolfo Acuna, and Armando Navarro attribute America's size and wealth to its lust for conquest. Acuna's standard textbook, assigned in numerous American schools and colleges, is titled *Occupied America*. The title refers to America's acquisition of half of Mexico, and also to Hispanic reoccupation of America. What these activists want is a restoration of land that was taken, not necessarily to Mexico but to American Hispanics. And if the whites don't give it, these activists believe that the Hispanic population will soon become the majority group in the Southwest. Then it will be in a position to take it. Immigration—legal and illegal—is the mechanism that today's progressive organizers are counting on to undo the consequences of the Mexican War, and make the dream of Aztlan a reality.

Hispanic activists offer different versions of the Aztlan solution. In Albuquerque, New Mexico, I met Charles Truxillo, a former professor at the University of New Mexico, to interview him for the *America* film. Truxillo conceded that, strictly speaking, the Aztlan idea is a myth. The Chicanos of the 1960s, he says, talked about how they were originally Aztecs and how they wanted to recover the territory of the Aztec empire. Even today, he says, many Hispanics get together to do Aztec dances and re-live the Aztec fantasy. But the Aztecs, Truxillo points out, did not inhabit what is now the southwestern United States. They were farther south, in present-day Mexico. Yet Truxillo says Aztlan represents a "metaphorical" truth. The Southwest—what Americans call the Southwest—is actually El Norte, the northern part of Mexico that America stole by force.

This theft, Truxillo says, has to be rectified. For many years he flirted with a land grant solution. This would require the United States to restore to Mexicans the lands originally granted by the Spanish government when Spain ruled Mexico. Essentially Hispanics would be given large tracts of land in the United States, similar to Indian reservations. Hispanics, like native Indians, would become an autonomous "nation within a nation." Today, however, Truxillo has a new solution. His new solution is for the United States and Mexico to combine into a single great nation. Over time, he excitedly says, this would become a Hispanic nation, not an Anglo or white nation. Moreover, this solution doesn't require a war; it is, in a sense, happening naturally, through immigration and higher Hispanic birth rates. Truxillo assures me that eventually the border between the United States and Mexico will simply disappear. History, he concludes, has a way of settling old scores.

Armando Navarro is chairman of the Ethnic Studies Department at the University of California at Riverside. He sports a drawing of Che Guevara in his office, and also a photo of him posing with Fidel Castro. In 2001 Navarro led a group of Chicanos and Mexicans at the Zapatista March into Mexico City. He said he wanted to "demonstrate our solidarity with the indigenous people of Mexico." Navarro argues that Mexicans "were victims of an imperialism by which Mexico lost half its territory." Today, he says, the Latino vote is powerful enough to be the swing vote in elections; tomorrow, it will be in a position to realize Aztlan. After all, the end of the Soviet empire created new possibilities, from the breakup of Yugoslavia to reassertions of Chechen independence. The same could happen here. "Imagine the possibility that Mexico recovers the lost territories, or that a new Republic of Aztlan is established."

Navarro calls for Hispanics to do to the Americans what the Americans did to their Mexican ancestors. The Americans took the land by force, and now the Hispanics can take it back. Navarro does not consider himself a secessionist. His point is that the Mexicans, unlike the Southerners, never agreed to join the American union. Since the original conquest was illegitimate, the establishment of Aztlan is justified, however it is obtained. Hispanics are not seceding from America; they are simply getting back what originally belonged to them. America is the usurper that is being compelled to return its stolen territory.

There is, however, an irony to these calls for land repatriation. I alluded to it in my chapter on native Indians, but it re-emerges here even more strongly. America, in a sense, is being accused of a double theft. Allegedly we stole the country from the Indians, and then we stole a large part of Mexico from the Hispanics. Yet if the two continents of North and South America once belonged to the native Indians, then how did the Hispanics become owners of that land? There is a simple answer: they conquered it. Historian Patricia Limerick points out in *The Legacy of Conquest* that "the Hispanic presence in the Southwest was itself a product of conquest. The Pueblo Indians found themselves living in Occupied America long before the Hispanics did."[1] The term "Hispanic" refers to Spain, and "Latino" derives from the term Latin. So these terms refer to Spanish people from Europe who see themselves as descended from the Latin-speaking Romans. These Spanish then interbred with the locals, producing a mestizo or mixed-race Latino group. Hispanics, or Latinos, are a mixed-race people who trace their ancestry to the Spanish conquest of the Americas. Yet if the Spanish illicitly seized the land from the Indians, then the land doesn't actually belong to them. If America cannot claim title to land by conquest, then neither can the people from whom it was taken, who themselves took it from someone else.

We often think of the Mexican War as one between the powerful Americans and the poor, defenseless Mexicans. In this progressive narrative, the Americans are intoxicated by the Monroe Doctrine and Manifest Destiny, seizing land as they expand west, building the new country through the age-old mechanism of seizure and confiscation, and then dominating and exploiting the other nations of Central and South America. In his book *The Audacity of Hope*, Obama railed against the Monroe Doctrine, which he defined as "the notion that we could preemptively remove governments not to our liking." And recently Secretary of State John Kerry announced in a speech to the Organization of the American States that, as far as the Obama administration was concerned, "The era of the Monroe Doctrine is over."[2]

Both Obama and Kerry seem ignorant of what the Monroe Doctrine really means, or the context in which it was articulated. In reality, America, having freed itself from British colonial rule, had to contend with a continent that was the playground of empire, with the British, the French, and the Spanish all vying for land and supremacy. The Monroe Doctrine was a defense of the independence of the nations of the Americas from new attempts at European colonial rule, the doctrine stating that the United States would consider such impositions of foreign rule as belligerent actions to which the United States would have to respond. It was not an assertion of United States ownership of the Americas, but rather a warning to the European powers to leave the New World alone.

Progressives insist that, in practice, the United States became the behemoth of the Western hemisphere, regarding the Caribbean and Latin America as its "backyard." Yet if this is so, why does America have so little control over its backyard? Why are there so many independent nations in Central and South America—not to mention Mexico itself—that enjoy full sovereignty and frequently defy their powerful neighbor to the north? By the end of the Mexican War, American troops had captured Mexico City. The whole country was in the possession of the United States. So from one perspective the United States took half of Mexico; from another, the United States returned half of Mexico which it could have kept for itself. We cannot assess the legitimacy of these actions—and the claims for reparations that inevitably accompany them—without examining what really happened. And recalling our effort to do "history from below," we must throughout these inquiries concentrate on the fate of the little guy.

"Manifest Destiny" was a term first used by John O'Sullivan in 1845 in the *Democratic Review*. Sullivan argued that if America expanded from the Atlantic Ocean to the Pacific, this would increase both its security and prosperity. Sullivan said it was America's "manifest destiny to overspread the continent allotted by Providence for the free development of our yearly multiplying millions." Sullivan's point was that tens of millions of people were being ejected from Europe as a consequence of famine and hardship, and they were landing in America in search of a better life. Why, he asked, did these teeming millions from Ireland, Scandinavia, and elsewhere have any less right to land than the Spanish whose only claim was that they conquered it first? Admittedly at the time Sullivan wrote this, Mexico had fought off the Spanish and won its war of independence. Still, Mexico was controlled by mestizo oligarchs, themselves of partial Spanish descent. Abraham Lincoln described the Mexican government as a mixture of tyranny and anarchy. The life of the ordinary Mexican was difficult and insecure, not only because of poverty but also because of government-sanctioned corruption and seizure of land and goods. Property rights were based on an antiquated land grant system that was capriciously enforced. Political rights were few, and Civil Rights non-existent. So despite Mexican independence, the Mexicans themselves had virtually no rights that they could count on.

The Mexican War began with Texas. Since gaining its independence from Spain in 1821, the Mexican government had through land grants and other incentives encouraged Anglo settlers and traders to relocate to Texas. Many people from the American South and West did so. The Mexicans wanted the Anglos to help revitalize the economy and—as they were reputed to be rough, combative types—to help them fight the Comanches and other warlike Indian tribes. The Anglos did all that but they also brought with them their own sense of political and legal rights. Mexican attempts to encroach on those rights they regarded as tyranny.

In 1830, the Mexican government halted Anglo immigration into Texas, imposed customs duties, reorganized the governmental structure of Texas, and set up new military garrisons there. By this time, a majority of the people in Texas were Anglos, not Mexicans. Historian Daniel Walker Howe estimates that in 1830 "Anglos in Texas outnumbered Hispanic *tejanos* by more than two to one."[3] Sam Houston, who had emigrated to Texas from Tennessee, wrote President Andrew Jackson about the difficulty of dealing with the Mexican government. "Mexico is involved in civil war. The federal constitution has never been in operation. The government is essentially despotic." Led by Houston, the Texans decided to break away from Mexico. They weren't being ornery or recalcitrant. Historian H. W. Brands reminds us that the Americans who moved to Texas had been induced to do so as settlers. Mexico's ban on new immigration meant that "Texas could remain a frontier society indefinitely." But according to Brand, "Very few Americans—even among westerners—loved the frontier for its own sake. They migrated to the unsettled regions because they could afford land there, but no sooner did they purchase their plots than they wanted the frontier to look like the settled regions back east. . . . Nearly all the Americans in Texas had assumed that more of their compatriots would follow them there, and that the Texas frontier would fill with towns and eventually cities and the rising standard of living towns and cities entailed."[4] In sum, these were poor settlers who were looking for a better life, and that prospect seemed thwarted by the actions of the Mexican government, which was centralizing authority at the expense of Mexico's states.

In 1836, the Texans revolted, proclaiming Texas the "Lone Star Republic." This wasn't purely a white or Anglo rebellion. Historian David Montejano points out the rebellion was "brought about through an alliance of the newcomer Anglo colonists and the established Texas Mexican elite."[5] Originally the Texan revolt was not an attempt at secession. Rather, the rebels demanded that Mexico live up to the Mexican constitution of 1824, which granted the states a large degree of autonomy. But General Antonio Lopez de Santa Ana, Mexico's dictator since 1829, was not about to do this. It was only when Mexico ignored the Texan demands, responding with force, that the Texans decided on a complete separation from Mexico. There is an interesting echo here of the American Revolution which began as a protest against British misrule—the deprivation of "the rights of Englishmen"—but eventually became a movement for full independence and to affirm the universal "rights of man." In the same vein, the Texans started out by trying to be good Mexicans and when that didn't work they broke away and drafted a new constitution modeled on that of the United States.

The Texans petitioned the United States for help in their war against the Mexican government. Oddly enough, none came. President Andrew Jackson—despite his reputation as an expansionist—rejected intervention on behalf of the Texans. Even when the Texans won and became a republic, the U.S. refused to admit Texas as a state, largely because of Northern concerns that the admission of Texas would strengthen the slave power of the American South. So Texas remained an independent republic for about a decade. Finally in 1845 Texas received admission into the United States. Now it was a matter of settling the border between Texas and Mexico.

It was the disputed claims between the Texans and the Mexicans—over where Mexico ended and Texas began—that set off the Mexican War. Mexico claimed the border was the Nueces River, while Texas insisted it was the Rio Grande. On balance, the Mexicans appear to have had the stronger case, yet for almost a decade they made no effort to enforce it, allowing Texas free access to the larger territory it claimed. Upon admitting Texas as a state, President Polk sent a delegation of U.S. troops to the Rio Grande to "inspect" the border. The Mexicans ambushed an American patrol, thus precipitating the Mexican War.

The Mexican War, though popular among the American people, was controversial and divided the country's leaders. The abolitionist Frederick Douglass was opposed, attributing it to America's "cupidity and love of dominion." Ralph Waldo Emerson thought it unwise and imperialist. Thoreau refused to pay his Massachusetts poll tax on the grounds that it would help fund the Mexican War. (He was jailed for a night while a relative paid the tax and obtained his release.) By contrast, Walt Whitman argued that Mexico was the aggressor and therefore "Mexico must be thoroughly chastised."[6]

Congressman Abraham Lincoln opposed the war, as did his mentor Henry Clay. The Whig position was against expansion—Whigs generally believed that America should set an example of a free republic rather than expand its boundaries. In the 1844 presidential election, the Whig candidate Henry Clay lost to the Democrat James Polk in part because Clay opposed admitting Texas to the Union. Clay later condemned the Mexican War as motivated by a lust for conquest and "a spirit of universal dominion."[7] By contrast, the Democrats favored extending freedom by enlarging the boundaries of the United States, through purchase and treaty when possible, through force when warranted. This debate was complicated by the slavery issue: Southerners wanted the country to get bigger so they could add more slave states; Northerners wanted to ensure that any additions to America would be free states rather than slave states.

Lincoln contended that President Polk had found an excuse to go to war with Mexico by falsely claiming that Mexicans had shed American blood on American soil. Lincoln introduced sarcastic "spot resolutions" demanding that Polk identify the precise spot on which that blood had been spilled. Even so, Lincoln's position had its own nuance. Lincoln never disputed that the Mexican government was tyrannical, or that the Texans had a right to assert their independence. If Americans had a right to revolt against British rule, surely the

Texans had the right to throw off the tyranny of the Mexican oligarchs. Later, in his Mexican War speech on January 12, 1848, Lincoln would proclaim the Declaration of Independence to be "a most valuable, a most sacred right—a right which, we hope and believe, is to liberate the world."[8] Lincoln's argument in opposition to the war was merely that it had been started under false pretexts, and that Polk had gone beyond defending Texas to coveting Mexican territory.

The war was short and decisive. The Mexicans were commanded by General Santa Ana, who had led the successful Mexican revolt against Spain. But Santa Ana was no match for the United States forces, led by Generals Zachary Taylor and Winfield Scott. Taylor would later become president of the United States, and Scott the highest ranking general in the army. Junior officers in the American army included such familiar names as Ulysses Grant, George McClellan, Stonewall Jackson, Robert E. Lee, and Jefferson Davis—future Civil War adversaries, now fighting on the same side.

The war ended in 1847, when the Mexican capital fell to the United States. The United States flag flew over Mexico City, which was occupied by the U.S. army for nine months. Ultimately the Americans withdrew and the peace was secured by the Treaty of Guadalupe Hidalgo, which settled the Texas border and granted the United States a vast area extending from the present states of New Mexico to California to Wyoming. America, however, could have kept all of Mexico. The United States decided to keep half and give half back.

How to assess the Mexican War? I don't feel sorry for the Mexican government, which started the war and lost the war. Nor will I deny that this was in part an American war of conquest that added a million and a half square miles to the territory of the United States. Who suffered as a consequence of the war? Howard Zinn, performing "history from below," focuses on the small number of American soldiers who refused to fight because they opposed America's involvement in the war. Motivated by opposition to the war, and also by land grants offered to defectors by the Mexican government, around three hundred American soldiers joined the Mexican army. So a small contingent of soldiers quit or switched sides—who cares? The real issue is the impact on Mexicans who were directly affected by the war. We have to consider what became of them and their descendants.

Consider the claims we hear today about how Mexicans merely want to return and work on their own land that was unjustly taken. But no land was taken from them at all. After the war, the United States immediately recognized as valid the property rights of Mexicans who were now part of U.S. territory. The change was not in any individual's land ownership but in the fact that people who were once Mexicans now became Americans.

Normally it is a lengthy process to become an American citizen— I know, because as an immigrant I went through it myself. Yet according to the Treaty of Guadalupe Hidalgo, the Mexicans who ended up on the American side were immediately made American citizens. Article IX of the Treaty guaranteed them "all the rights of the citizens of the United States." This itself is historically unique: of the three main "involuntary" minority groups—American Indians, blacks, and Mexicans—only Mexicans were offered immediate American citizenship. They were granted more rights, including more secure property rights, than they had ever enjoyed before.

There is probably some truth to Robert Rosenbaum's claim that, as a consequence of the war, "most mexicanos in the United States lost their freedom to live as they wanted to live." Rosenbaum is the author of *Mexicano Resistance in the Southwest*. He documents several cases—not numerous but significant—in which Mexicans fought against American occupation. Rosenbaum also notes that "full citizenship and property rights did not result in economic opportunity or social integration for mexicanos." Besides the differences in language and culture, there was nativism and discrimination to contend with. Even so, Mexican Americans enjoyed more opportunity to improve their lives than they would have had in Mexico. They now enjoyed the whole set of rights under the U.S. Constitution, including the right to self-government. Political scientist Harry Jaffa writes, "The accessions of parts of Mexico to the United States did not mean a denial of self-government to the inhabitants of these regions but the first effective assurance of self-government they would have had."[9]

Mexicans have always enjoyed a preferred status in U.S. immigration policy, and not just because of the country's proximity to America. In the 1920s the United States passed immigration restrictions, imposing quota limits on immigration from most countries, but there were no limits on Mexican immigration. Mexicans, in fact, were racially classified as "white" for the purposes of immigration policy. Today, despite the high number of legal immigrants America takes from Mexico, a majority of illegal immigrants also come from that country. Remarkably, had America retained control of all of Mexico, those illegals wouldn't have to cross the border; they would already be U.S. citizens. While progressives deplore American aggression, one wonders whether there are Mexicans who wish America had been more aggressive. What we do know is that the vast majority of Mexicans who ended up on the American side of the border, following the Mexican War, never attempted to return to Mexico. And neither have their descendants.

CHAPTER 8

THEIR FOURTH OF JULY

Other revolutions have been the insurrection of the oppressed; this was the repentance of the tyrant.[1]
—RALPH WALDO EMERSON

I n 1862, Abraham Lincoln spoke to a group of African Americans about his plan, at the conclusion of the Civil War, to relocate blacks to a new country that they could call their own. He noted that more than ten thousand free blacks had already emigrated to the nation of Liberia. As Lincoln knew, Congress had at his request appropriated $600,000 in funds for black relocation—what at the time was called "colonization." Lincoln established a special colonization office in the Department of the Interior. That office had solicited and received several proposals for relocation. Among the areas considered were British Honduras, British Guiana, Colombia (in what is now Panama), and an island off the coast of Haiti.[2]

In his speech, Lincoln acknowledged before his black audience that "your race is suffering in my judgment the greatest wrong inflicted on any people." Even so, he said that many whites—including whites fighting on the Northern side—detested blacks, and blacks returned that hatred. Lincoln remarked, "It is better for us both, therefore, to be separated." Lincoln invited free blacks to volunteer to be the first to relocate. He recognized that asking free men to move to another country was a burden. Yet he said, "For the sake of your race you should sacrifice something of your current comfort." After all, "In the American revolutionary war, sacrifices were made by men engaged in it."[3]

It may seem surprising to see Abraham Lincoln—the great emancipator—promote a colonization scheme that today seems wrongheaded and even racist. Yet colonization was an idea that predated Lincoln by almost a century. In fact, it was an idea first advanced by blacks, and it was supported by several American Founders. Thomas Jefferson raised it as a possibility, and James Madison and Daniel Webster offered early colonization proposals. Madison's scheme involved selling land acquired from American Indians to newly arriving European immigrants and using the money to repatriate blacks to Africa.[4]

The American Colonization Society was founded in 1816, and it had white and black members. The Society convinced President Monroe to send agents to help found the country now known as Liberia—its capital city was named Monrovia in honor of the American president. Lincoln's mentor, Henry Clay, was a member of the American Colonization Society. The concept of colonization was supported by a number of Northern Republicans, including abolitionist leader Thad Stevens. Prominent newspapers like the *New York Times* and the *Chicago Tribune* editorialized in favor of it. Black supporters of colonization included the abolitionist pamphleteer J. Willis Menard, physician and writer Martin Delany of Pennsylvania, political activist Charles Babcock of Massachusetts, and New Yorkers Junius Morel, a journalist, and the abolitionist preacher Highland Garnet of Shiloh Presbyterian Church.[5]

Frederick Douglass, the best-known black abolitionist leader, opposed colonization. In an 1894 speech, Douglass insisted colonization was abhorrent for the Negro because "it forces upon him the idea that he is forever doomed to be a stranger and a sojourner in the land of his birth, and that he has no permanent abiding place here." Instead, colonization condemns the Negro to "an uncertain home" someplace else. "It is not atonement, but banishment." Douglass resoundingly concluded that "the native land of the American Negro is America" and "we are here and here to stay."[6]

Yet a few decades earlier, this same Douglass told a white audience in his famous Fourth of July oration, "This fourth of July is yours, not mine. You may rejoice, I must mourn. To drag a man in fetters into the grand illuminated temple of liberty, and call upon him to join you in joyous anthems, were inhuman mockery and sacrilegious irony. I have no patriotism. I have no country. What country have I? The institutions of this country do not know me, do not recognize me as a man. I have not—I cannot have—any love for this country, as such, or for its constitution. I desire to see its overthrow as speedily as possible."[7] Douglass here is committing treason, but it is honorable treason. He is saying that one cannot be a good citizen in a bad country. Many abolitionists agreed with him, and they routinely denounced the American founding and burned copies of the Constitution which abolitionist leader William Lloyd Garrison termed a "covenant with death and an agreement with hell." The abolitionist view, shared by Garrison and Douglass, was that on account of its compromise with slavery, America was ill-founded and the American Founders were craven hypocrites.

The alleged hypocrisy of the Founders was a major theme of British scorn directed against America at the time of the American Revolution. Typical was Samuel Johnson's retort, "How is it we hear the loudest yelps for liberty among the drivers of Negroes?" The same criticism of the Founders was taken up by Supreme Court Chief Justice Roger Taney in the *Dred Scott* decision. Taney reasoned that the Founders said "all men are created equal" but they could not have meant it, since they allowed slavery in the Constitution and some of them personally owned slaves. Therefore, Taney concluded, the Constitution gives blacks "no rights which the white man was bound to respect." And Senator John Calhoun—the intellectual architect of the pro-slavery doctrine of the South—declared that "all men are created equal" constituted "the most false and dangerous of all political errors."[8]

While disavowing the Confederate cause, progressives today generally agree both with Northern abolitionist critics of the Constitution and pro-slavery Southerners that the Founders could not have meant what they said about all men being created equal. Many progressives hold, with Douglass, that slavery is America's "original sin," and that the Founders are guilty because they allowed it. Slavery—the argument continues—represents a two and a half century program of looting black labor without paying for it. America was built with the labor of the slaves, and the disadvantages imposed by slavery continue to keep blacks far behind whites in wealth and opportunity. In the view of some progressives, America today owes a huge debt of reparations to African Americans because as a group they are vastly worse off as a consequence of the enslavement of their ancestors.[9]

Can the progressive claim for reparations be sustained? Slavery is indeed a system of stolen labor, and historically slaves were taken as captives in war. Having conquered a nation or tribe, the victors would either kill or enslave the defeated group. From the dawn of mankind, every culture has had slavery. There was slavery in ancient Greece and Rome, in China, in Africa, and in India. American Indians had slaves long before Columbus arrived. What is uniquely Western is not slavery but the abolition of slavery. "No civilization once dependent on slavery has ever been able to eradicate it," historian J. M. Roberts writes, "except the Western."[10]

Moreover, from the founding through the end of the Civil War, there were black slave-owners in America. I am referring to free blacks who themselves owned black slaves. While the existence of black slave-ownership is known, its magnitude is surprising. A review of the relevant scholarship shows that in 1830 there were 3,500 American black slave-owners who collectively owned more than ten thousand black slaves. In *Black Masters*, Michael Johnson and James Roark tell the remarkable story of William Ellison, a free black planter and cotton gin maker in South Carolina, who owned more than a hundred slaves. Himself descended from slaves, Ellison did not hesitate to buy slaves and work them in the same manner as white slave-owners. Johnson and Roark write, "Ellison did not view his shop and plantation as halfway houses to freedom. He never permitted a single slave to duplicate his own experience. Everything suggests that Ellison held his slaves to exploit them, to profit from them, just as white slave-owners did." When the Civil War broke out, most black slave-owners like Ellison joined their white counterparts in supporting the Confederacy.[11]

Obviously black slave-owners in America represented a tiny fraction of the total number of slave-owners—I mention them because so little is known about them, and because they illustrate the universal conquest ethic that sustained slavery from its beginnings. This conquest ethic is further confirmed by the fact that when Britain and France in the early to mid-nineteenth century considered abolition proposals, tribal leaders in Gambia, the Congo, Dahomey, and other African nations that had prospered under the slave trade sent delegations to Paris and London to vigorously protest against them.[12] One African chief memorably stated that he wanted three things—foodstuffs, alcohol, and weapons—and he had three things to exchange for them—men, women, and children.

Slavery became controversial for one reason: the influence of Christianity. In my part-time career as a Christian apologist, I have debated this point with leading atheists, and they are reluctant to admit it. The atheists say that for many centuries Christians allowed slavery and it was only in the modern period—the period of the Enlightenment—that slavery came into question. The implication is that Enlightenment egalitarianism, not Christianity, propelled the anti-slavery cause. This, however, is simply false. Slavery was widespread during the Roman Empire which lasted until the fifth century. This was the period of pre-Christian Rome. Then slavery disappeared in Europe between the fifth century and the tenth century. Slavery was replaced by serfdom. While serfdom imposes its own burdens, serfs are not slaves. They own themselves, they can make contracts, they have a measure of freedom to work and marry that simply does not exist for slaves. The advent of serfdom was a huge change and a big improvement. It occurred during the so-called Dark Ages, when Europe was completely and thoroughly Christian. So what, if not Christianity, caused the extinction of slavery in Europe?

Unfortunately slavery was revived in the modern era, not so much in Europe as in America. This occurred for economic reasons: there was work to be done in the new world, and there were people who could be made to do it for free. There was a flourishing slave trade in Africa, supplying slaves to Asia and the Middle East, with an apparently inexhaustible supply of captives waiting to be sold.

This "supply" found a new "demand" in the plantations of North and South America. Slavery was profitable for the planter class, and also for the Africans who engaged in the trade. Yet the institution once again became controversial, and once again it was Christians who took up the cause of getting rid of slavery. It is a fact of great significance that only in the West—the region of the world officially known as Christendom—did anti-slavery movements arise. There is no history of an anti-slavery movement outside the West.

Even the atheists admit that the anti-slavery movements in England and America were led by Christians. I am not suggesting that the Christians were the only ones who disliked slavery. From ancient times there had been another group that disliked slavery. That group was called slaves. So there were always reports of runaways, slave revolts, and so on. What Christianity produced was an entirely different phenomenon: men who were eligible to be masters who opposed slavery. This idea is beautifully expressed in Lincoln's maxim, "As I would not be a slave, so I would not be a master."[13] Lincoln understood this to be nothing more than an application of Christ's golden rule: do unto others as you would have them do unto you.

As Lincoln realized, there is a deep connection between the movement to end slavery and the American founding. Both, it turns out, are built on the same Christian foundation. Christianity had always held that all humans are equal in the eyes of God. Starting in the early eighteenth century, a group of Christians—first the Quakers, later the evangelical Christians—applied this belief directly to the slave trade between Africa and the New World. They interpreted human equality in God's eyes to mean that no man has the right to rule another man without his consent. We see here that the moral roots of the anti-slavery movement are the same as the moral roots of democracy and America's founding. Both are based on the idea that no person is justified in ruling another without consent.

The idea of consent is critical to understanding why slavery is so bad; it is also critical to understanding why slavery could not be immediately abolished by the American Founders. Lincoln understood this in a way that abolitionists and modern progressives never have. Lincoln agreed with abolitionists that slavery was abhorrent; he disagreed with them on how to fight it. In fact, he regarded their strategy as one that would help slavery. Lincoln's understanding of slavery was built on two principles: the principle of self-ownership and the principle of consent. "I always thought that the man who made the corn should eat the corn," Lincoln said. For Lincoln, the greatness of America—what made it "the wonder and admiration of the whole world"—was that "there is not a permanent class of hired laborers amongst us" and that "every man can make himself." Lincoln envisioned a society in which people don't merely command the price that their labor brings, but they also go into business for themselves. Thus "the hired laborer of yesterday, labors on his own account today, and will hire others to labor for him tomorrow." The evil of slavery is that it is "a war upon the rights of all working people." The black slave has "the right to eat the bread, without leave of anybody else, which his own hand earns." In this respect, "he is my equal and the equal of Judge Douglas and the equal of every living man." Slavery was based on "the same tyrannical principle" that Lincoln expressed this way: "You work and toil and earn bread, and I'll eat it."[14]

Let's analyze Lincoln's argument. We own ourselves, so therefore we own our own labor and have a right to pursue happiness for ourselves. The means we employ is consent. We agree to sell our labor for a price that we agree upon, and we agree to be ruled by leaders whom we elect by our own free choice. In a representative democracy, consent takes the form of majority rule. In a free market, consent takes the form of agreement to work for a price, or contracts consented to by the parties involved. Without consent, there is tyranny. Slavery is wrong not because the work is hard and humiliating—immigrants in the North were doing work no less hard or humiliating—nor is it wrong because the slaves are not paid for their labor. I might agree to work for you and not be paid; this does not make me a slave. Slavery is wrong because the slave has not consented to the terms of employment. Against his will, he is made to work for free. We see here how Lincoln unifies the arguments for democracy, capitalism, and emancipation. They are all, at bottom, based on the primacy of individual consent.

Now we can answer the question: If the Founders really believed all men are created equal, how could they permit slavery? That the Founders were flawed and self-interested men of their time it is impossible to deny. Many were slave-owners, Jefferson being one of the largest. (Jefferson owned more than two hundred slaves, and unlike Washington, never freed them.) Yet Jefferson's case is revealing: far from rationalizing plantation life by adopting the Southern arguments about the happy slave, Jefferson the Virginian vehemently denounced slavery as unfair and immoral. "I tremble for my country when I realize that God is just; that his justice cannot sleep forever."[15] So the remarkable thing is not that a Southern planter owned slaves, but that this slaveholding planter nevertheless insisted that "all men are created equal."

If Jefferson and the Founders knew that all men are created equal, why not outlaw slavery from the outset? The simple answer is that had they done so, there would never have been a union. Historian Eugene Genovese states the obvious, "If the Constitution had not recognized slavery, the Southern states would never have entered the union." So the choice facing the Founders in Philadelphia was not whether to have slavery or not. Rather, it was whether to have a union that temporarily tolerated slavery, or to have no union at all.

The continent of North America might then have become an amal-
gam of smaller nations—vulnerable to the depredations of foreign
empires—and slavery might have continued longer than it actually
did.

The Founders' conundrum can be expressed in a deeper way. The
Declaration of Independence says that "all men are created equal"
and the Founders believed this. But the Declaration also says that
governments must be founded by the consent of the governed. These
are the core principles of democracy. The problem arises when a
substantial segment of the people, perhaps even a majority, refuses
to give their consent to the proposition that "all men are created
equal." In that case, how should the wise statesman respond? The
progressive answer—which was also the abolitionist answer—is
simple: forget about democracy. If the people aren't ready to get rid
of slavery—if they do not know what's right and good—then force
them. The Founders knew there was no way to do this, but even if
they could, in doing so they would have destroyed democracy in its
infancy. Slavery would be abolished, but tyranny would have to be
established to do it.

The Founders decided on a different course. They set a date a
few years ahead for the ending of the slave trade—no more importa-
tion of slaves. They prohibited slavery in the Northwest Territory
(essentially the modern upper Midwest, including Wisconsin, Michigan, Illinois, Indiana, and Ohio). Most important, they established
a union on anti-slavery principles that nevertheless temporarily
tolerated the practice of slavery. Nowhere in the Constitution is the
term "slavery" used. Slaves are always described as "persons," imply-
ing their possession of natural rights. The three-fifths clause, which
some today think represents the Founders' view of the worth of
blacks, was actually a measure to curb the voting power of the slave-
owning South—it helped over time to swing the balance of power

to the free states. Many of the Founders believed that this approach would prove sufficient because slavery was losing its appeal and would steadily die out. In this the Founders were mistaken, because Eli Whitney's invention of the cotton gin in 1793—which the Founders had no way to anticipate—revived the demand for slavery in the South.

Still, the Founders' efforts did undermine slavery. Before 1776, slavery was legal across America. Yet by 1804 every state north of Maryland had abolished slavery either outright or gradually; and Congress outlawed the slave trade in 1808. Slavery was no longer a national but a sectional institution, and one under moral and political siege.

Lincoln not only perceived the Founders' problem, he inherited it. Lincoln sought to distinguish the principles of the founding from its compromises. Yet he also knew that the compromises were not merely base calculations to advance self-interest; rather, they were accommodations to prudence, and to the popular consent that is the cornerstone of democratic self-government. Lincoln too deferred to the Founders' compromise, by saying he would not oppose slavery in the states where it existed, but would merely block slavery from coming into the new territories.

During the Lincoln-Douglas debates, Senator Stephen Douglas—sounding like Calhoun, and just as telling, like a modern progressive—ridiculed the idea that the Founders believed all men are created equal. Calhoun went even further; for him, the equality clause of the Declaration was not self-evidently true but rather self-evidently false, since people are obviously vastly different in size, in speed, in intelligence, and even in moral character. Lincoln sought to defend the Founders against these calumnies. Commenting on the Declaration, Lincoln responded on behalf of the Founders:

They intended to include all men, but they did not intend to declare all men equal in all respects. . . . They defined with tolerable distinctness in what respect they did consider all men created equal—equal in certain inalienable rights. They did not mean to assert the obvious untruth, that all were then actually enjoying that equality, nor yet, that they were about to confer it immediately upon them. . . . They meant simply to declare the *right*, so that the *enforcement* of it might follow as fast as circumstances should permit.[16]

Remarkably Lincoln's position came to be shared by Frederick Douglass, who as we saw had once denounced the Constitution but who eventually reached the conclusion that it embodied anti-slavery principles. "Abolish slavery tomorrow, and not a sentence or syllable of the Constitution needs to be altered," Douglass said. Slavery, he concluded, was merely "scaffolding to the magnificent structure, to be removed as soon as the building was completed." Douglass came to understand what nineteenth-century abolitionists and twenty-first-century progressives do not—that the best anti-slavery program is not support for the grandest impractical scheme but rather "is that which deals the deadliest blow upon slavery that can be given at a particular time."[17]

It took a Civil War to destroy slavery, and some six hundred thousand whites were killed in that war, "one life for every six slaves freed," historian C. Vann Woodward reminds us. The real heroes of the Civil War are not the ones progressives idolize—former slaves like Douglass or Northern abolitionists like Walt Whitman, the Grimke sisters, and Charles Sumner. It is hardly a surprise that a former slave should oppose slavery, and Douglass ended up gaining fame and fortune for his worthy abolitionist strivings. Northern abolitionists had the luxury of railing against slavery in pews and convention halls, but with the exception of John Brown—who put his life where his conscience was—very few paid the ultimate price for their convictions. The ultimate price was paid by the men—many of them recent immigrants—who died in the war to end slavery. I am thinking of the three hundred thousand or so Union men who never owned a slave and yet fought to the death to get rid of the institution.

When I recently visited Gettysburg, the guide showed us a church that was during the war converted into a Union hospital—this is where they bandaged wounds and performed surgeries and amputations. The carnage was so bad that they had to drill holes in the floor for the blood to drain out. If we are doing "history from below" let us remember the white soldiers who died in order to achieve freedom for the slaves. They owed the slaves nothing; the slaves owe them their freedom, a freedom that the slaves were not in a position to secure for themselves.

Did America owe something to the slaves whose labor had been stolen? I think it did, although Frederick Douglass, of all people, largely disagreed. Speaking to the Massachusetts Anti-Slavery Society just days before the Civil War ended, Douglass raised the question: What must be "done" for the former slaves? Here is Douglass's answer. "Do nothing with us! Your doing with us has already played the mischief with us. Do nothing with us. . . . If the Negro cannot stand on his own legs, let him fall. All I ask is, give him a chance to stand on his own legs! Let him alone. . . . If you will only untie his hands and give him a chance, I think he will live."[18]

And what about today? Does America owe blacks now living reparations on account of slavery? No more than it owes reparations to the descendants of whites who died in the Civil War. I don't mean this in the callous way of suggesting that what's done is done. Rather,

I mean that there is an enormous debt owed to the Northern men who died in the Civil War. But those heroes are dead, and their descendants are scattered. What is owed is more than money can pay; we discharge our debt by honoring and remembering. Similarly there is a debt owed to slaves whose labor was wrongly taken from them. That debt too is best discharged through memory, because the slaves are dead and their descendants—this will be a hard pill for progressives to swallow—are better off as a consequence of their ancestors being hauled from Africa to America.

Better off? The point is illustrated by the great African American boxer Muhammad Ali. In the early 1970s Muhammad Ali fought for the heavyweight title against George Foreman. The fight was held in the African nation of Zaire; it was insensitively called the "rumble in the jungle." Ali won the fight, and upon returning to the United States, he was asked by a reporter, "Champ, what did you think of Africa?" Ali replied, "Thank God my granddaddy got on that boat!" There is a characteristic mischievous pungency to Ali's remark, yet it also expresses a widely held sentiment. Ali recognizes that for all the horror of slavery, it was the transmission belt that brought Africans into the orbit of Western freedom. The slaves were not better off—the boat Ali refers to brought the slaves through a horrific Middle Passage to a life of painful servitude—yet their descendants today, even if they won't admit it, are better off. Ali was honest enough to admit it.

So was the black feminist writer Zora Neale Hurston. Of slavery she wrote, "From what I can learn it was sad. Certainly. But my ancestors who lived and died in it are dead. The white men who profited by their labor and lives are dead also. I have no personal memory of those times, and no responsibility for them. Neither has the grandson of the man who held my folks. . . . I have no intention of wasting my time beating on old graves. . . . Slavery is the price I paid for civilization, and that is worth all that I have paid through my ancestors for it."[19]

Our case is settled not by Ali or Hurston but by the actual choices made by African Americans from the end of the Civil War to the present. Here we get back to the American Colonization Society. Many of the free blacks who supported the idea of colonization held what we would today recognize as progressive assumptions. They held that America was founded as a white man's country and would remain a white man's country. They believed that blacks would never be able to call America home, and that they would never in good conscience be able to celebrate the Fourth of July. They insisted that the only way for blacks to be truly free was to found their own country, write their own Declaration of Independence, and build it themselves.

The idea of colonization disappeared after the Civil War because black leaders like Frederick Douglass realized that their premises were wrong. America was founded by white men, but it was not founded as a white man's country. America was founded on the principle of equality—not just equal dignity, but also the equal right of people to govern themselves and advance themselves and freely sell their labor. It took a bitter war to reconcile those principles and extend the pledge of equality to the enslaved African American, but hundreds of thousands of whites fought that war and paid in blood for their country's sin of slavery. The African slaves suffered horribly in their passage to America, and in the treatment that was too often meted out to them here, but their descendants enjoy something that no previous African did, and that few Africans do now. Today's African Americans, like all Americans, have the immeasurable benefit of living with freedom and opportunity in a country big enough to realize human dreams.

CHAPTER 9

"THANK YOU, MISTER JEFFERSON"

They were signing a promissory note, to which every American was to fall heir.[1]

—MARTIN LUTHER KING, "I HAVE A DREAM"

On September 18, 1895, the black educator Booker T. Washington spoke before an all-white audience at the Cotton States and International Exposition in Atlanta. He was the first African American invited to address this Southern group. In his speech, Washington said, "The wisest of my race understand that the agitation of questions of social equality is the extremist folly, and that progress in the enjoyment of all of the privileges that will come to us must be the result of severe and constant struggle rather than of artificial forcing. . . . It is important and right that all the privileges of the law be ours, but it is vastly more important that we be prepared for the exercise of these privileges." Remarkably the leading black statesman in the country gave an endorsement of segregation, saying in effect that blacks should focus more on self-improvement than on equality of rights under the law.

In the previous chapter, we focused on slavery. Here we examine what came after slavery—segregation and racism—and examine whether they are forms of theft. Consider the plight of the freed slaves and their descendants. They opt to stay in America, the only land they know, the land they have chosen as preferable to returning to Africa or going someplace else. Even so, in America they suffer systematic and virulent discrimination, both in the form of law and private conduct, especially in the South. This continues for a century. Only then, in the Civil Rights era of the 1950s and 1960s, is legal segregation finally ended and equal rights under the law finally affirmed.

Even so, racism continues to exist. For the *America* film, I interviewed the African American scholar Michael Eric Dyson, who teaches at Georgetown. I've debated Dyson a couple of times over the years—he's a gregarious scholar who calls me "Brother D'Souza." Dyson says that despite racial progress blacks continue to face serious obstacles that are the unquestionable product of past and present bigotry. Dyson infers this, in part, from the fact that blacks in America aren't doing as well as whites. Even non-white immigrants, he points out, are doing better than African Americans. Dyson presumes that this differential in black success is a measure of how much has been—and is being—taken from them. Dyson, like many progressives, contends that America has been and continues to be guilty of stealing the opportunities and labor value of African Americans. If this is true, he says, the thief must be held to account, and pay.

As for Booker T. Washington, he is regarded by progressives as a kind of sell-out, a so-called "Uncle Tom." Dyson is too kind to say this, but he is not a fan. And the sell-out accusation was even made at the time, by Washington's nemesis W. E. B. Du Bois. I focus on the Washington-Du Bois debate because it illuminates America's racial history from slavery to the present. It helps us to understand what it is about segregation and racism that constitutes theft, and what doesn't. Moreover, it is an illuminating study of how groups at the bottom can climb up the ladder.

Let's begin with segregation, the practice of separating the races that began after the Civil War. In slavery, of course, the races were very close together. But after the Civil War a humiliated South decided, once the Northern troops went home, to take it out on the blacks. The infamous Ku Klux Klan, for instance—begun after the Civil War as a secret paramilitary resistance group against Reconstruction, and then openly revived in the early twentieth century—visited lynchings and other horrors on African Americans. In the late nineteenth century, a coalition of Southerners—including the conservative ruling class of the region—passed laws mandating the segregation of the two races. As a consequence, railway cars, steamships, and ferries had separate sections for whites and blacks. So did post offices, prisons, restaurants, theaters, swimming pools, bowling alleys, and churches. Schools, hospitals, and retirement homes were also segregated. Blacks and whites used separate public toilets and drinking fountains.

Remarkably, for some Southern conservatives, segregation was a way to protect blacks from the wrath of the Klan and other radical racist groups. Historian Joel Williamson writes, "Conservatives sought segregation . . . to protect black people and their dignity. For conservatives, segregation meant giving the black person a very special place in which he would be protected. Far from putting down the self-esteem of black people, conservative segregation was designed to preserve and encourage it."[2] Today this seems incredible; it runs completely counter to the progressive propaganda against a uniformly racist South. But Williamson points out that there were different elements in the South—the radicals and the conservatives—and for the latter group, segregation was considered preferable to leaving blacks at the mercy of lynchings and flaming crosses.

Who fought segregation? Not the liberals; in the South, there were few outspoken liberals and their opinions were irrelevant. Rather, private streetcar companies mounted the only significant, albeit unsuccessful, opposition. Private companies were concerned about the higher cost of doing business under segregation. Economist Jennifer Roback, in her study of streetcar segregation, shows that companies did not want to provide separate cars for different racial groups. Some even refused to enforce segregation ordinances until they were coerced by the government into compliance through fines. Segregation was "free" for the government because any additional costs were simply passed on to the taxpayer. Segregation therefore, represented a triumph of government regulation over the free market.[3]

Under segregation, blacks had no alternative but to adapt, and the evidence shows they did. The most resourceful blacks realized that in a perverse way segregation created economic opportunity, because it kept whites out of businesses and professions that served the black community. Economist Thomas Sowell writes, "The reluctance of whites to minister to the hair, the bodies, or the souls of blacks created a class of black barbers, physicians, undertakers, and religious ministers." Black masons, jewelers, tailors, repairmen, and teachers made a modest living in the segregated Jim Crow world. In several Southern cities and towns, blacks developed flourishing banking, real estate, and insurance industries. In a few areas—notably entertainment and athletics—blacks were able to thwart segregation and achieve fame and affluence by catering to white audiences.[4]

While segregation represented a burden and imposition on blacks, it does not follow that segregation by itself constituted theft. Obviously there is no theft involved in voluntary segregation. People are free to associate with whomever they want, and if they choose not to associate with someone they are not thereby depriving that person of rights. This principle, of course, applies equally to blacks and whites. If a black man, for instance, wants to live in a predominantly black neighborhood he is not by that decision depriving anyone of his property or rights. By the same token, if a white man wants to have only white friends he is not thereby taking something away from blacks or anyone else. Voluntary segregation may be distasteful and even objectionable but it is not stealing.

State-sponsored segregation is a different matter. We are entitled as citizens to equal rights under the law. Therefore when legal segregation is imposed, it forcibly separates groups that have every right to live together, eat together, and work together. To the degree that segregation deprived blacks from freely interacting with whites, to their economic disadvantage, legal segregation did constitute a "taking" from blacks. This "taking" is undeniable, even if it is hard to quantify. Sure, blacks may have established productive niches within segregation, but undoubtedly at least some of them could have established even more productive enterprises that served both blacks and whites. Happily segregation was ended by the 1960s through a series of government and court decisions.

While segregation is now behind us by half a century, racism continues. Thus racism seems to constitute ongoing theft. Still, we should be precise with language. Strictly speaking, racism cannot be a form of theft because racism is a perspective or point of view. Racism is simply the doctrine or belief in the inferiority of another group, in this case African Americans. How can you steal from someone by thinking badly about them? What we are concerned about, therefore, is not racism but discrimination. Racism is the theory and discrimination is the practice. It is discrimination, not racism, that we should examine for the deprivations it imposes on blacks.

Racial discrimination, like segregation, can be voluntary or involuntary. To put it differently, discrimination, like segregation, can be private or state-sanctioned. Private discrimination is voluntary; it involves private persons or entities that choose to discriminate. State discrimination is compulsory; it involves laws that discriminate. As with voluntary segregation, it is hard to see how voluntary discrimination constitutes any kind of theft. Consider the example of a person or company that refuses to hire or rent to an East Indian. Is that person or company thereby stealing from the East Indian? Clearly not. When people enter into contracts to rent or work, the parties do so because of their mutual benefit. It benefits the landlord or employer on the one hand, and the renter or employee on the other. Either party, for any reason, may decline to make the contract. Private employers should no more be forced to hire employees than employees should be forced to work for employers against their will.

Now if an employer discriminates against any group—or refuses to hire members of that group—this is clearly to the detriment of members of that group. What is often missed, however, is that such actions are also to the detriment of the employer. Employers obviously benefit from having the widest pool of potential recruits, in order to be able to choose the most productive and competent employees. By excluding groups from consideration, discriminators narrow their own pool of selection. Therefore discrimination is good neither for employers or employees.

Is a worker who refuses to work for a particular company "stealing" from it? Obviously not. But why not? Perhaps the worker has valuable skills that could benefit the company. By depriving the company of his or her services—by "discriminating" against it—the worker could arguably be preventing the company from realizing its full profitability. Still, workers are not obligated to maximize anyone else's full profitability; they can work for whomever they want. The reason workers don't hurt companies by "discriminating" against them is that the company is not worse off than it was before. By the same logic, employers who discriminate against workers may indeed limit their options. But even if they refuse to hire them, without giving a reason, they are not leaving workers worse off than they were previously.

Stealing, by its very definition, means making someone worse off. If I have a valuable benefit to give to you, or a beneficial deal to make with you, but for whatever reason I withhold that benefit, or refuse that deal, you are in the same position as before. You are not *entitled* to that deal. You are entitled only to attempt to secure it through my consent. If I refuse consent, you have every right to be disappointed, but you cannot cry, "Thief!" I don't "owe" you the benefit or the deal. It is mine to give, and yours to take if you want it. Both sides have the same right of consent, and neither is robbing the other by refusing that consent.

Of course, we can all envision a serious problem if everyone refuses to hire a particular individual or group. Let's call this system-wide discrimination. This problem becomes especially acute when you consider the unfortunate predicament of former slaves who are now free in a country where widespread discrimination prevents them from getting jobs, housing, and other benefits that others take for granted. Many people think that America desperately needed a Civil Rights revolution—and strict laws mandating non-discrimination—because blacks were in precisely this situation. Yet even in the South, not everyone was opposed to hiring and associating with blacks.

How do we know this? Because of the very attempt to impose Jim Crow and segregation laws. The laws wouldn't be needed if everyone agreed not to hire or associate with blacks. The laws were necessary to force white Southerners to comply with rules they might otherwise have violated. If blacks after the Civil War had faced only private discrimination, quite possibly the discrimination would have eroded without the need for a Civil Rights movement, because whites who practiced racial discrimination would have been at a competitive disadvantage in terms of both employees and customers. This is essentially what happened in professional sports.

Blacks, however, faced another and more invidious type of discrimination: discrimination by the state. Here I refer to the segregation laws in Southern states and also to federal segregation in the military and other institutions. State discrimination, unlike private discrimination, does constitute a "taking" from African Americans. Why? Because the state is a monopoly and if the state doesn't do business with you, you don't have any alternative short of leaving the state or the country. As citizens, we are entitled to have our government—both state and local—treat us equally, and a government that doesn't do that is in fact infringing on our rights. A government that discriminates against some of its citizens is in fact "taking" from them something to which they are entitled. When there is a material deprivation, the "taking" can reasonably be described as "stealing."

The Civil Rights rulings and laws of the 1950s and 1960s were necessary and just in establishing equality of rights under the law. Somewhat weirdly, the Civil Rights Act of 1964 did not merely outlaw discrimination by the government; it also outlawed most forms of private discrimination. While I consider these restrictions on the private sphere to be unwise and unnecessary, they are also understandable. There was a powerful urgency about putting blacks on an equal footing with whites, and outlawing private discrimination was considered a price worth paying. Moreover, starting with President Nixon and continuing to the present, the federal government established a series of racial preferences in favor of blacks aimed at correcting for the wrongs and thefts of the past. Again, these preferences were unwise and unjust—they sought to cure discrimination by practicing it. Yet initially racial preferences could be defended as an extreme measure to kick in the closed door of entrenched state-sponsored discrimination.

Today, however, there is little reason to continue such preferences. The main reason is that racism today is vastly weaker than it used to be. One obvious proof of this is the election and reelection of President Obama. It is simply inconceivable that a white racist country would twice choose an African American to be its highest executive officer, in charge of its security and prosperity. Interestingly Obama seems to have endured virtually no discrimination while growing up. The best evidence is that his race worked in his favor. It is extremely rare, for instance, for someone to be able to transfer from Occidental College to an Ivy League institution like Columbia. Yet Obama did it with a mediocre academic record, and being African American was probably the deciding factor. Race may also have played a key role in Obama getting full scholarships to Columbia and Harvard Law School. As president, he enjoys a level of media sycophancy never before seen in American politics. If Obama were a white guy, is there any doubt that he would not be where he is today? None of this is a tribute to Obama. It's a tribute to how much Americans today want to see an African American represent them, and rise to the top, and succeed.

Racism—or the absence of it—can also be discerned in survey data about white attitudes not only toward black inferiority but also toward racial intermarriage.[5] Blacks know it too: ask blacks today to recall when they personally experienced racism—when for example

someone called them "nigger"—and many are hard pressed to give
a single example. While old-line activists continue to recycle horror
stories from decades ago, the new consensus is reflected by sociologist Orlando Patterson: "America, while still flawed in its race relations, is now the least racist white majority society in the world; has
a better record of legal protection of minorities than any other
society, white or black; offers more opportunities to a greater number of black persons than any other society, including all of Africa;
and has gone through a dramatic change in its attitudes toward
miscegenation."[6] Patterson wrote that in 1991 and it's even more
true today.

Among the younger generation, racism is virtually a non-issue.
This is not to say that racism isn't endlessly talked about in diversity
workshops and mandatory seminars in schools and colleges. Such
events, however, have assumed a surreal quality. The only race-based
discrimination that young people actually experience is affirmative
action policies that benefit blacks and Hispanics and disadvantage
whites and Asian Americans. If racist countries don't elect black
presidents, neither do they establish preferential policies benefiting
minority groups over the majority. So the persistence of affirmative
action over more than a generation is, like Obama's success, a testament to how far racism has receded in America.

Why did racism decline? It is tempting to answer: because of the
Civil Rights revolution. In reality, however, there wasn't much of a
"revolution." Ask yourself: If it was a real revolution, how come
hardly anyone died? The very fact that we can remember the isolated
incidents shows how isolated they were. Martin Luther King scored
an easy intellectual victory over the Southern segregationists and
racists. The best they could do against him was to unleash police
dogs and water hoses. Yet, dogs and hoses were no match for federal
troops that were eventually sent in to enforce court decisions and

federal legislation. So why didn't the South answer Martin Luther King? Why didn't Southerners say, "Of course we think blacks are inferior and we are justified in thinking that way." The simple answer is that racism had greatly eroded before the Civil Rights movement. The biggest reason for this is World War II. It was Hitler who helped to discredit the idea of racial supremacy, and ever since 1945 racism has been on the defensive.

Incredibly, there are Civil Rights activists who deny the magnitude of racial progress, and the massive falling-off in discrimination against blacks. I am not suggesting that we have reached the "end of racism," a title of one of my earlier books. That title was intended to convey a goal—where we are heading—rather than to announce racism's disappearance. Obviously, in a big country like America we can find examples of racism, but consider this: if you look at the crime statistics, there are innumerable black assaults on whites every day and no one notices; one black delinquent like Trayvon Martin gets shot and there is a national scandal. Perhaps the best way to summarize is that racism used to be systematic, but now it is merely episodic. Racism today is not strong enough to prevent blacks or any other group from achieving its aspirations.

Still, racism used to be a very powerful force in America. For the first half of the twentieth century black inferiority was pretty much taken for granted. In the early 1920s, the Ku Klux Klan had more than two million members. The group organized a march in New York that attracted more than fifty thousand Klansmen. Today the Klan could scarcely drum up a hundred marchers, and they would be vastly outnumbered by protesters against the Klan. So things have changed for the better. During the very heyday of racism, however, two very different strategies emerged for combating it. These were the protest strategy of W. E. B. Du Bois and the self-help strategy of Booker T. Washington.

Du Bois argued that blacks in America face a single problem: white racism. And he recommended a simple strategy to fight it, summed up in a phrase first used by Frederick Douglass: "agitate, agitate, agitate." As Du Bois himself wrote, "We claim for ourselves every single right that belongs to a free American, political, civil and social, and until we get these rights we will never cease to protest and assail the ears of America."[7] In keeping with this approach, Du Bois was one of the founders of the National Association for the Advancement of Colored People (NAACP), which quickly established itself as the leading Civil Rights organization in America. Its approach could easily be summed up in that slogan, "agitate, agitate, agitate."

Booker T. Washington argued that blacks face two problems in America. One was racism, and the other was black cultural backwardness. As Washington put it, "The Negro should not be deprived by unfair means of the franchise, but political agitation alone will not save him. . . . He must have property, industry, skill, economy, intelligence, and character. No race without these elements can permanently succeed." Washington believed in the ultimate triumph of the meritocratic idea. "Merit, no matter under what skin found, is in the long run recognized and rewarded. . . . Whether he will or not, a white man respects a Negro who owns a two-story brick house."[8] Here Washington is saying that just as important as rights is the ability to compete effectively and take advantage of those rights. Moreover, he added that black success and achievement are the best ways to dispel white suspicions of black inferiority.

When Washington pointed out shortcomings in the black community—such as the high black crime rate—Du Bois erupted with outrage. "Suppose today Negroes do steal," he thundered, "Who was it that for centuries made stealing a virtue by stealing their labor?" Washington never denied the bad habits cultivated in this way; his point was that they existed, and had to be changed. "In spite of all that may be said in palliation, there is too much crime committed by our people. . . . We should let the world understand that we are not going to hide crime simply because it is committed by black people." If Du Bois's motto could be summed up as "agitate, agitate, agitate," Washington's could be summed up as "work, work, work."[9]

The Civil Rights movement, led by the NAACP and by Martin Luther King, was based on the politics of protest. This movement was successful not because it represented a revolutionary departure from American principles, but because it made a direct appeal to those principles. When Martin Luther King declared he was submitting a "promissory note," and demanded it be cashed, we may pause to ask: What note? Did the Southern segregationists make him a promise and then renege on it? Of course not—the promissory note was none other than the Declaration of Independence. In other words, Martin Luther King appealed not for new rights but for the enforcement of rights already granted in 1776. Remarkably this twentieth-century black leader relied for his moral and legal claims on the charter of a white Southern slave-owner. Thank you, Mister Jefferson!

Today we hear from progressives that the Civil Rights movement is "unfinished," and they are right, but not for the reasons they think. Progressives are still chasing the windmills of old-style racism, whipping the nation into a frenzy every time there is some obscure incident. The reason blacks remain so far behind whites, however, has very little to do with racism. It has to do with African American cultural backwardness. Martin Luther King recognized this. In a statement that has gone largely ignored, he said, "We must not let the fact that we are victims of injustice lull us into abrogating responsibility for our own lives. We must not use our oppression as an excuse for mediocrity and laziness. . . . By improving our standards here and now, we will go a long way toward breaking down the arguments of the segregationist. . . . The Negro will only be free when he reaches down into the inner depths of his own being and signs with the pen and ink of assertive manhood his own Emancipation Proclamation."[10]

Here King places himself directly in the line of Booker T. Washington. But King's advice, just like Washington's entire philosophy, has been largely disregarded by the Civil Rights leadership. Even now that group continues with "agitate, agitate, agitate." But today Americans enjoy equality of rights under the law, and the challenge for black Americans is to compete effectively in school and in the marketplace. Rights by themselves have a limited value. What is the benefit of having the right to compete in the Olympics if you don't know how to run fast or swim well? More to our point here, what good is it to have a right to work at Google or Oracle if you don't know how to do software programming? Rights are a prerequisite to success but success also requires the skills to take advantage of those rights.

Even though Du Bois knew this, he didn't emphasize it. What he emphasized was discrimination and theft, and his solution was that the thief owes the victim and the thief must pay. Booker T. Washington's insight was deeper: even if there has been a theft, sometimes it is the victim who is in the best position to mitigate the damage and restore his opportunities. In other words, society may have put him down but he is in the best position to get up. Ultimately Du Bois became disgusted with America because he didn't see blacks achieve the same status as whites and other groups. Consequently Du Bois became an enthusiast of Soviet Russia—even an admirer of Stalin. He also tried to inject himself into the Third World anti-colonial movement, organizing a Pan-African Congress in 1945 for various African independence leaders. In 1961, Du Bois renounced his American citizenship and emigrated to Ghana. He was one of very few American blacks who actually took the step of going back to Africa, although he did it when he was ninety-three, two years before his death.[11]

While Booker T. Washington is ignored or reviled among the mainstream of the Civil Rights leadership, there is one group that is silently following his strategy of "work, work, work." That group is the non-white immigrants in America. I am thinking here of the Koreans and Haitians and West Indians and South Asians and Mexicans. These groups are all beneficiaries of the Civil Rights movement, as I am. Yet we seem to know, in a way many African Americans don't, that America has changed. Rather than protesting the remaining obstacles, we look for the broad vistas of opportunity. Rather than agitating for white sympathy and government largesse, we work our way up the rungs of success.

Today we can simply compare African Americans with non-white immigrants to see whether the protest strategy or the self-help strategy is better. This is one of the benefits of multiculturalism. It offers what Friedrich Hayek termed "a framework of competing utopias," and we can compare them to see what works and what doesn't. Today the verdict is clear—protest is a dead end when rights are already available to you. In twenty-first-century America, Du Bois is irrelevant and Booker T. Washington is indispensable. Consistent with Washington's philosophy, little guys of every race and color can move up from the bottom and through "work, work, work" write the charter of their own Emancipation Proclamation.

CHAPTER 10

THE VIRTUE
OF PROSPERITY

*There are few ways in which a man can be
more innocently occupied than in getting money.*[1]

—SAMUEL JOHNSON, *BOSWELL'S LIFE OF JOHNSON*

I
n 1893 the historian Frederick Jackson Turner published a
famous essay declaring that the American frontier was closed
and that the American dream based on the acquisition of new
land must finally end. Jackson argued that the frontier had defined
America from the beginning. But now, he said, we have reached the
Pacific Ocean and there is no more land to discover and occupy.
Jackson identified the specific traits the frontier brought out in
Americans. "The coarseness and strength combined with acuteness
and inquisitiveness, the practical, inventive turn of mind, quick to
find expedients, that masterful grasp of material things, lacking in
the artistic but powerful to effect great ends, that restless, nervous
energy, that dominant individualism, working for good and for evil,
and withal that buoyancy and exuberance which comes with freedom—these are the traits of the frontier." One can see that Jackson

is not uncritical of frontier traits, but he also knows the role they played in building the country. Jackson declared that the closing of the frontier represented the end of an era. "Four centuries from the discovery of America, at the end of a hundred years of life under the Constitution, the frontier has gone, and with its going has closed the first period of American history."[2]

Jackson's thesis has been hotly debated. The first question I want to consider is whether he's right that there is no more frontier. I don't think he is. Jackson presumes that the American dream is built on land, and for more than a century, it was. People of limited means would move west in order to find someplace new. But now there is a new frontier, and it is new wealth and new technology. Instead of finding someplace new, we make something new. Today's wealth is not primarily in land; it is in making things that didn't exist before. I'm not just thinking about the wealth created by new communications technology—we have computers and cell phones now that didn't exist in 1893—but also of the countless innovations and amenities in medicine, recreation, work efficiency, and home life. Someone has to come up with this stuff, and in a way it's more difficult than simply to push west and develop new tracts of land. My point is that, under entrepreneurial capitalism, once the land is gone there are new ways for America to create wealth and opportunity. The frontier is never closed.

Progressive criticism of the Jackson thesis has focused on challenging his assumption that America has historically offered new land waiting to be discovered. The progressive view, as we know, is that America was already a fully occupied country and therefore "settlement" is another name for "theft." We have examined this argument in previous chapters. Now we consider whether capitalism, innovation, and free trade, the new forms of wealth creation that drive the American and the global economy, are also forms of theft. If they are, then the great mass of wealth now in America's possession is illegitimate, and should be placed at the disposal of progressive redistribution, both on a domestic and global scale.

In 1965, Barack Obama Sr. published an article in the *East Africa Journal* in which he considered the possibility of 100 percent tax rates.[3] It's worth asking, how can a sane person propose taxing people at 100 percent? In the 1980s, the economist Arthur Laffer pointed out that if the government imposes a 100 percent tax rate, it is likely to get just as much revenue as if it imposed a zero percent tax rate. If tax rates are zero percent, obviously the government gets no revenue. But Laffer noted that at 100 percent tax rates, no one has an incentive to work. Why work at all if you have to turn it all in? Consequently, no one produces anything and here too the government gets no revenue.

Why then would an intelligent person propose 100 percent tax rates? There is one scenario in which such rates make sense. Imagine if you came to my house and stole all my possessions. In that case, what's the proper tax rate for you? Well, 100 percent—because the possessions are not yours. Where theft is involved, no one cares what the effect of returning stolen goods may be on one's incentive to work. The stuff doesn't belong to you, so you had better give it back, and if you refuse, then the government has every right to take it back. The anti-colonial view is that capitalist wealth is stolen goods, and hence Barack Obama Sr. has no compunction about proposing that state power be used to confiscate it.

All of this may seem quite remote from President Obama, yet consider again what Obama said on the 2012 campaign trail:

> Look, if you've been successful, you didn't get there on your own. I'm always struck by people who think, well, it must be because I was just so smart. There are a lot of smart people out there. It must be because I worked harder than everybody else. Let me tell you something—there are

a whole bunch of hardworking people out there. If you were successful, somebody along the line gave you some help. There was a great teacher somewhere in your life. Somebody helped to create this unbelievable American system that we have that allowed you to thrive. Somebody invested in roads and bridges. If you've got a business— you didn't build that. Somebody else made that happen. The Internet didn't get invented on its own. Government research created the Internet so that all the companies could make money off the Internet.[4]

A similar theme was articulated by Senator Elizabeth Warren, darling of the progressives. "There is nobody in this country who got rich on his own. Nobody. You built a factory out there? Good for you. But I want to be clear: you moved your goods to market on the roads the rest of us paid for, you hired workers the rest of us paid to educate; you were safe in your factory because of police forces and fire forces that the rest of us paid for."[5]

What are Obama and Warren really saying here? Clearly they are not saying that entrepreneurs should go back and find their old teachers and give them a nice bonus. Rather, they are trying to create nihilism about the source of wealth—to detach effort from reward. In a way, their argument that we aren't entirely responsible for our own success seems indisputable. All success has preconditions—to build a house, we have to be allowed to get a permit to build a house—and also infrastructure—we cannot build houses without roads, police to protect us, schools to educate us, and so on. In this sense, it's uncontroversial that our success is only partly due to our own efforts.

But this, while true, hardly says much because the public roads are available to everybody. Apparently entrepreneurs make better use of the public roads than everyone else. The teacher that taught the successful entrepreneur in school also taught other students. Did they learn less than the entrepreneur did? Did they not put their lessons to a good use? Well, that would imply that the entrepreneur made better use of what he learned and deserves the rewards of that. Now of course entrepreneurs couldn't operate without some government infrastructure. They depend on essential government services like defense and fire-fighting. But again, all citizens benefit from those services, which is why we have a government in the first place. So why should entrepreneurs incur additional obligations to the government simply by virtue of having a successful enterprise? The government didn't build that; they did.

In any other context, Obama's and Warren's statements would seem nutty. Imagine if I told my daughter, who is now a freshman in college, "You didn't earn your SAT scores." Asked to explain, I point out that she used the public roads to go to her SAT test. Or that she could not have taken the test had she not received childhood vaccinations that prevented her from getting typhoid. Indeed I could go further. She could not have done what she did if she had been an orphan in a Third World country. Nor could she have produced good SAT scores had there been no oxygen in the earth's atmosphere, or had the sun not been eight light minutes away from the earth, giving humans the necessary warmth to live. Now if I said all this, she would think I had lost my mind. While there are obvious preconditions for achievement, it does not follow that the achievement is unearned. So from this point of view, Obama's and Warren's statements seem like pure stupidity.

Yet when intelligent people say something stupid, that doesn't make them stupid. Rather, they are actually trying to convey a different point. Here's what Obama and Warren really mean. They mean that capitalist wealth—all of it—belongs to the community.

No one specifically earned that wealth, and no one has an exclusive right to it. Wealth is produced collectively, and therefore everyone is collectively entitled to it. The problem, from this point of view, is that before the wealth can be widely claimed and evenly distributed, greedy entrepreneurs rush in and grab it. These selfish people think the surplus belongs to them. But it's not theirs, and the government has every right to seize it and distribute it however it wants. The government is not taking what's yours; it is taking what never belonged to you in the first place. Thus there is a close similarity between the ideology of the two Obamas, father and son. In fact, they both subscribe to the same creed.

The premise of the progressive argument is that wealth and profits in today's economy are being appropriated by greedy, selfish people who are taking more than their "fair share." This is a new type of attack on capitalism. In the twentieth century there was a lively debate between capitalism and socialism in terms of which system was more effective in creating wealth. Capitalism won that debate. Yet although capitalism won the economic debate, it never won the moral debate. Today's critique of capitalism, led by Obama, is not about how well it works; it's about how capitalists are the bad guys. In order to answer Obama, we have to consider the motives of capitalism. We also have to examine more closely what it is that entrepreneurs and workers actually do, and whether they deserve the money they make.

Many successful entrepreneurs seem to have internalized the progressive critique of capitalism, which has put them on the defensive. Years ago, Ted Turner was asked a probing question on John Stossel's TV show. Noting that Turner had pledged to give a billion dollars to the United Nations, Stossel asked him: Why give to such a dubious cause? Why not invest in your own businesses? This way, you could create jobs, and generate products, and arguably benefit far more people. Turner became so agitated that he ran off the set. Stossel pursued him. Finally Turner erupted, "I am simply trying to give back to the community."[6] And this is a standard justification for philanthropy. "I am giving back to the community." Yet whenever I hear this, I think to myself, "How much have you taken from the community?" The implication is that profits are illegitimate, and some of that loot now must be returned through a kind of obligatory philanthropy. Entrepreneurs like Turner seem to be pleading guilty to the charge of theft. At the very least, they seem unwilling or unable to make a moral defense of the system that enables their prosperity.

The moral conundrum of capitalism is, in one sense, a twenty-first-century phenomenon, but in another, it goes back to the very origins of capitalism.

The classic defense of capitalism was made in 1776 by Adam Smith in *The Wealth of Nations*. In that book, surprisingly enough, Smith takes a dim view of businessmen. He says they seldom meet in private except to fix prices. Moreover, Smith seems to *agree* that capitalism is based on selfishness. Smith writes, "It is not from the benevolence of the butcher, the brewer, or the baker that we expect our dinner, but from their regard to their own interest. We address ourselves, not to their humanity, but to their self-love, and never talk to them of our own necessities but of their advantages."[7]

Smith's argument is based on a paradox: individual selfishness can be channeled to the collective benefit of society. How is this possible? A half-century before Smith, Bernard Mandeville offered an even more flamboyant version of Smith's thesis. In a long poem titled *The Fable of the Bees*, Mandeville insisted that "private prices" produce "public benefits." Virtue, said Mandeville, is simply the province of "poor silly country people." Mandeville actually praised vices such as greed, selfishness, pride, and envy. Without them, he suggested, the engines of commerce would grind to a halt. Vice is what makes possible modern civilization.[8]

Smith repudiated Mandeville, and in place of Mandeville's terms "greed" and "selfishness," Smith used a more precise term: self-interest. For Smith, self-interest is not good, but neither is it bad. What's significant about self-interest, however, is that it works. Self-interest, mobilized in the right way, produces mass prosperity. But not by itself. Here is where Smith introduced his famous concept of the "invisible hand." Individuals may be thoroughly self-interested, but through the "invisible hand" of competition, they are motivated to improve quality and drive down prices and thus to promote the material welfare of the community. Smith notes that by activating self-interest through the mechanism of competition, the entrepreneur promotes the prosperity of society "more effectually than when he really intends to promote it."[9] Imperceptibly but surely, private self-interest promotes the public interest. Economist Gary Becker, a Nobel laureate, has termed this one of the most important ideas of the past two and a half centuries. Smith's defense of free markets, however, seems incomplete. While Smith vindicates capitalism—the system—he does not seem to vindicate capitalists—the people.

Greed and self-interest, Smith recognized, do not arise out of capitalism. They arise out of human nature. Capitalism, Smith writes, arises out the human "propensity to truck, barter and exchange." Workers, no less than employers and investors, are motivated by greed and self-interest. These are universal tendencies. Karl Marx famously disputed this, insisting that greed and self-interest were the products of societies that had private property. Marx held that in a communist society there would be no private property and therefore neither greed nor self-interest. In such a society, Marx rhapsodized, people would be motivated to work not for their own good but for the public good. Marx probably recognized how foolish this sounded, so he offered a vision in which the work itself would be light and sporadic. In his imagined society, people could do physical labor in the morning, fish in the afternoon, and do criticism in the evening.[10] Sounds like the life of a professor of romance languages at an elite American university! Even so, we recognize today that Marx's communism doesn't work. At best, it is a utopia, a "city in speech." No actual society can function that way. Actual societies must be built on human nature as it is, not as we wish it to be.

None of this is to suggest that Communism never works. There is a place where Communism works beautifully—in the family. The family, after all, is based on the Communist principle, "From each according to his ability, to each according to his need."[11] Right away we see that the charge that people work only for themselves—for their own greed and self-interest—needs to be modified. Most people work to support their families. In some cases, this is an extended family that includes older parents or other relatives. Why does Communism work in the family? Because there is a tight knot of affection that binds the community together, so that the interests of one are virtually identical with the interests of others. This bond is much harder to achieve in larger communities because our affections grow thinner as we move in concentric circles from the family to relatives to a local neighborhood to a wider community of countrymen. Patriotic though we may be, it's hard to feel about people we don't know as we do about people who are close to us.

Greed and self-interest may be features of human nature, but shouldn't an economic system that encourages these vices be morally condemned? To answer this question we must look closely at the motives of capitalism and also at what entrepreneurs actually do. Here we contend with a variety of contradictory positions. The philosopher Ayn Rand, for instance, published a book called *The Virtue of Selfishness*. Rand's position was: of course capitalism is based on selfishness, and that's wonderful, because selfishness is wonderful. "The attack on selfishness," Rand wrote, "is an attack on man's self-esteem." Of course Rand was being provocative. She too meant self-interest more than selfishness. Why then use the word "selfishness"? Rand's answer: "For the reason that you are afraid of it." Rand's advice: be not afraid. Her goal was to insist that it is ethical for people to do what's good for themselves.[12] In a sense, Rand took the familiar charge against entrepreneurs—you people are greedy, selfish bastards—and pleaded guilty. What's wrong, she asked, with looking out for Number One? I admire Rand's pugnacity, but ultimately I think her attempt to overturn two thousand years of Western morality is quixotic. Contrary to Gordon Gekko, greed is not good. As for self-interest, it may not be a vice but neither is it a virtue. We can understand a fellow who cares mainly or exclusively about himself or herself, but we cannot on those grounds admire such a person.

A different understanding of the motives of capitalism comes from technology guru George Gilder, who insists that capitalism is based on altruism. Giving—he says—is the moral center of the system. Gilder points out that many successful entrepreneurs have already made their money; they don't need to come to work every day. Think, for example, of Ted Turner, Richard Branson, or Mark Zuckerberg. Yet these guys continue to work. Why is that? Gilder says it is because they have the gift of creativity, and they want to share it with society. They are not primarily motivated by money; they are primarily motivated by love of what they do. Call this the eros of enterprise. Certainly these tycoons continue to harvest huge rewards. But the rewards are not—at least not now—why they continue to do it. Rather, Gilder says, these are creative gift-givers who put their big ideas and innovative products out there, and then they are gratified to see how well they are received. The consumer, in a sense, repays the entrepreneur for his generosity, and the entrepreneur measures his creativity by how well it is received in the market. Truly successful entrepreneurs, Gilder contends, recognize that "the good fortune of others is also finally one's own."

Obviously tycoons who don't have to work for a living are rarities. My focus is not on them but on ordinary people who start and operate businesses. Why do they do it? They do it to make a living. In this respect they have the same motivation as the workers they employ. But here is the difference. The worker to be successful has only to please his employer, but the employer to be successful has to please a much wider community of consumers. My point is simply that success under capitalism comes not through self-absorption but by attending to the wants and needs of others. Capitalists who make good profits do so not because they are especially self-interested but because they are especially good at empathizing with and serving other people.

Ironically it was Adam Smith who made empathy the central theme of his other book, *A Theory of Moral Sentiments*. Here Smith made a surprising observation. "To feel much for others, and little for ourselves, to restrain our selfish, and indulge our benevolent, affections, constitutes the perfection of human nature."[13] Smith, the great champion of the invisible hand and of capitalist self-interest, admits that the best of human nature is an orientation away from the self and toward others. Morality requires us to transcend and in some cases even repudiate self-interest. Smith failed to add, however, that this is precisely what successful workers and entrepreneurs do. They put themselves in the place of others. They ask: How can I provide a service that is really helpful to other people? How can I develop and improve my products so that they better meet what consumers want?

While self-interest may be the motive for capitalism, empathy is the operative virtue that is required for success under the capitalist system. And this I believe is the key to understanding why so many entrepreneurs and workers like what they do and take pride in it. In some respects, it seems strange to find people taking pride in being a doorman, or sweeping a floor, or adding up numbers, or selling widgets. The aristocratic attitude is to revile such petty and degrading activities. Oscar Wilde once wrote that to do manual labor, of the kind that a janitor does, is depressing enough; to take *pride* in such things is absolutely appalling. Marx too complained of the worker who is alienated from his labor. I suppose this feeling of lassitude, of boredom, of watching the clock and waiting for the weekend, is understandable enough. Yet many Americans understand that "the mind is its own place" and how you feel about your work depends on what attitude you bring to it. For many workers and entrepreneurs, even those doing "unglamorous" tasks, there is pride in a job well done. Clean floors, proper accounts, and useful widgets all improve the lives of others and there is a moral satisfaction in providing these.

Having empathy for others may not seem like such a big deal. Don't we all, as humans, display empathy in our professional dealings with others? Actually no. Except for the clergy and doctors, I don't know of any field that draws out human empathy as much as entrepreneurship. Consider, by contrast, the mentality of the intellectual. Years ago, when I worked at a research foundation—a so-called "think tank"—I asked one of my colleagues, who was finishing up his book, "What's your book about?" He informed me, "It's about the theories of the Physiocrats." I asked him, "Who besides you is interested in reading about the Physiocrats?" He looked at me with puzzlement. Clearly the question had not occurred to him. In other words, he was writing about what he cared about, and whether there was actually a market for his work was a secondary, almost irrelevant, question. Of course I would not be surprised to find the same fellow, once his book came out, bemoaning why there were not long lines to purchase his book at Barnes and Noble. But even then it occurred to me that no entrepreneur would think that way. No entrepreneur would go into the business of, say, selling soap without first asking, "Who are my consumers? How can I best satisfy their wants and needs?"

The most creative, and ultimately the most highly rewarded, entrepreneurs are those who carry empathy beyond meeting the demand of others. Instead, they are the ones who envision the wants and needs of others *even before they have them*. Many years ago, at a *Forbes* CEO conference, I met Akio Morita, the inventor of the Sony Walkman. Morita told me that before he thought of the idea, no one had requested a music box that was small, portable, and allowed for individual listening through earphones. No one even knew that would be a good idea. Morita said he got the idea himself when he took his family to the beach and had to endure the awful music that emanated from the boom boxes of teenagers. Morita asked his engineers to figure out a way to shrink a car radio so that people could hear their favorite music without inflicting it on others. The Sony Walkman was a huge success. Here is "supply side" economics in its classic form. Demand does not precede supply; supply precedes demand. The genius of Morita—this old Japanese man— was to recognize what millions of American young people wanted even though they had no idea they wanted it until it was made and offered to them.

I give the example of the Sony Walkman but I could just as easily have mentioned Facebook, Federal Express, or the iPhone. I could add very simple inventions, like roll-on luggage. I don't know who thought of that one, but I do know that for decades people went around airports lugging huge suitcases, until someone got the bright idea to put wheels on them. In each of these cases, entrepreneurs created demand by introducing a product that no one asked for, but millions of people wanted it once it was available. I call this "extreme empathy" because it's a case of entrepreneurs providing for the wants of consumers before consumers even know what they want. For these entrepreneurs—and entrepreneurs in general—profit is not a measure of how greedy or selfish they are. Profit is a measure of how well they have served the wants and needs of their customers.

In his book *The Passions and the Interests*, Albert Hirschman shows how capitalism, far from being a system of theft and looting, arose historically as an alternative to theft and looting. In fact, capitalism was built on a human proclivity entirely different from the desire to rob and pillage. Hirschman notes that in the ancient world—and even today, in many parts of the world—wealth was obtained by looting and conquest. If your group or tribe wanted possessions, you simply seized them. The impulse to conquest comes from what Augustine termed the *libido dominandi*, the lust for power. This powerful passion included not merely the desire for goods but also for slaves and concubines.

According to Hirschman, the early modern thinkers who advocated capitalism recognized this passion as destructive but also powerful. They also knew that merely preaching against it might not be sufficient. So they sought to curb or check the desire for conquest by opposing to it an equally powerful desire: the desire to accumulate. In their view, the "passion" for predatory conquest could be mitigated, and ultimately eliminated, by the "interest" in capitalist accumulation. Hirschman quotes Montesquieu's words, from the *Spirit of the Laws*: "It is fortunate for men to be in a situation in which, though their passions may prompt them to be wicked, they have nevertheless an interest in not being so." In both cases there is acquisition, but in the former case it is violent, involuntary, and socially harmful; in the latter it is peaceful, consensual, and socially productive.[14]

In other words, capitalism civilizes greed in the same way that marriage civilizes lust. Greed, like lust, is part of the human condition. These emotions cannot be eradicated, although some monkish sects have certainly tried. And to the degree that greed leads to effort and lust to pleasure, why should we seek to eradicate them? At the same time, it is widely recognized that these inclinations can have destructive effects. So they have to be channeled in such a way that they serve us, and society, best. The institution of marriage allows the fulfillment of lust, but within a context that promotes mutual love and the raising of children. Lust is refined and ennobled by marriage. Similarly capitalism channels greed in such a way that it is placed at the service of the wants and needs of others. Under capitalism, helping others is the best way of helping yourself. Capitalism provides a virtue to prosperity.

Newcomers to America on Ellis Island. Immigrants like me are a walking refutation of the idea that all cultures are equal. We are voting, in the most decisive way possible, against our native countries and in favor of America.

America the Inexcusable? Asked which country is the evil empire, Ward Churchill replies, "You're in it."

America (the film)

Former domestic terrorist Bill Ayers, whom I recently debated at Dartmouth, is now a respected academic. "Revolutionaries want to change the world...and teachers...want to change the world too."

AP Photo/Michael Dwyer

Howard Zinn, perhaps the most influential historian of the past half-century: "I prefer to try to tell the story of the discovery of America from the viewpoint of the Arawaks...the slaves...the Cherokees... socialists...peons in Latin America."

America (the film)

Michael Eric Dyson argues that "of course" America's wealth is based on theft—theft from Indians, theft from blacks, theft from Mexico, and theft from working people.

Everett Collection/Newscom

Anti-colonial writer Frantz Fanon: "The wealth of the imperial countries is our wealth too.... The wealth...was stolen from the under-developed peoples."

Alexis de Tocqueville admired America because he found the ordinary man to be "enterprising, adventurous, and above all an innovator."

Michel Foucault admired America because of its sexual freedom, including, as he put it, the opportunity "to die for the love of boys."

Is Noam Chomsky a "wage slave"? It seems as though he exploits MIT as much as MIT exploits him.

Charmaine White Face of the Sioux tribe wants to get rid of Mount Rushmore because it represents "oppression" and "genocide."

The arrival of Columbus forever altered the lifestyle of Indians who used to live in tepees and chase animals for their meals. How unfortunate! So why don't any Indians go back to that way of life now?

TECUMSEH.

"War now! War for ever!" "Let the white race perish," cried the Shawnee chief Tecumseh, upsetting the progressive myth of native Indians as peaceful, highly spiritual people.

The essence of slavery, according to Abraham Lincoln: you work, I eat.

The Founders, according to Lincoln, were not hypocrites. Speaking of the equality clause in the Declaration, he said, "They meant simply to declare the *right*, so that the *enforcement* of it might follow as fast as circumstances should permit."

For W. E. B. Du Bois, the Harvard sociologist, blacks faced one big problem, racism, and his solution was to "agitate, agitate, agitate."

For Booker T. Washington, the former slave, blacks faced a second problem, cultural backwardness, and his solution was to "work, work, work."

Upon his return from Zaire, Muhammad Ali was asked, "Champ, what did you think of Africa?" He replied, "Thank God my granddaddy got on that boat!"

Anti-colonialism, a Third World ideology, was imported into America during the Vietnam War and is now part of modern progressivism.

The coming of the robots: technological capitalism generates a "gale of creative destruction" that improves lives, even as it forces people to keep pace with change.

Excuse me, Obama, Steve Jobs didn't build that? The most successful entrepreneurs don't just meet wants; they figure out how to supply wants and needs that people don't even know they have.

The way of the world from time immemorial—what makes America different is that the Founders figured out a solution to the problem of wealth creation.

Saul Alinsky, mentor to Obama and Hillary, liked to boast that "I could persuade a millionaire on a Friday to subsidize a revolution for Saturday out of which he would make a huge profit on Sunday even though he was certain to be executed on Monday."

Why did Alinsky dedicate his book to the devil? Because, as it turns out, the Lucifer strategy also happens to be the Alinsky strategy.

Obama kept returning to Chicago because that was the center of Alinsky organizing. Below, Obama teaches Alinsky power techniques to community activists.

Hillary wrote her thesis on Alinsky, and incorporated his techniques, but she figured out something Alinsky didn't—how to take radical activism inside the corridors of power.

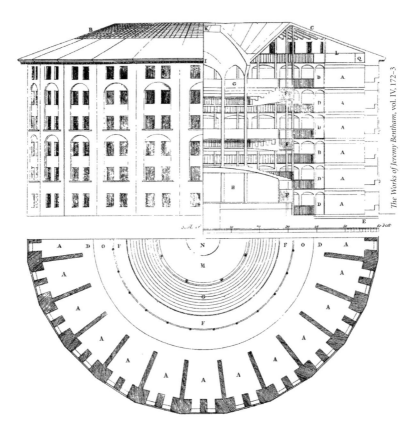

The Works of Jeremy Bentham, vol. IV, 172–3

Jeremy Bentham's Panopticon, a design for the "perfect prison," becomes a chilling reality when the government routinely spies on its own citizens.

CHAPTER 11

WHO'S EXPLOITING WHOM?

It is said that justice is equality, and so it is, but not for all persons, only for those who are equal.

—ARISTOTLE, *POLITICS*

In 2011, President Obama went on one of his periodic rants about capitalism. Obama said that in "most countries" teachers are paid "on par" with doctors and he bewailed the fact that we don't do that in America. A little research showed that Obama's factual claim was false—most countries pay doctors a lot more than teachers—but we can see where Obama is going with this argument. He's suggesting that capitalism may create abundance but its rewards are distributed without regard to merit. Obama's implication is that both teachers and doctors provide something indispensable to society and therefore they deserve to be paid a comparable wage. In his book *The Audacity of Hope* Obama makes a similar argument about CEO pay. He says that CEOs are now paid much more, compared to those who work for them, than was the case in the past; then he declares that there is no economic rationale for this: "It's cultural."[1] One of Obama's key objectives as president is to change the culture so that reward is in proportion to merit and people are paid their "fair share."

The puzzling aspect about Obama's "fair share" talk is that our solomonic president never says what anyone's fair share actually is. This is not an unreasonable thing to ask of a liberal: In what society would he be a conservative? If a liberal wants people to have more, he or she needs to specify how much more. Obama, however, seems to believe that there is some Platonic definition of "fair share" out in the Empyrean. He simply *knows* that people aren't getting their due. Presumably his confidence on this score arises from a conviction that American society distributes rewards so unequally. We live in a country where the top 1 percent owns more than a third of the wealth. The top 10 percent has two thirds. And this of course means that the bottom 90 percent controls only about a third of the wealth. Yet Obama's comment about teachers and doctors seems to imply more than the claim that there is inequality and we should strive to reduce it. Rather, Obama seems to say that some people are getting too much for what they do and others too little. Consequently, the pie must be carved differently not just to equalize outcomes but to give people what they truly deserve. Obama's argument does not appeal to compassion or even to pure egalitarianism; it appeals to just deserts.

Obama's claims about teachers and CEOs gets to a broader puzzle about how a capitalist society assigns rewards. At first glance, it seems that there is no relationship between merit and reward. Athletes and entertainers, who provide services much less indispensable than teachers and doctors, earn vastly more than either of those two professions. Earlier I mentioned the example of the parking lot guy who parks all the cars and makes money for the resort, yet he gets a pittance of that money. From his point of view, there is no relationship between work and reward. He does the work, and "they" get the profits. This is pretty much how workers feel in a variety of occupations. They are the "makers" and their bosses are the "takers." In a truly fair and merit-based society, they should get more and the bosses should get less.

These arguments are, whether their proponents recognize it or not, anchored in Karl Marx's notion of "surplus value." Marx is largely discredited today, because Communism proved a failure, and Marx's prophecies proved dead wrong. Still, Marx's core argument about the injustice of capitalist distribution remains hugely influential, because it seems to reflect common sense. Marx argued that everything that is produced under capitalism is produced by labor. Even machines and technology, Marx pointed out, are simply the products of past labor, since it took human effort to make those machines and technology. Whether skilled or unskilled, labor is responsible for everything that is made and sold.

The way that capitalism works, according to Marx, is that entrepreneurs provide the initial capital and use this to pay workers for their labor. This is their cost of doing business. Products, however, are not sold for what it costs to make them. They are sold for the highest price the market will bear. The difference between what things are sold for, and what it costs to make them, Marx terms "surplus value." It is another name for "profit." Marx contends that capital by itself is worth very little—since money has a modest rental value called "interest"—and therefore once this interest is paid, workers are responsible for the full value of a product. Despite this, workers actually receive only the labor cost of that product, leaving the entrepreneurs or capitalists to make off with the difference.

Marx gives the example of a new enterprise in which an entrepreneur invests a fixed sum, say $100. This is the cost of hiring the labor. There are of course other costs: rent, raw materials, machinery, and so on. Let's say that these amount to $400. So the total investment is $500. Then the product is sold for $600. The profit is, of course, $100. Now most people might say that this is a 20 percent rate of profit, since profits are calculated based on the total investment. Yet Marx calculates the profit to be 100 percent, since it is double the cost paid to the workers. Marx insists that workers were deprived of one-half the value of their labor. In a sense, they gave a day's work and were paid for half a day. This Marx terms "the real degree of exploitation of labor." Marx's math may be suspect, but his general point remains. Essentially, from Marx's point of view, the capitalists are thieves, stealing from the worker the true value of what the worker has contributed. Marx is the original apostle of Obama's doctrine of "fair share."[2]

Many intellectuals are naturally sympathetic to these "fair share" doctrines. Years ago I debated a political scientist—very much a creature of the 1960s—on the subject of free markets. Our exchange illuminated one of the biggest reasons intellectuals detest capitalism. During our discussion, the political scientist said that free markets systematically undervalue intellectuals like, well, himself. Yet he acknowledged he drove a very nice car and employed a nanny. Even so, he fumed that "some fat Rotarian with a gold chain on his chest is taking in $2 million a year selling pest control or term-life insurance." So this well-published Ph.D. simply couldn't fathom why a society would want to pay ill-educated, culturally unsophisticated entrepreneurs so much and a guy like him so much less. His complaint wasn't a simple matter of envy; rather, it was one of injured merit. He wasn't getting his "fair share." (Of course, in reality, most professors get a subsidized share, as taxpayers pay part of all of their salaries at state schools or through federal research grants, a "benefit" the pest control or term-life insurance salesman doesn't get.)

Ordinarily these grievances about market distribution of rewards simmer below the surface; the reason they have become the central political question of our time is that economic inequality in America seems so much greater. We now live in a country where CEOs make several million dollars a year while their low-wage employees have trouble making ends meet; where tech entrepreneurs become billionaires in short order while ordinary families (their savings depleted and their homes under water) have virtually no accumulated wealth, where the great American middle class seems to have disappeared and America is now a nation of plutocrats on the one hand and wage serfs on the other. Technological capitalism appears to be the obvious culprit causing this inequality. To the degree that the inequality reflects an unjust distribution of wealth, technological capitalism can be viewed as a form of systematized theft. The people at the top seem to be ripping off the people at the bottom. This is the moral force behind Obama's success.

Let's begin by considering the parking lot guy. He thinks that he is the one doing the work in parking the cars. But in fact, the actual value of parking a car is close to zero. The physical labor involved is negligible, and the benefit to the guy who owns the car is virtually nil. If you offer to come to my house and park my car every time I get home, I would pay a dollar or two for the service. Why, then, do patrons of a resort pay $25? They do so because they are *at a resort*. They want a vacation experience, or a convenience so that they can rush to their business conference, and in this situation they are willing to pay much more for parking than they normally would. The value of this convenience cannot be properly measured by simply considering the labor of parking the car. Someone had the idea for the resort. Someone raised the money. Someone secured and paid for the permits. Someone then designed the property, including the parking lot. Someone fitted the parking lot with its gates and struc-tures. Someone obtained and paid for insurance. Then came the hiring not only of the parking lot guy but a hierarchy of overseers and managers to make sure the entire resort functioned properly.

There are a few points worth making here. First, Marx is wrong that a business venture is simply capital plus labor. He fails to count the added value of the entrepreneur. What the entrepreneur brings to the project is, first, the idea. This is quite simply the most impor-tant element of any business—the original idea for doing it. An idea, of course, is hard to measure because it is abstract, it is ethereal, it is not a thing. Yet without the idea for delivering mail overnight there would be no Federal Express. A second, equally valuable, contribu-tion of the entrepreneur is the organization of the business. Ideas are fine by themselves but they don't get the job done. We all know people who have great ideas—for businesses, for new inventions, for books and movies—but they don't take the necessary steps to implement their ideas. A third entrepreneurial contribution is risk. While labor gets paid its fixed wage, the entrepreneurs take all the risk. Entrepreneurs might do well, but they might also lose money, ending up worse than they were before they started. The worker's risk is much lower: at worst, he's out of a job and doesn't get addi-tional wages. No one, however, asks the worker to receive wages only if the company does well, or to give back wages to help the company meet its obligations.

So these distinctive entrepreneurial contributions—ideas, orga-nization, and risk—are very different from "labor," indeed they involve the establishing of a system that then enables labor to func-tion. If labor gets paid "wages" in return for its contributions, entre-preneurs get paid "profits" in return for theirs. There is nothing inherently unfair about that, even when the profits are substantial, since without entrepreneurs, the workers would not have their jobs.

Moreover, the parking lot guy seems to be suffering from an optical illusion. He thinks that he is doing the work of parking the car, but he is merely the last man in a chain of employees who are getting this particular job done. The parking lot guy wonders, "All I got paid was $100. Where did the rest of the money go?" Well, it went to all the other people who created and designed, and continue to maintain and manage a resort property in which it is feasible to charge $25 per day to park a car. Instead of wallowing in his grievances, and voting for Obama, the parking lot guy would do better for himself if he asked, "How can I become one of the managers?" or "How can I start a company that builds and operates parking lots?"

In a way, the confusion of the parking lot guy is understandable—it derives from a basic misunderstanding of the principle of division of labor. We can understand this better by recalling Adam Smith's famous example of how pins are made. Smith intended to show that ten skilled individual pin-makers might each make one, or just a few, pins a day, while as workers in a pin factory they could make thousands of pins—Smith estimated "upwards of forty-eight thousand pins a day." How? "One man draws out the wire, another straightens it, a third cuts it, a fourth points it, a fifth grinds it," and so on. Smith figured that "the important business of making a pin is . . . divided into about eighteen distinct operations." Now assume that the last of these eighteen operations is the act of putting the head on the pin. The guy who does that could easily say, "I finished the job. I made the pin." That guy—who is the equivalent of the parking lot guy—then demands that most or all of the profit derived from selling the pin should go to him. From that man's perspective, he got the job done, he made the pin; nevertheless, once we understand the full operation of pin-making, we see how myopic and mistaken he is. The money paid to the last man in the pin-making chain, just like the $100 paid to the parking lot guy, represent precisely the value that they are adding to a process that goes far beyond their narrow efforts.

This last point, however, requires clarification. How do we know that $100 represents the "merit" of the labor of the parking lot guy? Here we need to make an important distinction between "merit" and "value." In *The Constitution of Liberty*, Friedrich Hayek writes that "in a free society it is neither desirable nor practicable that material rewards should be made generally to conform to what men recognize as merit." Hayek acknowledges that "this contention may appear at first strange and even shocking." He gives the example of several people who are striving with equal intelligence and equal effort to create a new venture or to make a new discovery. Even though all have striven as meritoriously, he writes, we still give all the rewards to the ones who succeed.[3] In the case of the new discovery, success may be measured objectively, as when Watson and Crick figured out the structure of the DNA molecule. In the case of new ventures and new products, however, success is measured subjectively, by the amount that customers are willing to pay.

Consider an extreme example: let's say I can throw sharp objects into the air and catch them between my teeth. Am I going to get rich doing it? In some places this skill may be completely useless; at most, it would make me a barroom curiosity. In a capitalist society, however, I can put my skills up for public consumption. If for some reason millions of people are fascinated by my skill—and even more important, if they are willing to pay to watch me—then my peculiar talent, regardless of its intrinsic "merit," becomes marketable. Now it has the potential to make me rich. Luck may also be a factor here. A person with very good math skills who lived in the early twentieth century might have found those skills largely unmarketable; today, another person with the same skills would likely be in huge demand as a hedge fund analyst or a computer programmer. Of course the second fellow is simply lucky, compared to the first, but even so, he is entitled to the benefit of his luck, in the same manner that the lottery winner deserves his winnings even though it was mere good fortune that conferred them.

Here, as in all cases, the monetary value of a person's contribution is determined by the consumer. The consumer issues the final verdict and casts the deciding vote, using ballots that are otherwise known as dollar bills. So that's why athletes and singers get paid so much, vastly more than teachers and doctors. Obama may have a low view of the "merits" of their services, but their millions of fans feel differently and prove it by continually buying tickets for games and concerts. In this context I recall the response of baseball great Babe Ruth who was once asked why he deserved a higher salary than President Hoover. He said, "I had a better year than he did."[4]

The beauty of free markets is that the "value" of each provider is decided precisely by the guy who is going to pay for that provider. CEOs, for instance, are paid by boards that are typically made up of large investors in a company. (I am not speaking here of companies where CEOs are somehow able to put their own cronies on the board.) These investors stand to make money with a good CEO, and lose money with a bad one. In a competitive market, a difference between a good CEO and a bad one can be critical. It is analogous, in a way, to the difference between a good and a bad quarterback. Therefore companies are often willing to pay high prices to attract the right "quarterback." How preposterous it is for Obama to pontificate on what CEOs should be paid when he is not the one who is paying them! All that he brings to the subject are his prejudices. He has no more idea of what value CEOs provide to their companies than he has of what value a particular coach or quarterback provides to a team. That's something for the owners of the team to decide, not some outside observer who is ignorant of the team's needs and has absolutely no "skin in the game."

Intellectuals are particularly susceptible to such speculations. Recently I found myself at MIT, in the spacious office of the famous linguist and leftist Noam Chomsky. Chomsky was raging about how workers in America are really "wage slaves," and in this category he includes intellectuals. I sat there in amazement. Here is a guy who likes to spend part of his day on linguistics; the rest he devotes to politics, from blasting Israel to celebrating the "Occupy" movement to assorted other leftist causes. For these activities MIT pays him a six-figure salary and gives him a secretary and a team of student researchers. Now who is exploiting whom? Sure, MIT gets a distinguished linguist who is, at least part time, working on linguistics. But Chomsky gets well-paid to do something that he would probably do even if no one paid him—namely pursue his academic interests and advance his pet causes. Is MIT depriving Chomsky of his "fair share"? One could equally make the case that Chomsky has found himself a pretty good racket. Professors who teach a few classes a week for nine months out of the year and get comfortably paid for doing it somehow manage to count themselves among the ranks of the oppressed.

Is Chomsky getting his due from MIT? Of course he is. So is the CEO. So is the parking lot guy. How do we know that? We know it because they have consented to those terms of employment. If Chomsky thinks he's worth more, say double his current salary, he can approach Harvard or Dartmouth and see if they will pay it. If no one will, then he ain't worth it.

The point here is that the morality of capitalism, just like the morality of democracy, is rooted in consent. What gives Obama his legitimacy as president? The fact that Americans voted for him: our consent is the moral basis for representative government. Similarly, what gives capitalist transactions—from employment terms to the price of milk—their legitimacy is that all parties must agree or the transaction doesn't go through. Obviously Chomsky wouldn't take the job if he didn't consent to the terms. Obviously MIT as an employer also has to consent to those same terms. This mutual consent is what gives capitalism and trade their legitimacy. Why? Because consent is confirmation on the part of all parties that they are better off. If they weren't better off, they wouldn't make the deal. The ingenuity of capitalism is that people who are complete strangers can make deals with each other for mutual benefit. Multiply these deals across a society and we have that good and well-functioning institution called a market.

Now I turn to the general subject of inequality, a topic which President Obama has proclaimed "the defining challenge of our time." Here the reigning progressive mantra has been, "The rich are getting richer and the poor are getting poorer." Inequality is the persistent theme for columnist Paul Krugman, and it is also the theme of economist Richard Wolff's book *Occupy the Economy*. Wolff rages about "a widening in the disparity between rich and poor." This disparity, and also the alleged disappearance of the American middle class, is the subject of Robert Reich's book and accompanying documentary film, *Inequality for All*.[5]

This is a familiar chorus. Early in the twentieth century, Thorstein Veblen wrote that "the accumulation of wealth at the upper end of the pecuniary scale implies privation at the lower end of the scale."[6] It's the same old chant. And maybe it was true in the past— I mean, the very distant past, when wealth was primarily in land. But if we look at data for America over the past five or ten or fifty years, we see a different picture. In reality, the rich have gotten richer and the poor have also gotten richer, although not at the same pace.

Inequality is admittedly greater. But is inequality the problem— or are we using inequality as a synonym for poverty? Is it a problem, for example, if I drive a Jaguar and you drive a Hyundai? If you have a three-bedroom house, do you have cause to be outraged that your neighbor has a seven-bedroom house? Inequalities of this kind seem unobjectionable, and perhaps there is even a valid rationale for them. If we look at how America became more unequal, we see that on the balance it is a good thing. To see what I'm getting at, imagine a society in which everyone makes $20,000 a year—which we will call our poverty line. That's a truly egalitarian society in which everyone is poor. Now imagine that, over time, half of those people improve their situations and now they make $30,000 a year—which we will call our middle-class line. The rest continue at the poverty line of $20,000 a year. Clearly we now have a more unequal society, since it is now divided into the $20,000 "poor" group and the $30,000 "middle-class" group. Even so, the result is a positive one, as the first group is no worse off than it was before, while the second group is better off. Moreover, the second group didn't gain at the expense of the first. Rather, the overall wealth of the society is greater, and that's a good thing, even if it is not equally shared. Unequal prosperity is better than shared poverty.

Something like this has happened to America in the past few decades. In the period following World War II, most Americans were middle-class. There was a small number—say 10 percent—of poor people and a small number—say 5 percent—of rich people. Today the fraction of the poor is about the same, although the poor live much better now than they used to. At one time America had the kind of poverty we see in developing nations. Economists call it "absolute poverty." In America today, there is virtually no absolute poverty; there is only relative poverty. Indeed poor people in America have a standard of living that is higher than 75 percent of the world's population.[7] Not only are our poor better housed, better clothed, and better fed than average Americans were in the first half of the twentieth century, but in some respects—including the size of their living space—they live better than the average European today. Our poor people have automobiles, TV sets, microwave ovens, central heat, and cell phones. I know a fellow who has been trying for years without success to emigrate to America. When I asked him finally why he was so eager to move, he replied, "I really want to live in a country where the poor people are fat."

As for the rich, they are still around 5 percent of the population, although "rich" means something completely different than it used to. In 1945 you were rich if you had a net worth of a million dollars—that made you a millionaire—but today (and this has been true for a few decades now) you need an annual income of $1 million to be counted as rich. America even has a sub-category of the super-rich whose net worth is counted in the hundreds of millions or even billions. These people have resources that compare to the gross domestic product of small nations. Many years ago I visited a tycoon who lived in a mansion on the James River in Virginia. When I arrived he was in the process of moving his main house. I don't mean he was moving to another house. I mean, he was having his mansion lifted and moved elsewhere on his property. I asked him what such an imaginative venture might cost and he responded, "If you have to ask, you cannot afford it." These wealthy people have achieved a standard of affluence that, in the words of Tom Wolfe, would "make the Sun King blink."[8]

The big change in America has come not from the poor or the rich but within the middle class. Yes, the middle class has fragmented, just as progressives allege. What progressives fail to acknowledge, however, is that the American middle class has fragmented upward. What this means is that many people who previously were middle-class have moved up. They have joined the ranks of the well-off. We can measure this simply by looking at the ballooning of the affluent class. In 1980, according to Federal Reserve Board data, there were roughly six hundred thousand American families with a net worth exceeding $1 million. Today more than 10 million families are worth in excess of $1 million.[9] Even recognizing the effects of inflation—$1 million today won't buy what it bought in 1980—that is a stupendous increase in the ranks of the affluent.

Who are these people? I was on an airplane flight recently, and my Delta platinum status got me bumped up to first class. There I found myself seated next to a Hispanic plumber who was taking his second wife to St. Kitts. There she was, sitting across the aisle from him. Actually, the man wasn't just a plumber, although he started out that way. He now owned a small plumbing business, and had several plumbers working with him. When we think of well-off people in America, we think of people who are born with privileges or of people who go into medicine or software. But the typical well-off person in America is much more likely to be a sixty-two-year-old from Flint, Michigan, or Tucson, Arizona, who owns a car dealership or a mobile home park, or runs a welding, contracting, or pest-control business. While most of these folks are white, a surprising number are first-generation or second-generation immigrants; they are, in fact, an ethnically diverse group. These are not people who lucked out—who "chose their parents carefully"—they are people who chose their professions and businesses carefully. They got their money the old-fashioned way, by earning it.

While many progressives condemn American capitalism for fostering inequality, in reality American capitalism has helped to create the first mass affluent class in world history. Previously the great achievement of the West was to create a middle class. Middle class means that you don't lack for necessities—you have food and clothing and can take a modest annual vacation—but you don't have surplus income, and you don't have substantial accumulated wealth.

While most of the world struggled with basic food and shelter, the West was able to provide most of its citizens with middle-class comfort. But now America has topped that by creating mass affluence, extending to many what was previously possible only for few. Mass affluence means that you can afford a big house with a big kitchen and nice cars and expensive cruises and shopping expeditions and private school tuition, and you still have money left over at the end. Millions of Americans who used to be middle class now enjoy the luxuries of affluence, and how can that be considered a bad thing?

Now the reason why some in the middle class have moved up, while others have stayed put, is that economic change and opportunity always benefit those who have the required skills and resourcefulness to benefit from them. While the old middle class was comfortably situated in manufacturing, this was precisely the sector that declined over the past few decades. Suddenly old skills were obsolete. The decline of manufacturing did not, however, spell the decline of opportunity. Rather, opportunities blossomed with the emergence of new industries—primarily in technology, communications, and various service sectors. Americans who had the educational skills and the adaptability to move into the new sectors benefited handsomely. Others remained stagnant and some even fell behind. It should be emphasized that this result is not an anomaly of technological capitalism; rather, it is how the system operates, unleashing a "gale of creative destruction" that boosts those most in tune with its "animal spirits."

All of this, however, is in the short term. While technological capitalism can be faulted with permitting, or even creating, short-term inequality, in the long term technological capitalism creates deep and abiding equality among citizens. This is not obvious or intuitive, so let's consider some examples. In the late nineteenth century—just over a century ago—a rich man traveled by horse and carriage, while the poor man traveled by foot. Today the rich man might drive a Mercedes or BMW, and his poorer counterpart a Honda Civic or a Hyundai. A Mercedes is faster and more luxurious than a Hyundai, but still, there has been an enormous leveling of the difference between the rich man and the poor man in getting from here to there. Another example: in the early twentieth century, the rich could escape the bitter cold of winter by going to homes in warmer climates and avoid the sweltering heat of summer by going to cooler retreats. Meanwhile, the common man had to endure the elements. Today most homes, offices, and cars are temperature controlled, and the benefits are enjoyed by rich and poor alike.

These examples could be multiplied, but here is the most telling one. A hundred years ago, the life expectancy of the average American was around forty-nine years. The gap between rich and poor Americans was considerable: about ten years. It was not uncommon for a wealthy person to live into his late sixties or seventies but quite rare for a poor person to do so. A similar gap, of course, separated the United States from poorer countries like China and India. Today the average life expectancy in the United States is around seventy-eight years. There is a gap between the rich and the poor but it's negligible: two to three years. Poorer countries like China and India have also seen a sharp rise in life expectancy. India's life expectancy has almost doubled, from around thirty-five years to nearly seventy years.[10] That's still below the American average, but who can deny that there has been a remarkable closing of the gap and that this is an egalitarian achievement?

Now who is responsible for this achievement? The answer, remarkably, is technological capitalism itself. It is technological capitalism that produced the advances in medicine and food production that have reduced infant mortality, disease, and starvation. I am not denying that government policies and private philanthropy have also helped, but their impact is minimal compared to that of technological capitalism. Technological capitalism has not only equalized life expectancy, it has also equalized the availability of countless amenities that are now available to the rich and poor alike. Economist Joseph Schumpeter made this point in a general way when he wrote, "Queen Elizabeth owned silk stockings. The capitalist achievement does not typically consist in providing more silk stockings for queens but in bringing them within the reach of factory girls in return for steadily decreasing amounts of effort."[11]

How does this process occur? In America, we can see it by considering examples such as automobiles and computers. When the automobile was first invented, it was dismissed as a "rich man's toy." But not for long. Eventually Henry Ford introduced the Model T, and brought the price down so his workers could afford them. Similarly, computers were first thought to be just for big corporations, and then just for rich people, and pretty soon for everyone. Cars and computers took a while to go from rich people's contrivances to mass items, but the cell phone seems to have morphed within just a few years from an expensive curiosity to a universal necessity. Even Indians in remote villages and in urban slums now have cell phones. International phone calls that were once prohibitively expensive are now within the reach of ordinary folk.

None of this happened "automatically" or "by accident." Consider the example of phone calls. In 1920 it cost $20 to make a long-distance phone call from New York to San Francisco. No ordinary citizen could afford that, yet someone had to make phone calls at that price, or else there would have been no market for phone service. In footing the big initial bill, the rich paid the fixed cost of bringing long-distance service to the masses. Today a coast-to-coast phone call costs almost nothing. The same trend of improved technology at lower cost is equally true of cars and computers and advanced medicine. In each case, the rich pay the high initial price, which funds additional research and development, which in turn enables technological improvement, economic efficiency, and lower prices. Former luxury items are now within the reach of the common man. The broad spread of technology and medicine, far from representing a theft by the rich, represents a subsidy on their part that has greatly benefited the larger society. In the words of Friedrich Hayek, "Many of the improvements would never have become a possibility for all if they had not long before been available to some. . . . Even the poorest today owe their relative well-being to the results of past inequality."[12]

My conclusion is that technological capitalism is by far the best system for giving entrepreneurs and workers their "fair share." This fair share, whether measured in terms of profits or wages, is precisely what people are entitled to as a result of the value they create for their fellow citizens. While short-term inequality frequently results from the dynamic energy of a capitalist economy, that energy also produces mass affluence that ultimately raises life expectancy and living standards for everyone.

CHAPTER 12

A GLOBAL SUCCESS STORY

*The end of empire has been accompanied by
a flourishing of other means of subjugation.*[1]
—KWAME NKRUMAH, *NEOCOLONIALISM*

We live today in a world of economic globalization—a global marketplace that has been decisively shaped by America and the West. Progressives claim that the first step in this globalization was the direct colonialism of the British and the French, and it has been followed by America-led "neocolonialism," another form of economic exploitation that amounts to theft. To a generation that grew up in the Third World in the 1950s and 1960s, nothing seemed more obvious than that colonialism itself was theft on a grand scale. Britain, for example, took cotton and other raw materials from India, converted them into finished products in the factories of Manchester and Liverpool, and then sold those products domestically and internationally. Indians would end up buying shirts manufactured in England with Indian cotton—while the Indian handlooms closed down.

Yet for the British to purchase cotton at the Indian market price does not seem, by itself, to constitute theft. The Indian farmers had been selling at that price to the Indian handloom mills. Nor can the British be faulted for using the machines of the Industrial Revolution to efficiently convert cotton into cloth, nor for selling that cloth to Indians more cheaply than the Indian handlooms could. Not only were British manufacturers not stealing from the Indian people; they were actually giving them a better deal than they were previously getting from the Indian mills. Moreover, there is a deeper factual point that often goes unrecognized in the anti-colonial literature. In that literature we read innumerable claims to the effect that "the Europeans stole rubber from Malaya, and cocoa from West Africa, and tea from India." But as economic historian P. T. Bauer points out, before British rule, there *were* no rubber trees in Malaya, nor cocoa trees in West Africa, nor tea in India. The British brought the rubber tree to Malaya from South America. They brought tea to India from China.[2] And they taught the Africans to grow cocoa. In these cases, far from "stealing" native resources, the British deserve credit for introducing profitable crops that benefited the native economies as well as British global trade.

Even more broadly, it makes no sense to claim that the West grew rich by taking everybody else's stuff for the simple reason that there wasn't very much to take. Most Third World countries were desperately poor before colonization, so they could hardly be worse off in material terms after the colonizers went home. How, then, did the West become affluent if not by stealing from Asia, Africa, and South America? The reason is the West invented some new things that didn't exist before. These inventions were modern science, modern technology, and modern capitalism. Science here refers not merely to invention but to what Alfred North Whitehead terms "the invention of invention," a new mechanism for generating knowledge and converting that knowledge into usable technological products. Capitalism here refers not merely to trade but to property rights, contracts, courts to enforce them, and later limited liability, credit, stock exchanges, insurance, and the whole ensemble of institutions that Adam Smith outlined in the *Wealth of Nations*. Science, technology, and capitalism are Western institutions that developed due to internal causes, from the scientific revolution to the Industrial Revolution.

The impact of the West in transforming developing countries for the better was noted in the nineteenth century by, of all people, Karl Marx. Marx credited colonialism with transforming feudal society into modern industrial society. "England has broken down the entire framework of Indian society," Marx acknowledged. In particular, "It was the British intruder who broke up the Indian hand-loom and destroyed the spinning wheel." Marx added, "This loss of his old world . . . imparts a particular kind of melancholy to the Hindu." Even so, Marx emphasized that the Hindu had been living in a village system based on the hierarchy of caste and economic and social oppression. Moreover, "These idyllic village communities, inoffensive though they may appear, have always been the solid foundation of Oriental despotism." Marx pointed out that through such mechanisms as railways and steam power, Britain unified India and integrated her into a global system of trade. Marx termed this a "fundamental revolution in the social state of Asia," a positive development that he characterized as a "regeneration."[3]

Progressives today reject this aspect of Marx, because Marx seems to say that while colonialism is theft, the theft was historically necessary as part of the modernizing process. Marx didn't justify colonialism or capitalism but he sought to transcend them. Progressives, however, want to reverse them, and their abhorrence for Marx's views in these areas is part of the reason many on the left have soured on Marx. Today's progressivism is less indebted to Marx than it is to Lenin. Lenin "rescued" Marx by arguing that colonialism represented the final crisis of capitalism. In Lenin's view, the Communist revolution had not occurred in Europe because European leaders found a temporary solution to their domestic problems. They ameliorated internal class conflict by conquering other countries and exploiting the workers there. Lenin called on people in the colonies to drive out the colonizers. This, he concluded, was good not only for the self-determination of the colonies but also to accelerate the crisis and collapse of European capitalism.[4] This double benefit helps explain why the otherwise foreign ideology of anti-colonialism became so attractive to many leftists in the West.

Marx might have disappointed the progressives, but was he right? On this particular issue, I think he was. No one, least of all Marx, suggested that the British came to India with purely noble intentions. Some Englishmen, like Macaulay and Kipling, spoke of the "white man's burden" to share civilization with the lesser peoples, but today such rhetoric is rightly dismissed as a rationalization for conquest. Like previous conquerors—the Afghans, the Persians, the Arabs, the Mongols—the British ruled largely for their own benefit. In order to administer the empire, however, the British had to build roads, railways, and ports. They also built the major cities of India: Bombay, Calcutta, and Madras. (The subsequent re-naming of these cities does nothing to change the historical fact that they were founded and built by the British.) The British also had to educate a native class of Indians. This required teaching them English. Education exposed Indians to new ideas that were largely alien in traditional Indian culture: modern science and technology, self-government, the rule of law, property rights, human rights, individualism, and self-determination. Ultimately the Indians learned the very language of political liberation from their captors.

Since India's independence in 1947, Indians have been reluctant to acknowledge the benefits of empire. Years ago I wrote an essay in the *Chronicle of Higher Education* titled "Two Cheers for Colonialism" and it stirred up a big controversy when it was republished in India. Even some of my relatives were outraged, with one of my aunts advising me, "We Indians are not supposed to say things like that." She was right; I was violating a national taboo. But that's changing. Recently India's Prime Minister Manmohan Singh spoke at Oxford University and there he did something no previous Indian politician dared to do—he praised the British legacy in India. "Today with the balance and perspective offered by the passage of time and the benefit of hindsight, it is possible for an Indian prime minister to assert that India's experience with Britain had its beneficial consequences. Our notions of the rule of law, of a constitutional government, of a free press, of a professional civil service, of modern universities and research laboratories have all been fashioned in the crucible where an age-old civilization met the dominant Empire of the day."[5]

Why did it take more than fifty years for an Indian leader to state the obvious? The reason is that, for most of this time, India failed to take advantage of what it gained from the British legacy. In this respect, India was similar to many other former colonies in Asia and Africa. Ironically this failure is due to the leadership of these nations falling under the anti-colonial spell. The anti-colonial ideology, forged in the colonies and subsequently embraced by many in the West, blamed the West for the poverty and underdevelopment of the "Third World." So the new leadership of many independent countries adopted a resolutely anti-Western stance. Because the West was opposed by the Soviet Union, these leaders were putatively non-aligned but in practice pro-Soviet. Because the West was capitalist, India and others decided to go in the socialist direction.

This was, as we now know, a disastrous mistake. We can see this by comparing, say, South Korea and Kenya. When Kenya became independent in the early 1960s, it was at the same economic level as South Korea. But Kenya took the socialist road and South Korea took the capitalist road. Today South Korea is many times richer than Kenya. Sure, there are important cultural differences between the two countries. But we can also verify the superiority of capitalism to socialism by comparing South Korea with North Korea. Same people, same culture. Yet North Korea remains desperately poor while South Korea is a comparatively rich country. India suffered the same fate as other socialist nations—it had a stagnant economy, and indeed for nearly half a century India was symbolized by the "begging bowl."

During this period—the second half of the twentieth century—the former colonies bewailed the continued economic strength of the West and pressed for foreign aid, foreign loans, and other handouts to alleviate their poverty and backwardness. Sometimes this aid was urged on the basis of compassion; mostly it was demanded as a matter of entitlement. Over a period of several decades there was a huge inflow of aid and loans to India and the poor nations of Africa. Nevertheless, none of this assistance made a significant difference. There are various reasons for this, including government misappropriation of foreign money. Perhaps the main reason, however, is that foreign assistance solved short-term famine and poverty but did nothing to enable the poor countries to become self-reliant. Basically, the poor countries used up the aid and then demanded more, or they spent the loans and then asked for new loans to repay the old ones. Until the late 1980s, it seemed that the world would long remain divided into an affluent West and an impoverished non-West.

What a difference a couple of decades makes. Between the late 1980s and today, the world has changed dramatically. Countries once termed "Third World" have now become "developing countries" or even "emerging markets." These emerging markets are growing at a rate three to five times faster than that of the West. While the economies of Western countries are growing at around 2 percent a year, the emerging markets are growing at 6 to 10 percent a year. China, once a backward economy, stands in the next decade or so to become the world's largest economy. India, while trailing behind China, could become the world's second largest economy by the middle of the century. Brazil, another large and once-backward nation, is also on the move and quickly becoming a serious economic contender on the world stage.

How did these once-impoverished countries gain economic traction? They did so by exploiting what may be termed "the advantage of backwardness." At first it seems crazy—or at least paradoxical—to assert that backwardness can possibly be an advantage. Poor countries themselves had long regarded their backwardness as a serious impediment. This point of view was clearly expressed by the African writer Chinweizu. In his book *The West and the Rest of Us*, Chinweizu wrote, "The poor have no way of influencing or changing the world market prices to their benefit."[6] Chinweizu's assumption was that the rich countries are powerful enough to set world prices and the poor countries have no choice but to go along.

Actually Chinweizu was wrong. There was never a problem with the rich countries having too much bargaining power. Rather, the problem was that, other than supplying some basic raw materials, the poor countries made little or nothing that anyone else wanted to buy.

What launched the "emerging markets" and changed the whole global economic picture? It was an epiphany on the part of China, India, and other countries. China was the first country to get there, and India second. China and India had long been considered "problem" countries on account of their large populations. In fact, overpopulation was considered the main reason those two countries were so poor. But under Deng Xiaoping, China realized that population need not be a liability; it can become an asset. If a poor country can put its large population to work and make stuff that the rest of the world wants, then it can undercut the world price and grab a substantial share of the world market. China has, in the last few decades, made itself the manufacturing capital of the world, and businesses in every country must now figure out how to beat—or at least contend with—the "China price." India followed China but not so much in manufacturing prowess as in deploying its educated, English-speaking, and technologically sophisticated middle class to provide needed global services at an unbeatable price. Together China and India in the past two decades have driven the global engine of economic growth.

Here we get to a tremendous irony. By exploiting the advantage of backwardness within a global economy, China and India have together lifted hundreds of thousands of people into affluence, and hundreds of millions of people from poverty into the middle class. Thanks to globalization, the United Nations Millennium Development goal of reducing world poverty by half by 2015 is likely to be met. Beyond the economic gain, the ordinary person in China, India, and other emerging countries now has an increased sense of self-worth and possibility. The future no longer looks like a bleak replica of the past. So these are not only material improvements, they are also moral gains. For progressives, this comes as a surprise. For decades progressives have advocated anti-poverty programs in poor countries. The main mechanisms for this were foreign aid and loans. These did little good, while technological capitalism has proven to be the greatest anti-poverty scheme ever invented. As one Indian entrepreneur put it, globalization and technological capitalism are finally helping to achieve Gandhi's dream of wiping a tear off every Indian face.

Even so, some progressives portray globalization as a form of exploitation of poor workers. The basic idea here is that large American corporations hire workers for a few dollars a day—vastly lower than the minimum wage in America. Moreover, they subject these workers to terrible working conditions, similar to those in locally owned factories. Yet Kishore Mahbubani, an Indian scholar based in Singapore, points out that local companies in emerging countries can no longer get away with low wages and sub-human conditions. It is no longer easy to attract people to work long hours in claustrophobic cubbyholes. The reason for this is the foreign companies pay more and offer better conditions. The American companies are at the top of the scale. Certainly the wages and working conditions are not what one would find in Milwaukee or Dallas, but they are nevertheless high by local standards. Mahbubani writes that $5,000 a year may be a scandalously low wage in America, but it is a small fortune to someone in Jakarta, Manila, or Kolkata. The people who take those jobs used to make $500 a year or less working in rural agriculture.[7] No wonder that there are long lines and long lists of applications when companies like Nike advertise openings. If globalization were a form of exploitation, one would expect there to be strong anti-globalization sentiment in developing countries. In fact, there is no significant anti-globalization movement in countries like China and India. That's because the Chinese and the Indians know much better than American progressives what's good for them.

Because globalization is good for workers in poor countries, it helps to reduce immigration from poor countries to rich countries. Largely as a consequence of globalization and free trade, Mexico is more prosperous today than it was a couple of decades ago. Consequently Mexicans have more opportunities in their own country, and they are less likely to hazard the difficulties of illegally crossing into the United States. India, too, offers vastly better chances to young people than it did when I left in the 1970s. Many Indians of my generation were "pushed out" because of the lack of economic opportunity at home. There is no longer that same pressure to leave now; in fact, some developing nations now provide incentives for their talented runaways to come back.

In a way that is not often recognized, globalization is also a force for peace among nations. The simple logic of this was noted centuries ago by figures like Adam Smith, David Hume, and Montesquieu. They knew that countries that trade with each other become mutually dependent. Thus they are less likely to fight. This is clearly true of America and China today. We get along with China vastly better than we used to get along with the Soviet Union. One reason, clearly, is that we routinely do business with China. We need them for the stuff we live by, and they need us to buy their stuff. Global trade doesn't just change the calculus of conflict; it also creates a new type of culture among people. As a result of the prosperity produced by globalization, for instance, many Indians spend less time grousing about Pakistan and more about their new business ventures. Across the world, globalization has people more interested in improving their lot through their own industry than through national conquest.

Like everything else, globalization has costs as well as benefits. Progressives are on stronger ground in claiming that globalization disadvantages some workers in America and the West. This is undeniable; the question is whether it constitutes exploitation. Consider a young person who has been raised in a steel town like Pittsburgh or an auto city like Detroit. For more than a generation, those places provided steady employment at a decent wage. Pittsburgh and Detroit were two of the most prosperous cities in America, gleaming illustrations of the American dream. And undoubtedly there were fathers who told their sons and daughters that if they worked hard and played by the rules, in the manner their parents did, they too would have a stable and prosperous future. Yet today Pittsburgh is no longer the steel capital of the world, and Detroit has lost its dominance in the global auto industry. What can we say to the young man or woman who is trained in steel work or auto work but no longer has a good job available to him or her? Has America failed these people? Has globalization stolen their American dream?

It is a fact that today steel can be made more cheaply outside America. This is also true of many other products: shoes, shirts, toys, and so on. Cars are different—Detroit's prosperity plummeted because auto executives made bad decisions and overpaid their workers. Consequently others figured out how to make cars better and more cheaply not only in Korea and Japan, but also in other states like North Carolina. There is unintentional comedy today in watching Michael Moore's film *Roger and Me*, in which Moore chases around the head of General Motors to find out why he closed the Flint, Michigan, plant in which Moore's father used to work. Moore thinks that the plant was closed because greedy bosses like Roger Smith wanted to keep more profits. He fails to mention that unions, like the one his dad belonged to, pressured GM to raise wages so high that GM cars just cost too much. Hardly anyone wanted to buy mediocre cars that were so expensive. Either GM had to keep losing market share, or figure out how to make cars more cheaply. So if Moore wanted to find the greedy fellows who caused the Flint plant to close, he should have started by interviewing his dad.

The bottom line is that in a globalized economy, the job goes to the people who can do it best and at the most affordable price. This is an iron law of capitalism, and it has been true in America for a long time. Globalization only changes the narrative in that the rest of the world also competes to provide the cheapest and best goods and services. This is bad news for unions that want to bid up wages beyond what the market will bear, and bad news for American workers if they cannot compete in terms of price and quality.

One option, of course, is to protect unions and American workers by restricting or blocking globalization. Remarkably some progressives who style themselves as compassionate and defenders of the little guy support such measures. And so do some conservatives on patriotic grounds. The patriotic impulse to protect America's workers and American manufacturing is understandable. Yet to block globalization is to block the greatest engine of global uplift that has ever been devised. It is to inhibit poor people from developing self-reliance and entering the middle class, not through handouts, but through selling things that others want to buy. So anti-globalization efforts are really measures to protect people who make $20 an hour at the expense of people who make a few dollars a day. Whatever we call this, we can't say it's helping the little guy.

I don't think that anti-globalization is a form of patriotism, because while it helps some Americans it hurts many others. Consider the guy who used to make shoes in Cincinnati and got paid $20 an hour. Now that guy is in trouble, because Walmart contracts to make shoes in the Philippines or Thailand, and pays those workers $5 a day. Consequently shoes that would otherwise cost $85 are now sold at Walmart for $20. Who benefits from that? American consumers! So while globalization penalizes inefficient American workers, it benefits cost-conscious American consumers. Globalization hurts the overpaid worker and benefits the silent majority of American consumers.

While it is easy to blame foreign workers for "taking" American jobs, let's remember that the greatest thief of American jobs is not foreigners—it's technology. Consider those travel agents who used to make a good living booking airline flights. Now they are mostly obsolete. It's cheaper and easier to book your own flights online. So should we "protect" travel agents by outlawing internet flight bookings? The very idea is absurd—no one has even proposed this. Similarly, there are now robots that can do things much faster and cheaper than human hands. Should we not build those robots in order to protect American jobs? China is already building millions of robots to replace human workers. So what happens to America's global competitiveness when other countries use robots and other forms of advanced technology while we don't?

Clearly there is no alternative to doing things in the best and most efficient way, whether it's through technology or outsourcing. This is what capitalism does to societies, and globalization is just capitalism in a single global market. There is an answer to what should be done by American workers who find that their old jobs are gone— they have to get new skills and find new jobs. I admit this is not easy. For many, the concept of a lifelong career is destroyed; time's arrow is bent if not broken. This may seem like an insufferable burden, but let's remember that this is what previous generations of Americans have uncomplainingly accomplished for themselves.

Just a century ago, most Americans worked on farms. Agriculture was America's leading occupation. Today less than 5 percent of America is employed in agriculture. What a sight it is to see a single guy in a tractor, with his headphones plugged in, farming a huge tract of land using the latest in modern technology and fertilizer products! So what happened to all those farming families that once lived off the land? They figured out that times had changed. They recognized that America no longer needs more than half its workforce to feed the American people. Instead of whining about it, they accepted that their old way of life was over. They got off the farm and learned how to do something else. What we need today is the same spirit that enabled earlier generations not only to adapt to change but to thrive in it; that's how America can compete effectively on the global track.

CHAPTER 13

EMPIRE OF LIBERTY

Americans need to face the truth about themselves,
no matter how pleasant it is.[1]

—JEANE KIRKPATRICK

I n 1946 the American diplomat George Kennan wrote a famous "long telegram" to the U.S. State Department proposing a strategy for dealing with Soviet expansionism. The strategy—subsequently elaborated by Kennan in a 1947 article in *Foreign Affairs*—came to be known as "containment." Basically Kennan argued for drawing a tight cordon around Soviet expansionism so its growth could be stopped. Kennan's ultimate goal wasn't just to corral the Soviets; it was to bring down the Soviet empire itself. Kennan argued that empires require expansion in order to survive; contain them and they will collapse. Kennan urged America to "choke" the Soviet empire and, by doing this, to cause the empire to implode. And this is exactly what happened. In one of the most stunning events of the twentieth century, in the late 1980s and early

1990s the huge, seemingly invincible Soviet empire disintegrated. Containment worked.

Now containment is being tried again, by President Obama. Only this time the country he is attempting to contain is his own. Obama's foreign policy may be neatly summarized by the phrase "self-containment." I get this phrase from a recent article by Douglas Feith and Seth Cropsey.[2] It may seem odd for a president who is the commander in chief, who takes an oath to protect and defend the interests of the United States, to self-consciously and deliberately seek to reduce America's power and influence. For Obama, however, it is good for America to have less influence. In tune with his progressive and anti-colonial ideology, Obama regards the American empire as the only remaining empire in the world. While America exalts democratic and universalistic ideals, in reality its foreign policy has been based on self-interest and plunder. America has used its power irresponsibly, to dominate others and to control their oil and other resources. Consequently Obama seeks to end America's neocolonialism, its large-scale global theft. To do this, he has to end America's tenure as the sole global superpower. Obama wants America to be a normal country, and to play a shrunken, more modest role in the world.

How is the Obama team doing this? One way is by sharply reducing America's nuclear arsenal. Obama has taken America's nuclear arsenal down from 6,000 to 1,500 warheads and now he wants to go to 1,000 and eventually to zero. He says he wants a world free of nuclear weapons, which seems like an admirable goal, except that no other nuclear power is interested, and the only country whose nuclear weapons Obama is in a position to dismantle is his own. As several leading strategists have pointed out, nuclear weapons are the main way that American maintains its global military superiority; by shrinking our nuclear arsenal Obama ensures that America's relative global strength is diminished. So is America's ability to protect its allies.[3]

Ultimately an alliance of, say, Russia and China will be able to checkmate America. This is not well understood; some people think it's sufficient to have a handful of nuclear bombs because those are enough to blow up half the world. Anyone who has studied nuclear strategy knows how foolish this is. Here's why. Imagine a scenario in which America has 300 nuclear warheads, and so do Russia and China. (Russia currently has more than 1,500 warheads and China has around 250.[4]) Russia and China make an alliance with each other, and each agrees to launch 150 warheads against America in a first strike. True, America's entire arsenal won't be wiped out; some of the Russian and Chinese warheads may miss, and some of our warheads are carried on submarines and bombers that are much harder to target.

Let's assume America has enough warheads left to destroy a dozen Chinese cities and a dozen Russian cities. America can strike back, to be sure, but if it does, the Russians and the Chinese have an additional 150 warheads each with which they can level every American city. The point is that America is now deterred from striking back, because it fears a completely devastating second strike that would basically end America as we know it. These are not wild speculations; they are precisely the "war games" that the Pentagon has played since the dawn of the nuclear age. The Cold War is over, but the logic of deterrence has not changed. So Obama's plan for self-disarmament is far more dangerous than people realize.

Another way Obama curtails America's global influence is that he undermines our allies while enabling our adversaries to consolidate their power. Obama's brusque treatment of England and Israel I have covered in earlier books and won't revisit. Here I want to focus on how Obama has been diminishing American power in the Middle East. While Obama slashes America's nuclear arsenal, he has done virtually nothing to curb Iran from getting nuclear bombs. Recently Obama agreed to reduce sanctions against Iran in exchange for Iran agreeing not to move further on its nuclear program. Since Iran's word means very little, this seems like a way of consolidating Iran's progress, helping its economy by lifting sanctions, and allowing Iran to move ahead on its nuclear program by stealth.

Obama's attitudes toward allies and enemies can be seen in two glaring double standards that have defined his foreign policy. While Obama refused to back the democracy movement in Iran in 2009, doing nothing to assist the Iranian people to rid themselves of our common enemies the Iranian mullahs, he staunchly backed the democracy movement in Egypt and helped get rid of our ally President Hosni Mubarak. Obama then cheered the rise of the Muslim Brotherhood in Egypt and provided aid to its government, even though Egypt was now in the hands of the largest organization of radical Islam. In the process of backing the Muslim Brotherhood, Obama alienated the Egyptian military. When the military ousted the increasingly repressive Brotherhood government, Obama's policies ensured that the military, which previously had been heavily supported by the United States, now looked at America with suspicion.

In the same manner, Obama supported the removal of the dictator Muammar Qaddafi in Libya on the pretext of "genocide" even though, at the time, only 250 or so people had been killed in the uprising in that country. By contrast, Obama for months refused to help the rebels fighting to get rid of dictator Bashar Assad in Syria's much bloodier civil war in which well more than 125,000 men, women, and children have been killed by government forces. Obama has been content instead to let Syria's ally Russia take the lead, reaching an agreement with Syria to eliminate its stockpile of chemical weapons. Obama has used this agreement as a pretext to continue to deny aid to the anti-Assad rebels. What then is the main difference between Qaddafi and Assad? The main difference is that Qaddafi was a dictator who had at least partially reformed from his anti-western ways and was doing business with America while Assad is an enemy allied with Iran.

As a consequence of Obama's actions, what America does in the Middle East now hardly seems to matter. In Asia, the Obama administration has done nothing to cultivate India, South Korea, and Japan as allies to check the growing power of China. Consequently India, South Korea, and Japan are building alliances with China for their own self-protection. While Russia bullies its neighbors, such as Ukraine, Obama does little more than growl like a toothless tiger. Everywhere—even in South America—the United States seems impotent or at best uninvolved. Obama is now little more than an international totem; in a sense, he has made himself irrelevant. This is not weakness; rather, Obama is implementing his larger objective of diminishing American power and ending American hegemony.

Obama is not alone in wanting America to play a more modest role in the world. There are many conservatives who agree, for instance, that America over-extended its involvement in Iraq and Afghanistan, that "nation-building" in these countries was an impossible task, that we should never have invaded Iraq in the first place or what we should have done in Afghanistan and Iraq was swiftly topple the regimes there and then just gotten out, ideally leaving behind a pro-American regime, whether democratic or not, in the two countries.

The difference is this, however: conservatives don't want America overextended because they want to protect American interests. Conservatives want America to be strong and powerful, and believe that unnecessary foreign entanglements have the effect of eroding America's economic and military strength. Conservatives distinguish between America's vital interests and foreign expeditions that are unnecessary and wasteful. By contrast, Obama and the progressives don't want America to be self-interested. They do not seek to conserve America's strength and power. They oppose American intervention in places like Iraq precisely because America has strategic and commercial interests there. Progressives prefer interventions in places like Haiti and Rwanda where America has nothing much to gain. They want the American giant cut down to size so that he can no longer be a force for global rampage and pillage. Moreover, many progressives contend that America should make amends and pay reparations for the harm it has done and the wealth it has stolen.

Given that the Obama administration—with the aid of Hillary Clinton, Obama's former secretary of state—has been scaling back America's influence and redistributing power away from this country to the rest of the world, it's worth examining their premise: Is America a force for global rampage and pillage? Does America owe reparations to other countries? Germany, for instance, has taken steps in the past half-century to eradicate the legacy of Nazism and to restore to Jews who fled Germany their ancestral property and possessions. This, however, was not reparations to Jews as a group but to specific Jews whose possessions were taken. The reparations, in other words, were to actual victims.

My family lived for generations under British rule; should I submit a bill for reparations to the British government or to the queen? I could do that—the British are actually paying reparations to Kenyans tortured during the Mau-Mau uprising, for example—but I'm not sure that in my case it would be fair. The British were not the only invaders who conquered parts of India. Before the British, India was invaded and occupied by the Persians, by the Afghans, by Alexander the Great, by the Arabs, by the Mongols, and by the Turks. Depending on how you count, the British were the seventh or eighth colonial power to invade India. Indeed ancient India was itself dominated by the Aryan people who came from the north and subjugated the dark-skinned indigenous people.

If reparations are due on the basis of conquest or domination, then the list of people needing to pay reparations is virtually endless: Should Normans—or Romans—pay reparations to the English? Should the Persians, Macedonians, Muslims, Mongols, Arabs, Chinese, Aztecs, Mayans, and innumerable others pay reparations to all the peoples they conquered or enslaved? Those of us living today are taking on a large project if we settle on a rule of social justice based on whose ancestors did what to whom. The conquest ethic was too pervasive historically for its effects to be reversible without creating new victims and new forms of injustice.

In any case, what does any of this have to do with America? America started out not as an empire but as the colony of an empire, and fought an anti-colonial war to gain its independence. Jefferson termed America an "empire of liberty."[5] He said this not to promote American empire, but rather to insist that, if America be termed an empire, it would be an empire unlike any previous one. While other empires extended their influence in the name of acquisitiveness and power, America would extend its influence on behalf of liberty. America, in other words, would be an empire that promoted self-rule rather than foreign rule. In 1821, John Quincy Adams—then secretary of state—asserted that America "goes not abroad in search of monsters to destroy," adding that America is a friend to liberty everywhere but the custodian only of her own. We see here the distinctly un-imperial objective of American foreign policy. Unlike virtually every other empire, America seeks to eschew conquest and show others the way of liberty and national independence.

This reluctance—and this objective of promoting liberty—extends throughout the twentieth century right up to the present.

America was certainly reluctant to get into World War II. Even this "good war," to defeat Nazi expansionism, was one in which America refused to intervene. Sure, Churchill wanted America to help Britain, and President Roosevelt was sympathetic, but still the forces of non-interventionism were too strong. Only when Japan attacked America directly at Pearl Harbor did America get into the war. Certainly America's motives had nothing to do with looting or theft. America was protecting itself, and the best way to do that was to defeat the totalitarian alliance of the Nazis and the Japanese. While America's motives were certainly self-interested, America's actions also helped the world by ridding it of two expansionist tyrannies, that of Nazi Germany and Imperial Japan. Who can deny that the world was better off because of what America did? One shudders to think what may have transpired had America not gotten involved, or had there been no America to get involved.

After World War II, America reconstructed Germany and reorganized the Japanese system so that today both countries are capitalist democracies allied with the United States. Our former enemies are now our friends. This is worth remembering not only as an unrivalled example of American munificence—it is very rare in history for a victorious nation to level its enemy and then rebuild it—but also as an example of how America can use its power to advance both its ideals and its interests. Consider the Marshall Plan. Admittedly it was in the long-term interest of America to have trading partners in Europe. Even so, there is something incredible in the idea of America investing to rebuild not just the nations of Europe but of its former enemies Germany, Austria, and Italy. Instead of taking what it could from a defeated opponent, a victorious America instead helped Germany become a postwar economic powerhouse. This is the very opposite of theft—it comes close to a rare case of philanthropy.

Germany and Japan benefited not merely from American financial assistance but from the adoption of American ideals and American-style free institutions. We hear from President Obama that democracy cannot be imposed at the point of a bayonet. Obama writes in *The Audacity of Hope* that "when we seek to impose democracy with the barrel of a gun" we are "setting ourselves up for failure."[6] Some progressives say there is something contradictory in attempting to force other countries to be free. Yet we imposed democracy at the point of a bayonet on both Germany and Japan—we forced both countries to establish free institutions—and the results have been excellent.

After the war, America actively pushed for the dissolution of European empires, in particular the British Empire. In the Suez crisis, for instance, America backed the Egyptian leader Gamal Abdel Nasser over the British. Both publicly and privately, America sought self-government for the nations of Asia, Africa, and the Middle East, just as it had for South America with the Monroe Doctrine. This liquidation of European power is precisely what James Burnham termed the "suicide of the West." In the sense just described, America did indeed aid the suicide of the West. America's willingness to push its wartime ally Britain to jettison its worldwide colonies was especially brave considering that America was starting to fight a cold war with the Soviet Union. Many of the newly independent nations declared themselves "non-aligned" states that were often socialist or even pro-Soviet.

Nevertheless, the United States and its Western allies won the Cold War, as Margaret Thatcher put it, "without firing a shot."[7] The remarkable success of this victory, achieved without the usual carnage that accompanies war, has caused many to forget what enormous resources, what determination and patience, and what intelligent strategy, went into defeating the Soviet empire. Again,

America fought the Cold War primarily for reasons of self-interest. We didn't want to be at the receiving end of the Soviet Union's nuclear missiles. Russia still has a lot of missiles, but they are less menacing than they used to be when the trigger fingers on the other end belonged to the grim members of the Soviet Politburo. So Americans can breathe a little easier, the people of Russia and Eastern Europe are vastly freer and better off, and Russia, while still dangerous, no longer poses an expansionist Communist threat to the peace and security of the world. America's role in the Cold War, far from being a case of imperial looting, was one of protecting ourselves while extending liberty to a sizable fraction of humanity, both inside and outside Russia.

What, then, of more recent involvements, from America's alliance with unsavory Middle Eastern dictators to its role in Vietnam, the Gulf War, and the Afghanistan and Iraq invasions? Many progressives point out that America has long allied with dictators like the Shah of Iran and the Saudi royal family in order to maintain access to oil supplies. By doing this, we become part of the "gang of thieves" exploiting the people. We even allied for some years with Saddam Hussein, before turning against him. During the Soviet War in Afghanistan, the United States supplied weapons to Osama bin Laden. These facts seem to suggest, on America's part, an amoral mercenary foreign policy, a vindication of the progressive allegation that America's actions are motivated by power-seeking and theft.

Progressives are certainly right that America makes these alliances to protect its self-interest. In the Middle East, that self-interest is oil. Now America is not stealing and has never stolen that oil—we purchase it at the world market price. America, however, seeks to avoid hostile regimes or instability in the region that might cause a disruption in the oil market. Progressives don't seem to realize that there is nothing wrong with this. Some years ago I debated a leftist professor who harangued me, "Mr. D'Souza, will you admit that the main reason America is in the Middle East is because of oil?" I replied, "I certainly hope so. I cannot think of any other reasons to be there, can you?" The audience laughed. My opponent looked sullen. I could see he wasn't convinced. And in a sense he was right. The question he was wrestling with was not self-interest per se. Rather, he was asking: In protecting America's self-interest, are we making the overall situation in other countries better or worse? This is a legitimate question.

In order to answer it, we must consider the central principle of foreign policy—the principle of the lesser evil. This principle says it is legitimate to ally with the bad guy to avoid the worse guy. The classic example of this was in World War II. The United States allied with Stalin—a very bad guy—because another bad guy, Hitler, posed a greater threat at the time. In the same vein, the United States was right to support the Shah of Iran, and when under Jimmy Carter we pulled the Persian rug out from under him, we got Khomeini. The Shah was a pretty bad guy, a dictator who had a secret police, but Khomeini soon proved himself a far worse guy. American and Iranian interests would have been better served if Khomeini had been prevented from coming to power. During the 1980s, the United States briefly allied with Saddam Hussein. This was during the Iran-Iraq war. Again, Saddam was the bad guy and Khomeini was the worse guy.

When America provided arms to Osama bin Laden, he was part of the mujahedeen, a Muslim fighting force seeking to drive the Soviet Union out of Afghanistan. The mujahedeen could never have succeeded without American aid. Soviet withdrawal from Afghanistan was the beginning of the end of the Soviet empire. It was a spectacular triumph of American foreign policy. Of course no one knew that bin Laden and his minions would subsequently make

America their main target. We see here a danger of "lesser evil" thinking: lesser evils are still evils. The bad guys you support today may turn against you tomorrow, as bin Laden did. Bin Laden may have been a "good guy" in fighting the Soviets, but he remained a "bad guy" seeking the eventual destruction of both the Soviet empire and what he took to be its American equivalent. So was America wrong to back the mujahedeen? No. At the time, radical Islam was not a major force in the world and we did not know bin Laden's intentions. Foreign policy does not have the privilege that historians have—the privilege of hindsight. And even in hindsight America was right to do what it did.

What went wrong in Vietnam, and more recently in Afghanistan and Iraq? In Vietnam, America miscalculated its self-interest. Of course the South Vietnamese were threatened by the North. Of course Vietnam would be worse off if it went Communist. But America committed large numbers of troops because it believed its vital interests in deterring Communist aggression were at stake. In fact, America had no vital interests in Vietnam; it was a drain on American resources rather than an intelligent use of them. So Vietnam was a stupid war, but it was not a wicked war. America had no intention to rule Vietnam, or to steal the resources of the Vietnamese people; America had no colonial designs on Vietnam. Still, Vietnam was an irresponsible use of American power—on this the progressives are right.

The Iraq War, undertaken by George W. Bush, was also a mistake. I supported the war at the time, because I believed the Bush administration's claim that Iraq had "weapons of mass destruction" (WMDs). In retrospect, that proved to be false. I don't understand how a country can invade another country based on the suspicion that they have WMDs. We should not have gone in unless we *knew* they had WMDs. Having said that, the Bush administration assiduously sought to rebuild Iraq after Saddam's ouster. The problem was that this proved to be a difficult and costly enterprise. Far from stealing from Iraq, America returned to the Iraqis the keys to the oilfields, and invested hundreds of millions of dollars in restoring order and commerce to that country. Far from acting like a colonial occupier, America's intention from the beginning was to get in and get out.

Over the past few decades, America has intervened in a half-dozen countries, from Libya to Grenada to Afghanistan to Iraq. In every case, America has acted in a most un-colonial way. First, America did not take resources from those countries; rather, it expended resources to improve them. Second, America was planning its exit almost immediately after its intervention, looking for the quickest, safest way to get out. Progressives don't seem to recognize this. They often make lists of countries America has invaded and occupied. But they never consider the simple question, "If America was the evil colonial occupier of all these countries, why don't we own them?" The reason is that Americans have no interest in acquiring foreign real estate. We never have, and I'm convinced we never will. As Colin Powell memorably put it, the only ground America has sought abroad in the aftermath of war is sufficient ground to bury our dead.[8]

At its core, American foreign policy is based on two simple precepts: (a) don't bomb us and (b) trade with us. This is all that Americans want from the rest of the world. A more benign foreign policy can hardly be imagined. America should not and does not oppose the rise of other powers, as long as they are peaceful trading powers and not violent conquering powers. In the future, America should be more cautious about committing troops abroad. How then can we assist other countries to become free? The people in those countries must take the initiative. They must recognize the value of freedom. In general, we won't fight for their freedom. They must fight, but we can help. This was precisely the Reagan Doctrine of the 1980s. The mujahedeen in Afghanistan and the contras in Nicaragua are the ones who fought tyrannical regimes in their own countries. America did not send troops, but we did assist in other ways. And both resistance movements were successful. The Reagan Doctrine provides a good rule for America in the future: it steers a healthy middle course between reckless intervention and irresponsible indifference.

In the beginning of this chapter, I quoted Jeane Kirkpatrick's wry remark that "Americans need to face the truth about themselves, no matter how pleasant it is." Kirkpatrick meant this half-jokingly, but only half-jokingly. On the balance, America has been a great force for good in the world. From World War II to the Cold War to innumerable smaller involvements, America has simultaneously protected its self-interest while also making the world a better place. While America has made its mistakes, in no circumstance over the past hundred years has it gone abroad to conquer and plunder. In no case has America stolen the wealth of any other country. The allegation of some progressives that America is an evil empire is not simply wrong—it is obscene. For foreigners to make such allegations is one thing; for Americans to falsely accuse their own country is another. If America declines, new powers will rise to take its place. Then the world—and perhaps even the progressives—will miss the leadership of the kindest, gentlest superpower in world history.

CHAPTER 14

THE BIGGEST THIEF OF ALL

Any government which robs Peter to pay Paul
can always depend on the active support of Paul.[1]

—George Bernard Shaw

There is a scene in the movie *Casablanca* in which a suspicious-looking man approaches a tourist and warns him about the danger of pickpockets. He says there are "vultures everywhere" and, while the tourist nods appreciatively, the man reaches into the tourist's jacket pocket and takes his wallet. In this chapter, I examine the institutional equivalent of that thief: the federal government. While posing as the pursuer of thieves, and the restorer of stolen goods, the government is actually the biggest thief of all. In fact, progressives have turned a large body of Americans—basically, Democratic voters—into accessories of theft by convincing them that they are doing something just and moral by picking their fellow citizens' pockets.

Imagine a fellow who has worked hard to achieve a good position in a company or who has built a successful firm. He is watching TV one evening when policemen show up at his door and start carrying away his furniture, his TV, and his other possessions. When he demands to know what's going on, they inform him that he is a thief. Since he has never been convicted of anything, the man is non-plussed, but the police assure him that, while the specific time of the theft is unclear—it could have been through his business, or through his country's actions abroad, or through something his ancestors did—nevertheless he is no longer entitled to what he has, and the government is now going to confiscate it. Such a man, accused of robbery, will naturally feel that he is being robbed. In the name of correcting a supposed injustice, a grave injustice is being inflicted on him. Such is the situation facing all successful people in the age of Obama. The biggest thief—they are beginning to suspect—is not America or capitalism but the suave scoundrel in the White House. Moreover, he and his fellow progressives are turning honest Americans into thieves.

How does an honest man become a thief? Consider a person who works hard loading luggage at an airport or cleaning the floors of an office building. When such people leave work, they see successful people being driven around in limousines or eating in fancy restaurants. Immediately they wonder, "Why does that guy have what I don't?" This question is immediately followed by feelings of frustration and inferiority. These are very powerful and natural feelings, and they are worth examining more closely.

We feel inferior to others when we realize we are not as good as they are. Now in an aristocratic society, this type of feeling is actually rare. Aristocratic societies impose superior and inferior status on people, but this does not make the ones lower down feel inferior. If this is a surprise, it shouldn't be. In caste-bound societies, the lower orders know they are simply there because of birth or ill luck. They just got the short end of the stick. Consequently they can console themselves by thinking: if I were lucky like that other guy, I'd be just as rich and accomplished as he is.

In a free and competitive society, where there are equal rights under the law, and where people perform to the extent of their abilities, such consolations are not available. A society of free competition is like a race where everyone starts on the same line: the guy who hits the finishing tape first really is better. It's hard for losers to deal with this. Not only do they feel inferior, this feeling makes them hate those who are successful. Thus they begin to secretly nurture the emotion that will guide their political behavior from now on, the emotion of envy. In a sense they become like Iago, who says of Cassio, "He hath a daily beauty in his life that makes me ugly."[2] Because Cassio is beautiful, Iago must bring him down in order to bring himself up, to make himself feel better.

Back to the hard-working fellow who, rather than hate himself for being inferior, begins to resent his successful fellow citizens. At first this resentment is inarticulate, and has no legitimate outlet. Then along comes the progressive, the Obama type. This Obama is no less envious than the ordinary worker. Why? Not because Obama isn't talented. It's because Obama isn't talented in any of the things that it takes to succeed in a commercial society. Obama cannot do what Steve Jobs does. He cannot run a business; never has. Even with the full resources of government, he could not put up a working healthcare website. Consequently Obama develops a fierce envy toward his entrepreneurial superiors. He knows that he has talents, but they are other talents: the talent for rhetoric and mobilization, an ability to work up the mob. He decides to put these talents to use to bring down the hated entrepreneur, to establish his superiority through government control.

So the envious Obama type says to the envious person: You are actually not envious; you are indignant. (This is precisely how he feels himself.) And you have good cause to feel resentful and even enraged. That successful person has been stealing from you. You work just as hard as he does, and yet he makes off with all the gains. Actually you have produced just as much as he has, and so the gains belong equally to you. And I am here to restore you to justice. If you vote for me, I will use the power of the government to take away the other man's possessions. I will then give some of those possessions to you. Obama omits to mention, of course, that through this process he becomes more powerful. He, not you, exercises the levers of government control. He is using you to achieve his own objective, which is the conquest of the wealth creators. Yet to assuage your envy and resentment you recruit him to go to work for you, to take money from others and put it into your pocket.

This is how a righteous man becomes a thief. His envy is an invisible vice that had previously traveled in secret. The progressive contribution is to give that envy political cover, to permit it to travel under the passport of morality. Now the man who felt bad about himself gets to feel good about himself, *even while indulging his envy*. In a triumph of vice masquerading as virtue, the fellow eagerly supports progressives in using the power of the state to confiscate and seize the earnings of those who have contributed the most and earned the greatest rewards. The result is most pleasing: the envious get to enjoy some of that loot, all the while thinking they have struck a blow for social justice. As for the government, in the name of fighting theft—a theft we have shown to be largely nonexistent—it has under progressive rule become itself a burglar. This is burglary of a kind that is normally found in Third World countries; the burglars have the police on their side.

Since Obama was elected, conservatives and libertarians have been making elaborate critiques of government, critiques that seem to go nowhere. Let's examine why this is so. The first critique is that government is inefficient. This is obvious, as any visit to a post office, department of motor vehicles, or immigration office can easily demonstrate. Government is notorious for wasting money and this is not simply the consequence of bad government; it is a problem intrinsic to government itself. Basically, whatever the government does, it does badly. This is just as true of the Defense Department as of the Housing or Labor departments. Part of the reason is that government means bureaucrats spending someone else's money. Naturally they are profligate with it; it's not their money. Besides, they are not subject to market forces—consequently, there is no "bottom line." Private investors who make bad decisions get punished for them; bureaucrats who make bad decisions suffer no such consequences. Private initiatives that don't work get canceled, but with very few exceptions—to paraphrase Reagan—government programs are the closest thing to eternal life we'll see on this earth.

Another reason centralized government is so inefficient is that it just does not have access to the kind of information to make good decisions that people typically have at the local level. This is an argument made famous by economist Friedrich Hayek, and it has never been refuted. Consider this question: What's happening right now in New York at Lexington and Fifty-Fourth Street? Obama has no idea, and neither do his bureaucrats in Washington. But the guy who lives across the street, or the fellow selling hot dogs at that intersection, or the company that is considering opening a store there—these people have a much more detailed familiarity with what's going on. Consequently, they are able to make more informed decisions. Even if bureaucrats could be just as motivated as private sector actors to make wise and cost-effective decisions, they simply don't have adequate information to do so. The point here is that we need rules and decisions—in that sense, we need to be governed—but we are best governed by a decentralized network of private and state institutions.

Centralized government is simply ill-equipped to make the innumerable decisions that are best left to local people, local businesses, local civic institutions, and local government.

A second critique of government—one that I have previously made in the context of Obamacare—is that it purports to be fostering moral action among citizens while in reality its policies have nothing to do with morality.

My Obamacare argument will illustrate the point. During a recent debate I was asked why, as a Christian, I didn't support a program that was a fulfillment of our moral duty to be charitable to our neighbors. I responded with an example. Let's say that you and I are walking along the riverbank and I am eating a sandwich. You tell me you're hungry, and you demand half my sandwich. I give it to you. Now—I argued—that is a moral transaction all around. I have done a good deed, and can feel good about it. You are grateful, and perhaps someday if you have a sandwich you'd be inclined to share. But let's now consider a second case. The situation is just the same as before, but this time I refuse to share my sandwich. At this point, Obama himself shows up on a white horse. He dismounts, puts a gun to my head, and says, "Give that guy half your sandwich." And so I do.

The result—I pointed out—is identical to that in the previous case. In both situations, each of us has half a sandwich. But in the second one, the moral picture is completely different. I have no claim to virtue, because I didn't part with my sandwich voluntarily; I was forced to do it. You, the recipient, don't feel grateful; on the contrary, you feel entitled. Perhaps you are thinking, "How come I get only half a sandwich? That greedy selfish guy should have given me the whole sandwich." Obama's actions, which seem admirable when performed by the government, would, if he performed them as a private citizen, get him convicted of assault, extortion, and theft. My example was offered to illustrate how coercive government policies strip the virtue out of every transaction.

None of this is to suggest, of course, that government has no role to play in helping the disadvantaged. There is agreement across the political spectrum that it does. Here the problem with progressivism has to do with its utter inability to identify who the good guys are. Think of society as a bandwagon, with working Americans pulling the bandwagon. A wealthy society can afford to have some of its citizens—presumably those who are unable to pull—sit in the band-wagon. Historically that number was small, but in recent decades it has been growing. The more people who sit in the bandwagon, the harder it is for the rest to pull. Now one might expect a president to praise the people pulling the bandwagon, and thank them for what they are doing for their fellow citizens. Not Obama. He praises the folks sitting in the bandwagon, assuring them that they are the most morally wonderful people in America. Then he castigates the people pulling the bandwagon, accusing them of being greedy, selfish, and materialistic. Through their policies, Obama and the progressives create more incentives to sit in the bandwagon and fewer incentives to keep pulling. Naturally some of the people pulling the bandwagon are going to think, "Gee, maybe I should get in the wagon. It's so much better than pulling." So the bandwagon slows down, and at some point it could grind to a halt.

These critiques of government, while telling, have nevertheless not gotten very far. Why not? Because progressives have convinced people that they are fighting theft. If a greedy capitalist has looted your possessions, you would want the government to do something about it. An essential function of government is to bring thieves to justice and to restore stolen possessions to their rightful owners. If the progressive critique is valid, then it doesn't matter if government does it inefficiently, since there is no one else to do the job: inefficient justice is better than no justice. Moreover, when we ask the police to go after bad guys and repossess their stolen goods, we aren't concerned with whether we foster virtue among the "giver" and gratitude in the "receiver." That's because the giver isn't really giving; he's merely giving back, and the receiver has no cause for gratitude since he (or she) is merely being made whole. In this scenario, Americans who are sitting in the bandwagon have earned that right, and the people pulling are the thieves who deserve to be penalized and castigated. This is why I've devoted the bulk of this book to refuting the theft critique. If I've succeeded, then the whole progressive argument collapses and our federal government, far from being an instrument of justice, now becomes an instrument of plunder. This term may seem unduly harsh; in the rest of this chapter I intend to show that it is duly harsh.

Let's consider first the issue of plunder. How does progressive government plunder its citizens? It does so by illicitly transferring wealth from one body of the citizens to another. The mechanisms for doing this are confiscatory taxation, and also regulation and mandates. Taxation is quite obviously a form of "taking" but it's not so clear how regulation and mandates constitute theft. Imagine if the Obama administration were to say to an American family, "You must rent that extra bedroom in your house for $100 a month." The market value of that rental is $500 a month. By forcing you to rent for $100 a month, the government is stealing $400 of your money. Similarly when the Obama administration orders businesses to provide this or that benefit, it is basically stealing from the stockholders who have invested in that business.

Illicit taxation is also a form of theft. We are so used to being taxed in this way that we typically don't recognize this rip-off. So let's begin with some historical perspective. The core principle of slavery, according to Abraham Lincoln, is "you work, I'll eat." In his

Chicago speech of July 10, 1858, Lincoln called it "the same old serpent that says you work and I eat, you toil and I will enjoy the fruits of it." This, Lincoln said, is not only the essence of slavery; it is the essence of tyranny. It is the same argument "that kings have made for enslaving the people in all the ages of the world."[3]

For centuries in Europe, people understood that the very freedom of the serf—the main thing that distinguished serfs from slaves—is that serfs got to keep some of the fruits of their labor. Karl Marx points out that "the peasant serf . . . worked three days for himself on his own field or the field allotted to him, and the three subsequent days he performed compulsory and gratuitous labor on the estate of his lord." Marx appreciated the clarity of the system: "here the paid and unpaid part of labor were sensibly separated."[4] So at least the serf could recognize the degree to which he was being ripped off. And the thieves were the lords and aristocrats, who lived off the labor of the serfs. The serfs worked, and they ate.

America's tax rates, we may recall with some surprise, impose basically the same terms on successful citizens as those imposed on the medieval serf. The top federal tax rate is nearly 40 percent, and when other taxes are piled on, the top rate easily reaches 50 percent. What that means is that half of the labor of these citizens is confiscated up front; another way to look at it is that the first half of the year they work for the government, and only the second half they work for themselves and their families.

Obama and many progressives consider these tax rates unfairly low—they would like to raise them. Obama, with Alinskyite caution, never says how much. But progressive scholars are more specific. Former Treasury Secretary Robert Reich proposes a top marginal tax rate of 55 percent. Economist Richard Wolff nostalgically invokes the period immediately following World War II when the top marginal tax rate was over 90 percent. Wolff says that the rich, in paying a mere 40 percent currently, have enjoyed a massive "tax cut." He'd like to see the rates go back up toward 90 percent.[5] What this means is that successful people would get to keep 10 percent—10 cents of every dollar they earn. What's remarkable about this is that if you took away that 10 percent, they'd essentially be reduced to slavery. Slavery is a system based on a 100 percent tax rate.

Now obviously some of this money goes toward providing the necessary and appropriate services of government. These services include defense, the police, the highways, product safety, environmental protection, and basic research. Notice, however, that these are benefits that accrue to all citizens. Everyone benefits from the common defense. The highways are there for everyone to use, even if some choose not to use them. So these activities fall under what the Constitution terms the "general welfare." Contrast this with government transfer payments from one group of Americans to another. How does this promote the general welfare? Clearly it does not. It constitutes a forcible extortion from one group and an unearned benefit to another.

I acknowledge that we have moral obligations to our fellow citizens that go beyond equal treatment under the laws. Consider Bill Gates, who has a net worth of around $65 billion. Surely Gates can't spend the bulk of that money, and since there is such a huge surplus, doesn't he have an ethical duty to the needy people of America and perhaps also the world? Undoubtedly Gates's billions can help with what government has been doing: fund schools, build roads, bail out banks, send money to Egypt and Israel, and give more people monthly checks. Yes, Gates has an ethical duty, but I believe that he—not the government—should discharge that duty. First, it's his money and therefore he, not Obama or the U.S. Congress, should decide how much he wants to give away and who that money should go to. Gates may choose to buy mosquito nets for

Africans or sponsor health research, and this is his prerogative. Second, since Gates earned the money he is much more likely to disburse it wisely. It seems that the Gates Foundation has done more good for society than we could entrust Obama to do with comparable resources.

Why is it theft for governments to engage in large-scale wealth redistribution? Recall why people come together to form governments in the first place. According to the early modern philosophers, people enter into a hypothetical "social contract." They leave the state of nature and enter into society because they want protection from foreign and domestic thugs. This is the primary purpose of government. Yet it is not the only purpose. People together may also assign to government functions that promote the common good. The key feature of the common good, however, is that it benefits all citizens. It does not promote the common good for the state to require the people of the North to pay the mortgage bills of the people in the South. It does not promote the common good for the state to insist that successful people pay other people's medical bills. We see here why Obamacare is so outrageous. It would be one thing for Obama to urge government subsidies to provide insurance for poor people who can't afford it. Arguably that benefits the common good because we all benefit from a society with a safety net, a society that provides a minimal floor below which no citizen can fall. Obamacare, however, is not a safety net. Obama's healthcare law forces all Americans to buy insurance—even people who don't want it—and it imposes the additional cost of the premiums on Americans who already have insurance and are already paying for their own healthcare. Obamacare is a form of theft.

Progressive taxation is also theft. Of course, it is based on the claim that an earlier theft is being rectified. Absent the earlier theft, there is no legitimate rationale for the government to impose higher levels of confiscation on some citizens. Indeed, the only truly just form of taxation is proportional taxation. Proportional taxation means that everyone who is eligible to pay income taxes pays at the same rate. Of course the rich pay more, but they pay proportionately more. So above a certain floor, everyone pays a 10 or 15 or 25 percent federal income tax. Not only is proportional taxation consistent with the constitutional purpose of government—to promote the general, and not particular, welfare—but it also establishes a rule of fairness. It doesn't matter what level of taxation democratic majorities choose, through their elected representatives, as long as that level is imposed on everyone. Right now we have a system where people can happily vote to raise taxes on others while keeping their own taxes the same or even lowering them. The current system is a progressive delight because it encourages envy and promotes state-sponsored theft.

Consider this startling fact. While the top 1 percent of Americans pays more than one-third of all federal income taxes, and the next 9 percent pays another third, the bottom 50 percent of Americans pays no federal income taxes at all. This is grossly unfair. Obama is right about the unfairness of the system. In reality it is unfair to the successful! It is also unfair that so many Americans who are earning money and are not poor nevertheless pay no federal income tax at all. The American Revolution was fought, in part, to advance the principle of "no taxation without representation." Well, evidently half of the country currently has representation without taxation. This would seem to be a very troubling feature of our democracy, because we want citizens to have a stake in the system. Democracy is about self-government, not about making laws that affect only other people. Yet people who pay nothing into the federal income tax coffer are asked to make judgments about what constitutes a "fair share" for others and for themselves. No wonder that Obama's demagoguery falls on so many receptive ears. He is telling people that it is just and proper that they, who contribute nothing into the system, should get more out of it, while others, who contribute a lot, should pay even more. Here's the formula for Obama's success: "They work, and you eat."

CHAPTER 15

AMERICAN PANOPTICON

Someone must have been telling lies
about Josef K., he knew he had done nothing wrong
but, one morning, he was arrested.[1]

—Franz Kafka, *The Trial*

I n the previous chapter we saw how the government, in the name of fighting theft, has itself become a thief. In this chapter I show how the government is, through surveillance of American citizens, collecting the information that it can potentially use to carry out its theft. We think the government is spying on its citizens solely for the purpose of catching terrorists. For progressive government, I will show, there is a broader benefit. If the government has become a thief, then surveillance is nothing more than what thieves do. In other words, surveillance represents a case of our government *casing out the joint*. Government is assembling dossiers on its targets in the same manner that the thieves in the film *Oceans 11* cased out the casinos before robbing them. Spying on citizens also enables the government to have power over its citizens, power that can be used to enforce conformity and deter

opposition to government-sanctioned theft. In sum, the U.S. government is building the power not only to systematically steal from its
citizens but also to use terror against them if they oppose this theft.

Let's begin by recognizing that any state-sponsored theft is likely
to be popular with people who are the beneficiaries of that theft. If
a gang of thieves robs a bank and then distributes the loot to a group
of people, those people become very contented accomplices. Their
contentment turns to pure bliss if they become convinced that the
bank has long been stealing from them, and they are simply getting
back what originally belonged to them, or what they had been
unjustly deprived of. As George Bernard Shaw wryly put it a century
ago, in a line I quoted at the beginning of the previous chapter: "Any
government that robs Peter to pay Paul can always count on the
support of Paul."

Still, Peter is less likely to be enthusiastic or to go along with the
scheme. Peter knows he hasn't been stealing from anyone; he has
merely been outperforming everyone. So the progressives have to
go to work on him, and they do so in three ways. The first—the most
benign—is to try and convince Peter that he's a thief. The progressive
strategy here draws on Alinsky, and basically involves a radical
redefinition of terms. "Greed" no longer means an illicit desire for
something more than one's due; "greed" in the progressive lexicon
means "a desire to keep one's own money." The term "compassion"
undergoes a similar transformation: it no longer means "suffering
with or sympathizing with someone else's situation," rather; it now
means "taking away other people's money." The more a government
takes from its successful citizens, the more "compassionate" it is.
The more the citizens try and hold on to their money, the "greedier"
they are.

This is all a little preposterous, and not surprisingly this attempt
at persuasion doesn't often work. In that case, progressives attempt

to induce dissenters and uncooperative elements to join the progressive coalition for their own advantage and protection. Obama, for instance, convinced insurance companies to back his healthcare scheme for their own benefit. He said, in effect: I'll force Americans who don't want insurance to buy it, and you will have more customers. The insurance companies backed Obamacare, not realizing that Obama's ultimate goal is to have the government completely direct and control them. This technique is reminiscent of Alinsky's boast that he could cajole millionaires to support revolutionary schemes that lead to short-term profits but also to their ultimate execution.

Even so, not every Peter capitulates, and eventually the progressives have to deal with hard-core resisters. (I am a good example of a hard-core resister.) Now they have a solution: use the power of the state to spy on citizens and collect personal information from their phone calls, emails, and financial and personal records. This information-gathering involves some of the most powerful agencies of government, from the IRS to the National Security Agency. Various rationales are given for this spying and data-collection, from serving people better to fighting terrorism. I am more interested in how this information can be used for purposes other than the ones the government is telling us about. One such purpose is to keep tabs on citizens for the purpose of taking their money. Obviously if you are going to steal from someone it helps to know what he has and where he keeps it. So surveillance, whatever its other purposes, has the benefit of letting the government collect information for its heist. Second, the information collected through government spying can also be used to achieve social compliance. It can be used to identify citizens who are uncooperative or dissenters, and then audit their tax returns or accuse them of crimes. The benefit of having extensive reams of personal data is that almost anyone can be found to have fallen afoul of the rules sometime or other. So everyone—the whole citizenry—is vulnerable. And the government wants them to know they are vulnerable. Ultimately, dissenters and hard-core resisters will be forced to capitulate out of fear. Under the leadership of Obama and the progressives, this is where we are now heading.

The government, in other words, has not merely become an instrument of theft; it is also setting up the necessary apparatus to become a vehicle of terror. Just as progressives have figured out how to steal in the name of fighting theft, they are now acquiring the means to use terror against American citizens. Remarkably this power to inflict domestic terror is being accumulated in the name of fighting international terror. Defenders of government spying—on the left and on the right—insist that these are only potential dangers. Sure, the government may have the capacity to intimidate and prosecute its political adversaries and critics, but we can trust it will not use its power in this way. My own experience—detailed here—is that it can and will. Therefore I don't have a whole lot of trust in the goodwill of the government; in this respect, I think I am squarely in the camp of the Founders. My experience may be anomalous, of course, but if it proves typical, then no one is safe. If progressives like Obama continue along this path, they will make the U.S. government itself into a terrorist state, one that resembles Iran and other totalitarian states that terrorize their own citizens.

Obama is clearly attracted by the totalitarian temptation. In February 2014, touring Monticello, Obama said, "That's the good thing about being president, I can do whatever I want." It was said in jest, but it is also, frankly, how he has attempted to govern—indeed he boasted in his 2014 state of the union speech that he was going to bypass Congress whenever it blocked his wishes and act through presidential edicts. This was not a new departure for Obama. In his first term, he made the remarkable statement, reported in the *New York Times*, that "it would be so much easier to be the president of China."[2] Ah yes. And why would it be so much easier? Because the president of China is basically a dictator. He doesn't have to bother with checks and balances, or court approval, or even public opinion. The Chinese government can with impunity raid the bank accounts of its citizens, and also cow them into submission if they resist its policies. Now imagine what America would look like if Obama got his wish. We would be, like China, a state that did not shrink to use terror against its own citizens. This would be a different kind of terror than that of al Qaeda. It would be Alinsky-ite terror, involving intimidation and criminal prosecution rather than direct violence. Yet its reach would be much wider. While al Qaeda targets some Americans—mainly in an effort to strike out at symbols of American wealth and power—the U.S. government would target all Americans. Al Qaeda seeks to terrorize Americans through sporadic actions of violence, but these acts pose a very low probability of harm to any particular American family. The U.S. government by contrast would spy and collect information on all citizens; consequently, it would be in a position to intimidate, blackmail, or even arrest any American that stands in its way. Given the government's obvious capacity to harm each one of us, we must conclude that in such a scenario al Qaeda would pose a smaller potential threat to our individual safety and freedom than our own government would.

The government's mechanism for initiating a system of intimidation and terror is the American Panopticon. The term was made famous by the nineteenth-century British philosopher Jeremy Bentham. It was an architectural design for a prison. Bentham developed the concept on a 1785 trip to Russia with his brother. He was asked by Empress Catherine the Great to help her modernize the Russian penal system. Bentham obligingly designed his Panopticon. Bentham was a utilitarian, and he considered his Panopticon to be a model of progressive humaneness and efficiency. Catherine never implemented Bentham's idea. Yet today there are several prisons around the world—including a few in America—that use Bentham's architectural blueprint. None of them, however, fulfill Bentham's actual objective for the Panopticon. That objective, remarkably, may be fulfilled not in any prison system but in America as a whole. A scheme once intended for prisoners now chillingly describes what's happening to the American people.

Bentham's basic idea was to build prisons as circular multi-tiered structures with a guard tower in the center. Each cell would be well-equipped but also completely transparent. Thus every prisoner could be observed at all times from the guard tower. Even a single guard would be sufficient to keep track of pretty much everything that was going on. The building would be lit around the perimeter, so inmates could not see each other, nor could they see who was observing them. Bentham argued that in this way, through minimum effort, the state could monitor a large group of people at all times. Since prisoners would not know when they were being watched, they would have to regulate all their activities in fear that the authorities would know what they were doing. Bentham did not seek to limit his Panopticon to prisons. Rather, he proposed that this "simple idea in architecture" could be tried in prisons, and then, if it worked, extended to factories, schools, barracks, and hospitals.[3]

Bentham's disregarded Panopticon has now become a grim reality. Thanks to a single man—the whistleblower Edward Snowden—we know that the U.S. government now uses the latest technology to spy on its citizens. This surveillance has been going on for a dozen years, although it has become ever more detailed and sophisticated. What precisely has our government been doing to us? A clear and ominous picture is now emerging. The Obama administration has been collecting our emails and texts, observing our web behavior, monitoring our phone calls, downloading our contact lists, viewing our apps and personal photo files, gathering our financial and personal data, reviewing our online purchasing habits, even tracking our movements. This is all done through the collection of "metadata." The government stresses that metadata doesn't typically involve content—the government monitors who you are calling and when, but not what you are saying; it can track your email traffic, but it cannot read your email without court sanction. But as a number of web savvy critics have pointed out, a sufficiently detailed log of metadata can easily establish the most specific content of an individual's life.

It would be bad enough if the president himself were doing this. In fact, as Snowden said in an interview, "Any government analyst, at any time, can target anyone . . . anywhere."[4] The government has built huge data centers, such as a million-square-foot facility in Bluffdale, Utah, to assemble and process the information. The government even accesses the records of private companies such as Google, Yahoo, and AT&T to get the information it seeks.

It's hard for me to believe this is going on in America. When I first came to the United States, I discovered how much Americans cherish their privacy, their "personal space." Growing up in a heavily populated country, I had no sense of privacy or personal space. I remember once in high school leaning against someone's car and the guy came up to me and said, "Get off my car." I was puzzled; I didn't know what he was talking about. I soon learned that a man's car is a part of him, and keeping a certain distance from the car is a way of respecting a man's personal space. In America, we learn not to stand too close to another person, or else they say, "Get out of my face." Americans recognize that our privacy is part of our individuality and attempts to invade our privacy are experienced as an insult and a violation. Yet now our government has invaded our personal space. The most private precincts of our lives—our conversations—and of our minds—the things we watch and hear—are subject to covert government scrutiny. If you read this book electronically some government analyst at the NSA might be watching you do it. It's creepy.

Such comprehensive spying on American citizens would seem to flagrantly violate the constitutional prohibition of "unreasonable search and seizure." After all, the government is spying on law-abiding citizens who are not suspected of any crime. That would seem to make any searches *prima facie* "unreasonable." Admittedly in a 1979 case, *Smith v. Maryland*, the Supreme Court ruled that people who sign up with the phone company and receive a telephone number thereby relinquish their privacy right over the phone activity associated with that number. Still, it's one thing to give up necessary information to Verizon, or to share a credit card number with a company you are making a purchase from, and entirely another to expect your phone and credit card activity to be routinely monitored and stored by the U.S. government.

With privacy concerns in mind, Congress in 1976 set up a Senate Committee on Intelligence to review America's spy agencies. Yet, until Snowden's revelations, the Obama administration had not fully informed Congress about its spying practices. When Democratic Senator Ron Wyden asked Obama's intelligence director James Clapper, "Does the NSA collect any type of data at all on millions or hundreds of millions of Americans?" Clapper answered, "No, sir." It was, as Clapper later conceded, a brazen lie. Even now, Wyden says, he does not know the full extent of the Obama administration's spying on American citizens. Asked about specific actions—is the government downloading my Facebook photos?—Wyden typically replies, "What do I know? I'm only on the Intelligence Committee."[5]

Congress also set up special courts to review the government's espionage against American citizens. In 1978, Congress enacted the Foreign Intelligence Surveillance Act (FISA) which forbade intelligence agencies from spying on Americans unless they were agents of a foreign power. FISA courts were set up to oversee government actions. Yet the government typically does not provide to these courts the information necessary to make an independent judgment on the need for domestic espionage. The government makes its case, and there is no one to represent those who are the targets of the surveillance. So, in effect, the government pleads "national security" and the courts rubber-stamp its programs. All these proceedings are conducted in secret so there is no opportunity for the American people to know what is happening to them.

It took an independent judge, Richard Leon of the District of Columbia, to find the Obama administration's domestic spying "almost Orwellian" and to say that it flagrantly violates the protections the Founders built into the Constitution. Judge Leon wrote, "I cannot imagine a more 'indiscriminate' and 'arbitrary' invasion than this systematic and high-tech collection and retention of personal data on virtually every single citizen." Judge Leon considered the Obama administration's claim that warrantless phone tapping was necessary to thwart imminent terrorist plots. He found that there was not "a single instance in which analysis of the NSA's bulk metadata collection actually stopped an imminent attack or otherwise aided the government in achieving any objective that was time-sensitive."[6]

All of this, I regret to say, started under the Bush administration. Understandably the Bush people were in a panic over 9/11, and they demanded that Congress give the executive branch expanded powers to track terrorists. Bush officials were worried about the time delay in seeking warrants for spying. While the warrant was being pursued, there might be a terrorist attack. Congress, however, had no idea that this tracking apparatus would become a Leviathan of domestic surveillance, and that the government intended to spy on Americans who were not even suspected of any crime.

The Obama administration has not only continued the Bush administration's surveillance policies, it has also expanded them. Earlier in his career Obama was considered to be a defender of privacy and civil liberty. In his 2004 Democratic Convention speech, Obama spoke movingly about the danger of the government snooping in a library to find out what books Americans were reading. As a senator, Obama criticized what he then saw as excesses in the Bush administration's surveillance programs.[7] Now, however, Obama seems willing to adopt techniques far more sinister than library surveillance, and more expansive than the Bush programs he once objected to. Is it because Obama has come to a new realization of how sneaky and dangerous the terrorists are? I doubt it. Terrorism has never been his main concern. More likely he has come to see the benefits of government "having the goods" on the entire body of American citizens. I also believe he recognizes the value of Americans knowing what their government is doing; he wants them to know. People can only experience a "chilling effect" on their actions when they understand they are under scrutiny.

Obviously there is a national security rationale for tracking terrorists, and equally obviously, the state does not have to violate the privacy of 300 million Americans to do it. As Senator Rand Paul puts it, the big story here is not that the U.S. government is spying on terrorists—we expect that and want the government to do that—but that the U.S. government is spying on its own people. Now we know that Americans will endure reasonable invasions of privacy when there is a compelling rationale for it. When the Boston Marathon bomber was hiding somewhere in the area, many New Englanders willingly submitted to having their homes and yards searched to find the culprit. But imagine if the state, in order to catch a particular burglar—or even burglars in general—began a regular practice of entering and searching the homes of Americans. Imagine if the military or the police regularly showed up at your house for this purpose. There would most likely be a public revolt, because there is no clear connection between a program so widespread and extravagant, and the narrowly focused task of catching burglars. Similarly the government has not shown—has not even attempted to show— why it needs a nearly Soviet style of surveillance in order to keep tabs on the bad guys.

In the seventy years of the Bolsheviks, the Soviet Union attempted a comprehensive surveillance of the Russian people. The Soviets knew that to build a collective society and enforce the collectivist ideology, you must first collect information on the citizens. This practice reached its terrifying zenith under Stalin. Stalin used the information gathered through surveillance to murder political opponents, harass religious believers, relocate whole populations, and dispatch unwanted people to the labor camps in Siberia. Yet although Stalin's crimes were later exposed by his successor, Khrushchev, nevertheless the KGB continued to monitor the activities of the Soviet people. Dissenters, whether political or religious, continued to face harassment and prosecution. The Soviet methods were crude. Bugs were installed in homes and hotel rooms, "persons of interest" were followed, neighbors and children were encouraged to report on suspicious activities.

The writer George Orwell took the process to its grim logical conclusion in his dystopian novel *1984*. Orwell was prescient: he envisioned omnipresent telescreens with hidden microphones and cameras ("Big Brother is watching you"), he anticipated a Thought

Police, he portrayed the state feeding apathetic citizens a barrage of non-stop propaganda, he foresaw how the state might justify its regime of repression by contending that this was in the name of the people and for the people's own good. Orwell wrote, "There was of course no way of knowing whether you were being watched at any given moment. How often, or on what system, the Thought Police plugged in on any individual wire was guesswork. It was even conceivable that they watched everybody all the time. But at any rate they could plug in your wire whenever they wanted to. You had to live—did live, from habit that became instinct—in the assumption that every sound you made was overheard, and except in darkness, every movement scrutinized." Orwell concluded that "the possibility of enforcing not only complete obedience to the will of the state, but complete uniformity of opinion on all subjects, now existed for the first time."[8]

Notwithstanding his prescience, Orwell never imagined that technology would, just a quarter century after the year 1984, reach such a level of sophistication that citizens could be spied on and monitored without little bugs and treacherous neighbors and children. Orwell believed it would take massive torture and violence to sustain a Big Brother state. He symbolized such tyranny with the image of "a boot stamping on a face—forever."[9] In the case of American citizens, you don't have to worry about a boot stamping on your face, just an unwelcome knock on your door. There you will encounter not Big Brother but a couple of FBI agents there to ask a few questions. They will be responding to inquiries generated by analysts sitting in unmarked offices. America's spying strategy is different from Big Brother, yet no less effective in achieving its purpose. That purpose is obviously not the maintenance of an official Marxist ideology. Nor is it for the public adulation of the president. (Obama gets that from the media anyway.) Rather, the surveillance is to keep the entire citizenry in check, so that citizens who revolt against the progressive agenda can be identified and punished.

Sometimes this punishment can take the form of an IRS selective audit. We'll just add your name to the list. We know that this has happened to numerous Tea Party groups; their crime is not tax evasion, but organizing people to resist Obamacare and progressive policies. The IRS also came down on the producer of my film *2016*, Gerald Molen. Molen is the Academy Award winning producer of films such as *Jurassic Park* and *Schindler's List*. He also happens to be the producer of my new film *America*. Throughout his long career, Molen was unmolested by the IRS. Suddenly, around the time of the 2012 election, he came under IRS scrutiny. More recently the IRS has been harassing the Hollywood conservative group Friends of Abe. These are conservatives who seek anonymity in order to protect their careers. By forcing the group to release its donor and membership lists, the IRS is making it virtually impossible for the group to function effectively. These IRS shenanigans do not merely illustrate how government power can and does get abused. They also illustrate how progressives do not hesitate to use the government as their weapon of retaliation against their political enemies.

This kind of bullying is common in Third World countries, where the government uses tax audits and selective prosecution to intimidate its political foes. Americans, however, have never tolerated such behavior. The last time power was abused in this way—though not nearly to this extent—it was by Richard Nixon, and he was forced to resign because of it. Recently I was amazed to read that the Obama administration is going after Standard & Poor's in retaliation for the credit agency downgrading the credit of the U.S. government. At the time, Treasury Secretary Tim Geithner warned the head of the S&P that he was going to pay for embarrassing the Obama administration. Evidently the government is now making good on that threat.[10] And I myself have been charged with violating the campaign finance laws by reimbursing two friends who contributed $20,000 to the Senate campaign of one of my longtime friends from Dartmouth. There's a $10,000 limit in campaign contributions to a candidate. There is no allegation that I sought to benefit myself in any way. At worst, this was a misguided effort to help a friend in an uphill—and, as it turned out, unsuccessful—campaign against a well-heeled opponent. Even so, I am facing two felony counts that carry a maximum prison sentence of seven years.

There are hundreds—perhaps thousands—of federal laws, and the government has the ability to prosecute just about every citizen for doing something wrong. More precisely, the government has the power and discretion to decide whom it wants to prosecute. There is an obvious "danger posed to civil liberties when our normal daily activities expose us to potential prosecution at the whim of a government official." Those are the words of civil liberties attorney Harvey Silverglate, from his recent book *Three Felonies a Day*. Silverglate argues that the ordinary citizen goes about his life, from surfing the web to making investments to getting prescription drugs to buying stuff to donating money to charities, having no idea that these normal activities can be construed to be in violation of federal laws: drug laws, laws regulating financial transactions, laws regulating sales and purchases, "duty to disclose" laws, laws outlawing "leaks" and obstruction of justice, racketeering statutes, and anti-terrorism laws.

The government has used these laws to prosecute doctors who prescribe pain medication as being "drug dealers." Lawyers who protect the confidentiality of their clients have been hit up with "obstruction of justice." Journalists are prosecuted for failing to disclose their sources. Corporate officials carrying out their normal business functions, or peacefully demonstrating political activists, can be nailed on racketeering charges. Charitable donations by well-meaning donors can be linked to terrorist suspects or groups. Far from protecting law-abiding citizens, Silverglate writes that it is now routine for the government to target and prosecute them.

Quite often, you have no idea what you have done. Many of these laws are so vague that it's impossible to know in advance whether you are in compliance or not. I can testify to this. This vagueness benefits the government, because it gives government officials discretion to decide who they want to go after. In his introduction to Silverglate's book, civil liberties champion and Harvard Law professor Alan Dershowitz writes of "accordion-like criminal statutes" which can be expanded or contracted to suit political expediency. Silverglate notes that "the pliability of federal law makes it all too easy for a self-serving U.S. attorney to take down his or her political adversaries."

Federal prosecutors are not politically neutral. They are likely to serve the interests of the executive branch of government, since that's who appointed them. And getting charged is only the starting point. Even if you're innocent, Dershowitz writes, the government has ways to force you to plead guilty. Dershowitz points out that "federal criminal law carries outrageously high sentences, often with mandatory minimums. . . . The threat of high sentences makes it too costly for even innocent people to resist the prosecutorial pressure. That's why nearly all criminal defendants today plead guilty to 'reduced' charges rather than risk a trial with draconian sentences in the event of a conviction."

Silverglate writes,

Wrongful prosecution of innocent conduct that is twisted into a felony charge has wrecked many an innocent life and career. Whole families have been devastated, as have myriad relationships and entire companies. Indeed one of the most pernicious effects of the Justice Department's techniques . . . is that they wreck important and socially beneficial relationships within civil society. Family members have been pitted against one another. Friends have been coerced into testifying against friends even when the testimony has been less than honest. Corporations have turned against employees and former partners to save the companies from obliteration, following scripts entirely at odds with the truth. . . . Newspaper reporters have been pitted against confidential sources. Artists, including those critical of the government, have been subjected to Kafkaesque harassment. Lawyers and clients have found themselves adversaries, as have physicians and patients, where enormous pressure has been placed on the ill to turn against those in whose capable professional hands they placed themselves in search of treatment. No society can possibly benefit from having its government so recklessly attack and render asunder such vital social and professional relationships.

Silverglate writes, "Astute observers of the federal criminal justice system have long since given up believing that the guilty plea reveals true culpability: It's all too common for such pleas to be the product of risk avoidance at the expense of truth." No wonder Silverglate's book is subtitled, "How the Feds Target the Innocent." If you don't think these things happen in America, read Silverglate's book and wake up. You'll certainly become a believer when they happen to you. There is no disputing Silverglate's bottom line: "no field of work nor social class is safe," and the government now has the power to get you—if it wants to.[11] Surveillance is simply the means to ensure that no one is safe.

The screen of secrecy against government spying has been broken, yet the Obama administration is fighting hard to convince Congress and the Courts to let it keep its surveillance system, the American Panopticon. We need to curtail the system now, because in time it will expand so that even elected officials and judges will be too terrified to oppose it. After all, the government will have extensive files on them too. At this point America's checks and balances will have collapsed, and we will be living in a totalitarian society. If progressives enforce their agenda through total control and compliance, America will truly be an evil empire, and it will be the right and duty of American citizens to organize once again, as in 1776, to overthrow it.

CHAPTER 16

DECLINE IS A CHOICE

We are so used to the world being Western,
even American, that we have little idea
what it would be like if it was not.[1]

—MARTIN JACQUES, *WHEN CHINA RULES THE WORLD*

The post-American era, when it comes, will come as a surprise. The surprise is not in its coming; the surprise is in
what it will look like. I once heard Irving Kristol say, "Western civilization is in decline, but the decline will happen slowly, and
we can live well in the meantime." He was right, I suppose, in his
day, but Kristol is now dead. Decline does not always happen slowly.
Sometimes it happens very quickly: then it is called collapse. The
Roaring Twenties ended with the Crash of 1929. The booming prosperity symbolized by investors getting profitable stock tips from
newspaper boys ended with tales of men who had lost everything in
the stock market crash jumping out of windows to their deaths. We
expect our own decline, like that of our country, to happen gradually,
so that we can adjust to it; but life isn't always like that.

The former Soviet Union was declining for decades, yet the collapse came very suddenly—within just a few years. The Berlin Wall was toppled in 1989, a wave of rebellions across Eastern Europe penetrated the Soviet Union, and in 1992 the Communist Party abolished itself and the regime was gone. America's decline may be gradual—over a period, say, of fifty years—or it may be rapid. I am hoping for the former, but expecting the latter. The prospect doesn't just horrify me; it also fills me with a sense of responsibility. I don't want ours to be the generation that witnessed—and allowed—the end of the American era.

The end of the American era corresponds with the rise of the East—the rise of Asia. This rise is, historically speaking, a return. For most of history, Asia dominated the world. From the collapse of the Roman empire around the fifth century, until around 1750, China and India were the two largest, wealthiest, and most powerful civilizations. From around the eighth century, they were joined by the civilization of Islam, which although Abrahamic in its religion is also an Eastern civilization; that's why we call it the Middle *East*. Together these Asian powers dominated the world, accounting for three-fourths of the global domestic product, while Europe was a relative backwater, accounting for around 10 percent of global GDP.[2] Now for the past few centuries the West has dominated. We can date this period as the Western epoch, with the last half-century being the American era.

Talk to educated people outside the West and they sound as if the West is already finished; one of their stock phrases is, "After America. . . ." The debate abroad is not over whether America will be done, but what will replace America. The main candidates are Russia, Brazil, India, and China but the smart money is on China. According to Kang Xiaoguong, a professor at Renmin University, "People are now looking down on the West, from leadership circles, to academia, to everyday folks."[3] When I hear these people—their casual confidence, even arrogance—I am amazed. I grew up in an era when Western superiority—what in American schools is called Eurocentrism—was firmly established. For me, a schoolboy on the streets of Mumbai, it seemed no less secure than the law of gravity. And to a certain extent it made Western people seem superior and us feel inferior. Our inferiority was not due to racism—in post-independence India, there were no white people around to be racist. Western dominance injured our pride because we had to acknowledge that they had something we didn't. Their countries called the shots and ours didn't. Their lives and decisions had consequences in the world in a way that ours didn't. Even if they originally became dominant through conquest, they had obviously developed from their own resources the power to conquer everyone else. In other words, they must have been stronger before the conquest in order to be able to do the conquest.

Upon examination, we recognized that the real source of Western power, and of America's current hegemony, was economic strength. America's real power wasn't that it could pulverize everyone else, or even that everyone else admired American style and culture. Rather, America's military, political, and cultural power all derived from its affluence. America's wealth enabled the country to afford a more sophisticated military than anyone else. Similarly, wealth made Americans self-confident and creative, and this is why American culture exuded an irresistible allure—the allure of individuality and success. I now realize that, when America declines, not only will Americans have a lower standard of living, relative to others, but America's decisions will also matter less in the world, and American mores and American culture will become increasingly marginal and irrelevant. Think of the way Americans view Mexico, with a mixture of condescension and contempt. That's the way that we are going to be viewed. Correction: among many educated people outside the West, that's the way we are viewed now. This transfer of confidence from the West to the East, within my lifetime—this is what I find astonishing.

The rise of the East is, in a way, an American success story. It was the intention of the American Founders to create a new formula not just for Americans but for the world. This was the 1776 formula for the well-being of the common man. It was a formula invented here, but it was never a formula for the benefit of Americans alone. American exceptionalism was always linked with American universalism. That's why the Declaration of Independence doesn't say "all Americans," it says "all men." America wants to see other countries come up in the world, but it wants to see them succeed not through conquest but through wealth creation. China and India are rising because of wealth creation. They have learned well from their American tutors.

Now, as in the case of America, China's economic strength is going to translate into military strength and ultimately cultural power. It may seem hard to believe, but Chinese cars, Chinese fashion, Chinese music, and Chinese food are going to become cool. These changes will not be the result of Chinese conquest but of Chinese wealth creation. In this sense, China is enjoying earned success, and so to a lesser degree is India. In general, I'm delighted to see this success. The Chinese and the Indians have adopted for themselves some of the spirit of 1776.

I am also pleased to report that the rise of the East will also bring with it the end of progressivism. Part of this is natural: once a nation declines, many of its priorities and ideologies decline with it. In the past the Chinese, the Indians, and the Brazilians would attend international conferences and nod obligingly when Western progressives bloviated about their political preferences. But now the

reigning mantra in Asia, Africa, and South America is "moderniza-
tion without Westernization." The term "Westernization" here
means progressivism. The East has no intention of rejecting Western technology or Western economic structures. Rather, it is increasingly rejecting Western values. For the most part, these are not the
values of 1776; they are the values of 1968. The East doesn't want
to see the moral erosion, the family breakdown, and the vulgarity
of popular culture that it associates with America and the West.
These are not "American" traits; they are progressive traits. The
Asians agree with American conservatives: they reject progressivism
and want as much as possible to keep it out of their societies. "We
have healthy homes and healthy communities," one Indian told me.
"Why would we want to import all this filth?" At one time, the East
wanted to be modern and Western. Then it wanted to be modern
and didn't mind being Western. Now it wants to be modern without
being Western.

The real shock of Asian dominance for people in the West is to
see how differently the world is going to be run when America is no
longer running it. Our history, our maps, our sense of place and time,
will have to change. Right now our history books talk about World
War I and World War II. But those really weren't world wars; they
were European civil wars. I suspect that's how they will be remem-
bered a century from now, with Japan's part in the war treated
separately and given more importance. We are used to maps that
place Europe at the center of the world, China at the periphery. The
Chinese like to have maps that place China at the center. When the
Jesuits landed in China in the sixteenth century, they were amused
to see the Chinese maps. That was the beginning of the age of European expansion. But in an age of Chinese dominance, it will make
sense to everyone—not just the Chinese—to place China at the center and Europe and America at the margins. The maps will reflect

reality. In a Sinocentric world, our whole conceptual apparatus is going to have to change.

Many Americans, who know a China-dominated world is coming, console themselves by thinking that the Chinese are people who look Oriental but think like Americans. This is both ethnocentric and myopic. If we want to see what a world dominated by Islam would look like, it helps to see how the Muslims ruled when they did dominate the world. Similarly we can get clues about a Sinocentric world by looking at the world when China was its leading superpower. This is a project impressively undertaken in Martin Jacques's recent book *When China Rules the World*. Written by an informed scholar who has lived most of his adult life in the East, Jacques's book plumbs deep into Chinese history and the Chinese psyche to show that these are a distinctive people who intend to conduct global affairs in their own way. One thing is for sure, they are not Americans and their way is not the American way. Even so, there are aspects of China today that remind me of the way America used to be.

Jacques quotes Gao Rui-quan, a professor of philosophy at East China National University in Shanghai. "China is like the adolescent who is very keen to become an adult. He can see the goal and wants to reach it as soon as possible. He is always behaving as if he is rather older than he actually is and is constantly forgetting the reality of his situation."[4] Rui-quan means this as a criticism or rather, self-criticism. But in its mixture of excitement, anticipation, and confidence, I see in this attitude the spirit of 1776—the same spirit Tocqueville recorded in America a half-century later. The big question is, where is that spirit now? It can be found in China, India, and elsewhere, but where can it be found in America?

I will return to that question. For now, I want to stay with Jacques's portrayal of how Chinese hegemony will look different from American hegemony. Jacques points out that the Chinese "have a deeply hierarchical view of the world based on culture and race."[5] They are not democrats and egalitarians. Nor do they believe in "diversity." The Chinese want, and over time are likely to get, "a profound cultural and racial reordering of the world in the Chinese image." When the Chinese were down, they accepted and lived with their ethnic and cultural inferiority; when the Chinese come up, they are going to insist upon their ethnic and cultural superiority. The Chinese will demand that their currency, not ours, be the global currency. They will also push to have Mandarin replace English as the universal lingua franca. These, however, are the "small" changes; what Jacques is getting at is something much bigger.

Historically China did not seek to conquer other countries but to subordinate them into a Chinese order whose superiority they recognized and to which they paid tribute. Jacques expects the Chinese to re-establish that order. Basically the Chinese seek a restoration of colonialism, but this time in the Chinese style. The Chinese want to be the overlords of Asia, Africa, and South America, and ultimately also of Europe and America. Already the Chinese are making huge investments abroad, buying up land and mineral rights, getting their foothold in the same way that the British did a couple of centuries ago. The Chinese are shrewdly exploiting anti-American sentiments to make themselves look like the better alternative. Yet the Chinese want far greater hegemony, and are likely to demand a greater degree of obeisance from others, than Americans ever sought. Ultimately this domination might even extend to us. American presidents of the future may be forced to bow before Chinese officials before they get a hearing.

Moreover, the Chinese have no interest in shared global leadership. They will share as long as they have to, but their goal is singular hegemony. Here the Chinese motto is Deng Xiaoping's: hide our strength, bide our time. China is building its military power. It is modernizing its nuclear arsenal. China is building a powerful navy. And not surprisingly, given China's population, it can field by far the largest number of people on the battlefield. In an age of technology, numbers may not seem very significant, but as technology is equalized numbers become decisive. Consider this: while America has 2 million men and women in arms, China is capable of fielding well upward of 100 million! For the American military, half a million casualties would be horrific; if China faced that level of casualties, the nation would hardly notice. Jacques insists—and I agree—that China has no intention of actually fighting a war with America. Rather, its objective is to show that such a war would be absolutely suicidal for America, so that America will succumb to Chinese power without a fight. What the Soviets failed to achieve, China sees as a coming *fait accompli*. Just as America won the Cold War "without firing a shot," China intends to win the next war with America without firing a shot.

The Chinese, the Indians, the Brazilians, and the Russians are all getting richer and stronger due to wealth creation. Yet the leaders of these countries, while they appreciate wealth creation as one way to gain power, have never given up on the conquest ethic as another way to gain power. In fact, they see wealth creation as a way to increase their military power; then that power can be deployed to acquire more wealth through conquest. To see what I mean, imagine if we discovered a new planet rich in minerals and energy but inhabited by peaceful aliens. Would America regard it as right to conquer them and take their stuff? No, we no longer have the conquest ethic. But the Chinese do; they have never given it up. This is why the world still needs America. We remain the custodians of the idea that wealth should be obtained through invention and trade, not through forced seizure.

In terms of maintaining its leadership and strength, no one can deny that America faces a parlous challenge. Given this, the behavior of the Obama administration, and of progressives more generally, can only be considered surreal. I am tempted to say that they are like the violinists who played music while the *Titanic* sank. In this picture, Obama would be the strange conductor, obsessed with his tunes while missing the larger reality of the situation. This analogy, however, is unfair to the musicians on the *Titanic*. Their conduct was entirely rational. They knew the ship was going down and there was nothing else they could do. So they bravely resolved to play and give people what little cheer they could. In America's case, however, there is a great deal we can do. Yet Obama seems unwilling to do any of it. I am not saying he is ignorant of the global reality. In fact, he knows it quite well. His behavior is also rational, from the progressive point of view. If we think of the *Titanic* as symbolizing the American era, Obama wants that ship to go down.

Obama is the architect of American decline, and progressivism is the ideology of American suicide. Here's a way to think about what Obama and the progressives are doing. Imagine if they were in charge of a basketball team with a fifty-year track record of success. We hired them as coaches to keep the team winning. Yet they designed plays to ensure the team would lose. They didn't do so because they hated the team, but because they thought it was wrong for the team to win so much. The long previous record of victories, they argued, was based on exploitation, and it would be better for everyone if our team wasn't so dominant. If we had such a coaching staff, there is little doubt that we would get rid of them. We would ask ourselves why we hired them in the first place.

Even though we currently have such a coach, decline is not an inevitability; decline is a choice. We don't have to let Obama and the progressives take us down. We certainly don't have to hire another coach who is like Obama. Do we want to live in a country that no longer matters, where the American dream is a paltry and shrunken thing, where bitter complaint substitutes for real influence in the world, where we can no longer expect our children to live better than we do? The Greeks, the Turks, the French, and the English are all once-great nations that have had to cope with irrelevance, and although they have had time to adjust, the sense of defeat still shows on their faces. It's not so bad to be irrelevant if you've always been irrelevant. But to become irrelevant when you were formerly leading the world; that's a wound that permanently scars the psyche.

I pray this does not happen to America, sapping the optimism that built this country, and that I still saw when I came here a generation ago. And it need not happen: the crisis we face is also an opportunity. But we cannot delay—to delay is to convert a crisis into an irreversible situation. Then we will have not only failed ourselves, we will also have failed our children. We will have failed America when we were in a position to save her.

In fact, America is now in a situation that has arisen only a few times previously in history. This is a rare time when America's future hangs delicately in the balance, and when Americans can do something about it. This occurred in 1776, when Americans had to figure out whether to create a new country or live under British domination. This was the crisis of the creation of America. It occurred again in 1860, when Americans had to decide whether to preserve the union or let it dissolve. This was the crisis of the preservation of America. And now we have to choose whether to protect the American era and uphold America's example to the world, or to let the naysayers, at home and abroad, take us down. This is the crisis of the restoration of America.

Whether we like it or not, this is the American moment in world history. The American era cannot endure indefinitely, but it can last a lot longer. The spirit of 1776 is taking root around the world; this can happen with us in the lead, or without us. In previous crises there were great Americans who showed leadership, and ordinary Americans who showed commitment and heroism; together, they vindicated the American experiment. So what will be our legacy? Will we keep the flag flying, or will we submit to progressive self-destruction and go down with a whimper? I believe we will prove up to the task of restoration. But in any event, this is our turn at the wheel, and history will judge us based on how we handle it. Decline is a choice, but so is liberty. Let us resolve as Americans to make liberty our choice.

CONNECT
WITH
DINESH D'SOUZA

VISIT HIS WEBSITE:

DineshDSouza.com

FIND HIM ON SOCIAL MEDIA:

Like Dinesh D'Souza on Facebook
and follow him on Twitter at @DineshDSouza

LEARN

how you can see the film *America* at
AmericatheMovie.com

NOTES

Chapter 1: Suicide of a Nation

1. Robert Frost, "A Case for Jefferson," in Edward Connery Lathem, ed., *The Poetry of Robert Frost* (New York: St. Martin's, 1975), p. 393.
2. Albert Camus, *The Myth of Sisyphus and Other Essays* (New York: Vintage, 1991), pp. 3, 28, 31.
3. Abraham Lincoln, Lyceum Address, January 27, 1838, abraham lincolnonline.org.
4. Barack Obama, Inaugural Speech, January 20, 2009, whitehouse.gov.
5. Giacomo Chiozza, "America's Global Advantage," *Political Science Quarterly*, Summer 2011; Stephen Cohen and J. Bradford DeLong, *The End of Influence* (New York: Basic Books, 2010), pp. 6, 14, 143; Fareed Zakaria, *The Post-American World* (New York: W. W. Norton, 2009).
6. Kenneth Ragoza, "By the Time Obama Leaves Office, U.S. No Longer No. 1," *Forbes*, March 23, 2013, forbes.com; Stephen M. Walt, "The End of the American Era," *National Interest*, October 25, 2011, national interest.org.

7. Fawaz Gerges, *Obama and the Middle East* (London: Palgrave Macmillan, 2012), pp. 13, 152.

8. Tom Paine, *Common Sense*, Appendix to the Third Edition, ushistory.org; Alexander Hamilton, James Madison and John Jay, *The Federalist* (New York: Barnes and Noble, 2006), No. 1, p. 9; George Washington, letter to James Warren, March 31, 1779.

9. James Burnham, *Suicide of the West* (Washington, D.C.: Regnery, 1985), pp. 15–16, 20, 24.

10. John Milton, "Paradise Lost," in *John Milton: The Major Works* (New York: Oxford University Press, 2008), p. 370–71.

11. I get this phrase from Irwin Stelzer, "The Obama Formula," *The Weekly Standard*, July 5–12, 2010, weeklystandard.com.

12. Dinesh D'Souza, *Obama's America* (Washington, D.C.: Regnery, 2012), pp. 67–90.

13. Frantz Fanon, *The Wretched of the Earth* (New York: Grove Press, 1963), pp. 76, 101–3.

14. Howard Zinn, *A People's History of the United States* (New York: HarperPerennial, 2005), p. 10.

15. Howard Zinn, *A Power Governments Cannot Suppress* (San Francisco: City Lights, 2007), p. 23.

16. Cited by David Remnick, *The Bridge* (New York: Alfred Knopf, 2010), p. 265; Christopher Wills, "Obama Opposes Slavery Reparations," Huffington Post, August 2, 2008, http://www.huffingtonpost.com/2008/08/02/obama-opposes-slavery-rep_n_116506.html.

17. The "stolen goods" argument, attributed to Hardy Jones, is summarized in Robert Detlefson, *Civil Rights Under Reagan* (San Francisco: ICS Press, 1991), p. 54.

Chapter 2: A Tale of Two Frenchmen

1. Alexis de Tocqueville, *Democracy in America* (New York: Vintage, 1990), Vol. I, p. 244.

2. Edmund Burke, *Reflections on the Revolution in France* (New York: Penguin, 1982), p. 172.

3. Howard Zinn, *A Power Governments Cannot Suppress* (San Francisco: City Lights, 2007), pp. 57–61.

4. Tocqueville, *Democracy in America*, Vol. I, pp. 3, 94, 191–19, 292, 294, 303, 305, 334–35, 394, 427; Vol. II, pp. 22, 38.

5. James Miller, *The Passion of Michel Foucault* (New York: Anchor, 1994), p. 16, 20.

6. "Obamacare Freeing the Job-Locked Poets?" *New York Post*, February 7, 2014, nypost.com.

7. Noam Chomsky and Michel Foucault, *The Chomsky-Foucault Debate* (New York: New Press, 2006), pp. 39, 41, 51–52, 138–39.

8. Michel Foucault, "What Are the Iranians Dreaming About?" cited in Janet Afary and Kevin B. Anderson, *Foucault and the Iranian Revolution* (University of Chicago Press, 2005); see also Jeff Weintraub, "Foucault's Enthusiasm for Khomeini—the Totalitarian Temptation Revisited," *New Politics*, Summer 2004, jeffweintraub.blogspot.com.

9. Paul Hollander, *Political Pilgrims* (New Brunswick, NJ: Transaction Publishers, 1997).

10. Michel Foucault, *Foucault Live: Interviews, 1961–1984* (New York: Semiotext, 1996), p. 383.

11. Miller, *The Passion of Michel Foucault*, pp. 260–61, 264; Patrick Moore, *Beyond Shame* (Boston: Beacon Press, 2004), p. 72; David Macey, *The Lives of Michel Foucault* (New York: Vintage, 1993), p. 369.

12. Miller, *The Passion of Michel Foucault*, pp. 29, 350, 381; see also Roger Kimball, "The Perversions of M. Foucault," *The New Criterion*, March 1993.

Chapter 3: Novus Ordo Seclorum

1. Cited in John Richard Alden, *George Washington: A Biography*, p. 101, books.google.com.

2. Charles Beard, *An Economic Interpretation of the Constitution* (New York: Dover Books, 2004).

3. Noam Chomsky, "The U.S. Behaves Nothing Like a Democracy," salon.com; Howard Zinn, *A People's History of the United States* (New York: HarperPerennial, 1983), pp. 74, 85–86; Howard Zinn, *A Power Governments Cannot Suppress* (San Francisco: City Lights, 2007), p. 116.

4. James Fallows, "Obama on Exceptionalism," *The Atlantic*, April 4, 2009, theatlantic.com.

5. Thomas Jefferson, letter to Roger C. Weightman, June 24, 1826, in Merrill D. Peterson, ed., *The Portable Thomas Jefferson* (New York: Penguin, 1985), p. 585.

6. Cited by Harry Jaffa, *A New Birth of Freedom* (Lanham, MD: Rowman and Littlefield, 2000), p. 46.

7. Thomas Jefferson, *Notes on the State of Virginia* (Chapel Hill: University of North Carolina Press, 1954), pp. 120–21.

8. Alexander Hamilton, James Madison and John Jay, *The Federalist*, No. 84 (New York: Barnes and Noble, 2006), p. 474.

9. Ibid., No. 51, pp. 288–89.

10. Eugene Kamenka, ed., *The Portable Karl Marx* (New York: Penguin Books, 1983), p. 389.

11. Bob Young, "Obama's Big Time Fumble," *Arizona Republic*, May 17, 2009.

12. Confucius, *The Analects* (New York: Penguin, 1986), p. 74; Paul Rahe, *Republics, Ancient and Modern* (Chapel Hill: University of North Carolina Press, 1994), Vol. I, p. 44; Ibn Khaldun, *Muqaddimah* (Princeton, NJ: Princeton University Press, 1967), p. 313.

13. Forrest McDonald, *Novus Ordo Seclorum* (University Press of Kansas, 1985), pp. 11–12, 37.

14. Abraham Lincoln, "Lecture on Discoveries and Inventions," Jacksonville, Illinois, February 1859, cited in Michael Novak, *The Fire of Invention* (Lanham, MD: Rowman & Littlefield, 1997), pp. 53, 58–59.

15. Hamilton, Madison, and Jay, *The Federalist*, No. 10, p. 53; No. 12, p. 65.

16. Thomas Jefferson, letter to John Adams, October 28, 1813, in *The Portable Thomas Jefferson*, pp. 534–35.

17. Daniel Walker Howe, *What Hath God Wrought* (New York: Oxford University Press, 2009), p. 33; Angus Maddison, *The World Economy: Historical Statistics* (Paris: OECD Press, 2003), p. 261.

Chapter 4: America the Inexcusable

1. Bill Ayers, *Public Enemy* (Boston: Beacon Press, 2013), p. 18.

2. Bill Ayers, *Fugitive Days* (Boston: Beacon Press, 2009), pp. 114, 126, 162, 241, 265, 294–95; Ayers, *Public Enemy*, pp. 16, 18; Bill Ayers, speech at the University of Oregon, May 2, 2012, theblaze.com; Dinitia Smith, "No Regrets for a Love of Explosives," *New York Times*, September 11, 2001, nytimes.com.

3. Frank Marshall Davis, *Livin' the Blues* (Madison: University of Wisconsin Press, 1992), p. 277; Frank Marshall Davis, "How Our Democracy Looks to Oppressed Peoples," *Honolulu Record*, May 19, 1949;

Paul Kengor, "Obama's Surrogate Anti-Colonial Father," October 14, 2010, spectator.org.

4. Edward Said, *The Question of Palestine* (New York: Vintage Books, 1992), pp. xxi, 37, 143; Edward Said, *The Politics of Dispossession* (New York: Vintage Books, 1995), pp. xv, xxvii, 31, 70, 82, 138, 178; Stanley Kurtz, "Edward Said, Imperialist," *The Weekly Standard*, October 8, 2001, p. 35.

5. Roberto Mangabeira Unger, *The Left Alternative* (London: Verso, 2005), pp. xix, 80–81,128, 134–35, 143, 148, 164; David Remnick, *The Bridge* (New York: Vintage, 2011), p. 185.

6. Jeremiah Wright, "The Day of Jerusalem's Fall," *The Guardian*, March 27, 2008, http://www.theguardian.com/commentisfree/2008/mar/27/thedayofjerusalemsfall.

7. "Interview With David Kennedy," New River Media, pbs.org.

8. Allen Ginsberg, *Howl and Other Poems* (New York: City Lights , 1956), pp. 9, 22, 39–40, 43.

9. Tom Brokaw, *The Greatest Generation* (New York: Random House, 2001).

10. Ayers, *Public Enemy*, p. 39.

Chapter 5: The Plan

1. Saul Alinsky, *Rules for Radicals* (New York: Vintage Books, 1989), p. 12.

2. Gil Troy, *Morning in America* (Princeton, NJ: Princeton University Press, 2005), p. 36.

3. Richard Poe, "Hillary, Obama and the Cult of Alinsky," rense.com.

4. Stanley Kurtz, "Obama's Third-Party History," June 7, 2012, national review.com.

5. Alex Cohen, "Interview with Sanford Horwitt," January 30, 2009, npr. org.

6. Hillary Clinton, *Living History* (New York: Scribner, 2003), p. 38.

7. John Heilemann and Mark Halperin, *Game Change* (New York: Harper, 2010), pp. 218–19.

8. Sanford Horwitt, *Let Them Call Me Rebel: Saul Alinsky, His Life and Legacy* (New York: Vintage Books, 1992); Saul Alinsky, *Reveille for Radicals*, p. 25, books.google.com.

9. Nicholas von Hoffman, *Radical: A Portrait of Saul Alinsky* (New York: Nation Books, 2010), p. 82.

10. Alinsky, *Rules for Radicals*, pp. 184–96.
11. "Playboy Interview: Saul Alinsky," *Playboy*, March 1972.
12. Alinsky, *Rules for Radicals*, pp. ix, 25, 30–31, 36.
13. "Obama: Trayvon Martin Could Have Been Me," July 19, 2013, cnn.com; Jennifer Senior, "Dreaming of Obama," *New York*, September 24, 2006, nymag.com.
14. Barack Obama, *The Audacity of Hope* (New York: Three Rivers Press), 2006, p. 11.

Chapter 6: The Red Man's Burden

1. Robert Royal, *1492 and All That* (Washington, D.C.: Ethics and Public Policy Center, 1992), p. 19; Winona LaDuke, "We Are Still Here," *Sojourners*, October 1991, p. 16; Glenn Morris, "Even Columbus," *Wall Street Journal*, October 12, 1992, p. A-10; Stephen Greenblatt, *Marvelous Possessions* (Chicago: University of Chicago Press, 1991), p. 136.
2. Francine Uenuma and Mike Fritz, "Why the Sioux Are Refusing $1.3 Billion," PBS, August 24, 2011, pbs.org.
3. William McNeill, *Plagues and Peoples* (New York: Doubleday, 1976); Guenter Lewy, "Were American Indians the Victims of Genocide?" *Commentary*, September 2004.
4. Christopher Columbus, *The Journals of Christopher Columbus* (New York: Bonanza Books, 1989), pp. 33, 58, 116; Wilcomb Washburn, "The First European Contacts with the American Indians," Instituto de Investigacao Cientifica Tropical, Lisbon, 1988, pp. 439–43.
5. Bernal Diaz, *The Conquest of New Spain* (New York: Penguin, 1963), p. 229; Howard Zinn, *A People's History of the United States* (New York: HarperPerennial, 2003), p. 11.
6. Mario Vargas Llosa, *Wellsprings* (Cambridge: Harvard University Press, 2008), pp. 125–26.
7. Lewis Hanke, *Aristotle and the American Indians* (Chicago: Henry Regnery, 1959), pp. 19, 37.
8. Frederick Douglass, *Life and Times of Frederick Douglass* (Park Publishing, 1882), p. 128, books.google.com.
9. Thomas Pangle, *The Spirit of Modern Republicanism* (Chicago: University of Chicago Press, 1988), p. 159.
10. John Locke, *Two Treatises on Government* (Cambridge: Cambridge University Press, 1988), pp. 285–302.

11. Alexis de Tocqueville, *Democracy in America* (New York: Vintage, 1990), Vol. I, p. 25; Paul Johnson, *A History of the American People* (New York: HarperPerennial, 1997), p. 352.

12. Ralph Lerner, *The Thinking Revolutionary* (Ithaca: Cornell University Press, 1987), p. 163; Zinn, *A People's History of the United States*, p. 125.

13. Johnson, *A History of the American People*, p. 271.

14. H. W. Brands, *Lone Star Nation* (New York: Anchor Books, 2004), p. 49.

Chapter 7: The Myth of Aztlan

1. Patricia Limerick, *The Legacy of Conquest* (New York: W. W. Norton, 1987), p. 255.

2. Barack Obama, *The Audacity of Hope* (New York: Three Rivers Press, 2006), p. 293; Joshua Keating, "Kerry: The Monroe Doctrine is Over," November 19, 2013, slate.com.

3. Daniel Walker Howe, *What Hath God Wrought* (New York: Oxford, 2009), p. 659.

4. H. W. Brands, *Lone Star Nation* (New York: Anchor, 2004), pp. 157, 191.

5. David Montejano, *Anglos and Mexicans in the Making of Texas* (Austin: University of Texas Press, 1987), p. 305.

6. Howard Zinn, *A People's History of the United States* (New York: HarperPerennial, 2003), pp. 154, 156.

7. Howe, *What Hath God Wrought*, p. 686.

8. Abraham Lincoln, Speech in the House of Representatives, January 12, 1848, in Roy Basler, ed., *The Collected Works of Abraham Lincoln* (New Brunswick: Rutgers University Press, 1953), Vol. I. p. 115.

9. Robert Rosenbaum, *Mexicano Resistance in the Southwest* (Dallas: Southern Methodist University Press, 1998), pp. 5, 7, 20, 157; Harry Jaffa, *Crisis of the House Divided* (Chicago: University of Chicago Press, 2009), p. 79.

Chapter 8: Their Fourth of July

1. Harold Bloom, ed., *Emerson's Essays*, p. 185, books.google.com.

2. Phillip Magness and Sebastian Page, *Colonization After Emancipation* (Columbia: University of Missouri Press, 2011).

3. Abraham Lincoln, "Address on Colonization to a Committee of Colored Men," Washington, D.C., August 14, 1862.

4. Letter from James Madison to Robert J. Evans, June 15, 1819, in Drew McCoy, *The Last of the Fathers: James Madison and the Republican Legacy* (Cambridge: Cambridge University Press, 1989), p. 280.

5. Magness and Page, *Colonization After Emancipation*, pp. 1, 29, 32, 43–44, 47.

6. Frederick Douglass, "The Folly of Colonization," January 9, 1894.

7. Cited in Philip S. Foner, ed., *The Life and Writings of Frederick Douglass* (New York: International Publishers, 1950), Vol. I, p. 126; Vol. II, pp. 188–89.

8. *Dred Scott v. Sanford* (1857), 60 U. S. 393; John Calhoun, Speech on the Oregon Bill, June 27, 1848, in Ross M. Lence, ed., *Union and Liberty: The Political Philosophy of John C. Calhoun* (Indianapolis: Liberty Fund, 1992), pp. 565–70.

9. Randall Robinson, *The Debt* (New York: Dutton, 2000).

10. J. M. Roberts, *The Penguin History of the World* (New York: Penguin, 1990), p. 727.

11. Michael P. Johnson and James L. Roark, *Black Masters* (New York: W. W. Norton, 1984), pp. 23, 132, 135–36, 141, 308; Kenneth Stampp, *The Peculiar Institution* (New York: Vintage, 1956), p. 194; Abram Harris, *The Negro as Capitalist* (New York: Arno Press, 1936), p. 4; John Sibley Butler, *Entrepreneurship and Self-Help Among Black Americans* (Albany: State University of New York Press, 1991), p. 43; Larry Koger, *Black Slaveowners* (Charleston: University of South Carolina Press, 1985); H. E. Sterkx, *The Free Negro in Antebellum Louisiana* (Rutherford, NJ: Fairleigh Dickinson University Press, 1972).

12. Basil Davidson, *The African Slave Trade* (Boston: Little, Brown, 1969), p. 255; L. H. Gann and Peter Duignan, *Africa South of the Sahara* (Stanford: Hoover Institution Press, 1981), p. 4.

13. Cited in Roy P. Basler, ed., *Abraham Lincoln: His Speeches and Writings* (Cleveland: World Publishing, 1946), p. 427.

14. Allen Guelzo, *Lincoln and Douglas* (New York: Simon & Schuster, 2009), p. 32, 82, 266–67.

15. Thomas Jefferson, *Notes on the State of Virginia* (New York: W. W. Norton, 1982), p. 163.

16. Abraham Lincoln, "Speech on the Dred Scott Decision," Springfield, Illlnois, June 26, 1857, in Mario Cuomo and Harold Holzer, eds., *Lincoln on Democracy* (New York: HarperCollins, 1990), p. 90–91.

17. Frederick Douglass, "Address for the Promotion of Colored Enlistments," July 6, 1863.

18. Frederick Douglass, "What the Black Man Wants," speech to the annual meeting of the Massachusetts Anti-Slavery Society, Boston, April 1865, lib.rochester.edu.

19. Zora Neale Hurston, *Dust Tracks on a Road* (New York: HarperPerennial, 1991), pp. 206–8; Zora Neale Hurston, "How It Feels to Be Colored Me," in Henry Louis Gates, ed., *Bearing Witness* (New York: Pantheon, 1991), p. 16.

Chapter 9: "Thank You, Mister Jefferson"

1. Martin Luther King, Jr., "I Have a Dream," August 28, 1863, ushistory.org.

2. Joel Williamson, *The Crucible of Race* (New York: Oxford University Press, 1984), p. 254.

3. Jennifer Roback, "The Political Economy of Segregation," *Journal of Economic History* 46 (1986), pp. 893–917.

4. Thomas Sowell, *Markets and Minorities* (New York: Basic Books, 1981), p. 61.

5. See, e.g., "The Rise of Intermarriage," Pew Research, February 16, 2012, pewsocialtrends.org.

6. Orlando Patterson, "Race, Gender and Liberal Fallacies," *New York Times*, October 20, 1991.

7. Philip S. Foner, ed., *W. E. B. Du Bois Speaks: Speeches and Addresses 1890–1919* (New York: Pathfinder Books, 1970), p. 4.

8. Booker T. Washington, *Up From Slavery* (New York: Penguin Books, 1986), pp. 41, 208, 229; Booker T. Washington, "The Awakening of the Negro," *The Atlantic Monthly*, September 1896.

9. Booker T. Washington and W. E. B. Du Bois, *The Negro in the South* (New York: George W. Jacobs, 1907), pp. 181–82; E. Davidson Washington, ed., *Selected Speeches of Booker T. Washington* (New York: Doubleday, 1932), p. 237.

10. Cited in James M. Washington, ed., *A Testament of Hope* (San Francisco: Harper, 1986), pp. 212, 246, 489–90.

11. Jacqueline Moore, *Booker T. Washington, W. E. B. Du Bois, and the Struggle for Racial Uplift* (Lanham, MD: Rowman & Littlefield, 2003), p. 117.

Chapter 10: The Virtue of Prosperity

1. James Boswell, *The Life of Johnson* (New York: Oxford University Press, 1933), Vol. I, p. 567.
2. Frederick Jackson Turner, "The Significance of the Frontier in American History," Annals of America, 1968, learner.org, http://www.learner.org/workshops/primarysources/corporations/docs/turner.html.
3. Barack Obama Sr., "Problems Facing Our Socialism," *East Africa Journal*, July 1965.
4. Barack Obama, "Remarks by the President at a Campaign Event in Roanoke, Virginia," July 13, 2012; "Obama to Business Owners: You Didn't Build That," Fox News, July 16, 2012.
5. Elizabeth Warren, "There Is Nobody in This Country Who Got Rich on His Own," CBS News, September 22, 2011.
6. "Greed," ABC News Special Report by John Stossel, February 3, 1998.
7. Adam Smith, *The Wealth of Nations* (Chicago: University of Chicago Press, 1976), Vol. I, p. 18.
8. Cited in Gertrude Himmelfarb, *The Idea of Poverty* (New York: Knopf, 1984), p. 28.
9. Adam Smith, *The Wealth of Nations*, Book IV, Chapter 2, adamsmith.org.
10. Adam Smith, *The Wealth of Nations* (New York: Penguin, 1999), p. 117, 443; Eugene Kamenka, ed., *The Portable Karl Marx* (New York: Penguin, 1983), p. 177.
11. Kamenka, *The Portable Karl Marx*, p. 541.
12. Ayn Rand, *The Virtue of Selfishness* (New York: Signet, 1964), pp. vii–xi, 17, 27, 31.
13. Adam Smith, *A Theory of Moral Sentiments* (Indianapolis: Liberty Fund, 1982), p. 25.
14. Albert O. Hirschman, *The Passions and the Interests* (Princeton, N. J.: Princeton University Press, 1977), pp. 32, 73, 132–33.

Chapter 11: Who's Exploiting Whom?

1.   Remarks by the president on August 15, 2011; "Teachers Paid on Par with Doctors?" August 19, 2011, factcheck.org; Barack Obama, *The Audacity of Hope* (New York: Three Rivers Press, 2006), p. 62.

2.   Eugene Kamenka, ed., *The Portable Karl Marx* (New York: Penguin, 1983), pp. 412–13, 415.

3.   Friedrich Hayek, *The Constitution of Liberty* (Chicago: University of Chicago Press, 1978), pp. 94–95.

4.   "Babe Ruth," baseballreference.com.

5.   Richard Wolff, *Occupy the Economy* (San Francisco: City Lights Books, 2012), p. 30.

6.   Thorstein Veblen, *The Theory of the Leisure Class* (New York: Penguin, 1994), p. 110.

7.   Branko Milanovic, *The Haves and the Have-Nots* (New York: Basic Books, 2011), p. 117.

8.   Tom Wolfe, "Aspirations of an American Century," speech to the American Association of Advertising Agencies, reprinted in *Advertising Age*, June 12, 1989.

9.   Robert Frank, "U.S. Is Minting Almost All of the World's Millionaires," October 9, 2013, cnbc.com.

10.   "Life Expectancy Table," 2011, data.worldbank.org; "Life Expectancy in the USA, 1900–1998," demog.berkeley.edu.

11.   Joseph Schumpeter, *Capitalism, Socialism and Democracy* (New York: HarperPerennial, 1976), p. 67.

12.   Hayek, *The Constitution of Liberty*, p. 44.

Chapter 12: A Global Success Story

1.   Kwame Nkrumah, *Neocolonialism* (New York: International Publishers, 1965), p, 52.

2.   P. T. Bauer, *Equality, the Third World and Economic Delusion* (Cambridge: Harvard University Press, 1981), pp. 67–68; P. T. Bauer, *Reality and Rhetoric* (Cambridge: Harvard University Press, 1984), pp. 2, 24.

3.   Karl Marx, "The British Rule in India," June 10, 1853; "The Future Results of British Rule in India," July 22, 1853; in Eugene Kamenka, ed., *The Portable Karl Marx* (New York: Penguin, 1983), pp. 329–41.

4.   V. I. Lenin, *Imperialism, the Highest Stage of Capitalism* (London: Pluto Press, 1996).

5.   Manmohan Singh, address by the prime minister at Oxford University, July 8, 2005, http://www.hindu.com/nic/0046/pmspeech.htm.

6.   Chinweizu, *The West and the Rest of Us* (New York: Vintage, 1975), p. 256.

7.   Kishore Mahbubani, *The New Asian Hemisphere* (New York: Public Affairs, 2008), p. 56.

Chapter 13: Empire of Liberty

1.   Cited by Chalmers Johnson, *Nemesis*, p. 75, books.google.com.

2.   Douglas Feith and Seth Cropsey, "The Obama Doctrine Defined," *Commentary*, July 2011, commentarymagazine.com.

3.   Douglas Feith, Frank Gaffney, James Lyons and James Woolsey, "Obama's Nuclear Zero Rhetoric is Dangerous," April 1, 2013, canada freepress.com.

4.   "Nuclear Weapons: Who Has What at a Glance," Arms Control Association, November 2013, armscontrol.org.

5.   See, e.g., letter from Thomas Jefferson to James Madison, April 27, 1809.

6.   Barack Obama, *The Audacity of Hope* (New York: Three Rivers Press, 2006), p. 316–17.

7.   "Margaret Thatcher, RIP," April 18, 2013, nationalreview.com.

8.   Colin Powell, Remarks at the World Economic Forum, Davos, Switzerland, January 26, 2003.

Chapter 14: The Biggest Thief of All

1.   Cited by Richard McKenzie, *Bound to be Free* (Palo Alto: Hoover Press, 1982), p. 90.

2.   William Shakespeare, *Othello*, Act 5, Scene 1, shakespeare.mit.edu.

3.   Abraham Lincoln, "Speech at Chicago," July 10, 1858, journal ofamericanhistory.org.

4.   Eugene Kamenka, ed., *The Portable Karl Marx* (New York: Penguin Books, 1983), p. 410.

5.   Robert Reich, *Aftershock* (New York: Vintage, 2013), p. 131; Richard Wolff, *Occupy the Economy* (San Francisco: City Lights, 2012), pp. 42–43.

Chapter 15: American Panopticon

1.   Franz Kafka, *The Trial* (New York: Tribeca Books, 2011), p. 1.

2.   Mark Landler and Helene Cooper, "Obama Seeks a Course of Pragmatism," *New York Times*, April 3, 2009, nytimes.com.

3.   Jeremy Bentham, *The Panopticon Writings* (London: Verso, 2011).

4.   Ryan Gallagher, "Edward Snowden: The Man Behind the NSA Leaks," Slate, June 9, 2013, slate.com.

5.   James Bamford, "They Know Much More Than You Think," *New York Review of Books*, August 15, 2013, nybooks.com; Ryan Lizza, "State of Deception," *The New Yorker*, December 16, 2013, pp. 48, 55.

6.   Charlie Savage, "Judge Questions Legality of NSA Phone Records," *New York Times*, December 17, 2013, pp. A-1, A-17.

7.   Peter Nicholas and Jess Bravin, "Obama's Civil Liberties Record Questioned," *Wall Street Journal*, June 6, 2013, wsj.com.

8.   George Orwell, *1984* (New York: Harcourt Brace, 1983), pp. 2, 138, 183.

9.   Ibid., p. 239.

10.   Bradley Hope and Damian Paletta, "S & P Chief Says Geithner Warned About U.S. Downgrade," *Wall Street Journal*, January 21, 2014, wsj.com.

11.   Harvey Silverglate, *Three Felonies a Day* (New York: Encounter Books, 2011), pp. xviii–xix, xxv, xxxvii, l, 28, 264–65, 267.

Chapter 16: Decline Is a Choice

1.   Martin Jacques, *When China Rules the World* (New York: Penguin Books, 2012), p. 12.

2.   Angus Maddison, *The World Economy* (Washington, D.C.: Brookings Institute Press, 2007).

3.   John Pomfret, "Newly Powerful China Defies Western Nations with Remarks, Policies," *The Washington Post*, March 15, 2010.

4.   Jacques, *When China Rules the World*, p. 128.

5.   Ibid., p. 341.

INDEX

973
DSouza

America

D'Souza, Dinesh